Truly Beloved

Love Letters from
The Divine Mother in You

Book I

Received by Sebastián Blaksley

Take Heart Publications

Take Heart Publications
13315 Buttermilk Bend
North San Juan, CA 95960
www.takeheartpublications.com
ISBN 978-1-58469-705-3
Interior layout based on an original design
by Alejandro Arrojo
Cover illustration, design and computer
production by Patty Arnold,
Menagerie Design and Publishing

Manufactured in the United States of America

Table of Contents

About the Truly Beloved Trilogy

The *Truly Beloved* messages comprise a path toward the full realization of mystical union. They are designed to bring us deeper into a direct relationship with God through lovingly listening to His voice in our heart. This is how we return to the state in which the soul and its divine Source communicate without interruption or interference, just as it was before time began.

We have never actually been separate from God. However, we have become filled with "voices" that have nothing to do with our true identity, voices that speak in ways that love would never speak. Voices that tire, confuse, and sadden. They need not stay with us. The central message of this work is that the time has come for a direct relationship between Heaven and Earth, the human and the divine—the time of the humanized Christ. Please understand that the word "Christ" simply refers to the true nature of each being's unique eternal identity, even while always united to its divine Source.

I recommend that you approach these works not as another source of information. The time of learning is over. The time of being is now. Allow your mind, heart, and soul to "be with" the Voice of Truth that these messages convey. Feel it, embrace it, allow it to move within you, for this is how we return to the state of unity, harmony, and peace with ourselves and all creation.

The unity of our human and divine nature is the cradle of the new Earthly Kingdom. Therefore, I sincerely hope that these revelations, which are a transmission from pure holy love, serve to give increasing space in your daily life to your humanized Christ in union with your brothers and sisters and all creation.

With love in Christ,
Sebastián Blaksley
February, 2024

CHRIST, a definition

Received through Sebastian, March 25, 2023

"Christ is the identity that all creation shares in God. It is what makes a tree a tree, a fish a fish, and a human a human. This Christ identity is what makes each being unique, eternal, immutable, and holy since it is the essence of each created being and its own identity, united to Source. It is the true nature of each being."

How This Work Originated

Today, September 23, 2019, seven days after finishing the transcription of the messages received and compiled in the seven-volume work Choose Only Love, I received the glorious visit of the Immaculate Mary. Immense joy and tenderness enveloped my heart in a serenity without comparison. She sweetly told me:

My beloved, I want to open the floodgates of my heart. I will do it in this particular way, through you, loving hand, scribe from Heaven that has chosen to live in the truth. I do it for my love of humanity and for my love of you who receive these words.

Drop by drop my messages will pierce the stone, softening hearts hardened from the despair of the world.

Each message will be like a drop of morning dew that descends from the sky and waters the Earth with love, or like blessed roses descending to Earth, scattered to beautify the minds and hearts of my children and the entire world.

My sons and daughters, the world has wanted to convince you that you are what you are not. But now you are in the perfect position to live in the truth. You are holiness personified. You are the beauty of God's love come true. Do not be fooled by the idea you have that your worth is below that of God. Your reality and that of the Creator of everything is one and the same. To live in harmony with this truth is to live in freedom, expressing yourself in the beauty of your being.

The benevolence, goodness, and beauty of your hearts are waiting to be expressed. Live in the holiness of love. Remain in my heart. In it you will find the refuge of your souls and the grace to love more. Your hearts will be filled with thanks and blessings. You will forever live a life in fullness. You will attract to yourself, your loved ones, and the whole world all the good, holy, and perfect from the very heart of God. We are a unit. Together we are the union of love.

I thank you for answering my call. I fill you with blessings. I love you with perfect love.

Sebastián Blaksley
Buenos Aires, Argentina
September 23, 2019

Editor's Note: God has no gender but languages do. The reader will note that the Deity is referred to in this work sometimes as masculine, sometimes as feminine, and sometimes as "Mother-Father God." The intent is to reflect the universality of the Divine while staying within the conventions of the English language to which most readers are accustomed.

Prelude to the Letters

Children of my heart,

I come to dwell with you in a particular way, clad in the glory of Heaven, and in union with God's angels and my divine son Jesus. By design of the Father of Lights, this work of wisdom and truth is a sign of His love for you. We love you with the perfect love that comes from the Source of life, the only true love, and the origin of all holy love. In my Immaculate Heart you will find what your soul seeks, because it is one with the Source of your being and of all true, pure, and perfect being.

Love is calling you as never before. These words are a sign, among many others, that this is true. I invite you to open the eyes of your heart to contemplate the wonders that God created for each of His children. Beyond all form is the true essence of things that cannot be nullified. Your reality need not be separate from holiness. What you are need not be hidden behind a wall of illusions. You are children of God, created in His likeness, in love and holiness.

Be not carried away by voices that would convince you that you are something else. In the highest heights of the Heaven of God dwells your true identity. Your reality dwells in the abode of Christ. Find it there.

I am the wind that blows souls to the highest heights of sanctity where there is perpetual light. I am the refuge of hearts seeking peace. I am Mary, the Queen of Concord, of harmony. Whoever calls me receives me. Whoever looks for me finds me. Whoever opens the doors of his or her being to me receives the grace of my embrace.

This gift of my unrivaled grace has never before been given to those who inhabit Earth, not because my daughters and sons did not previously receive my holy love, but because you are here at the time of the Second Advent. You have chosen to live in the world in this moment of human history by the perfect design of the eternal Father and the will of your being. Each era has its grace. At this time it is the abundant grace of Mary Immaculate.

Yes, children of my sweet heart, these are the times of Mary: times of sweetness and love, times of beauty and holiness, times when the divine joins the Earth in the beauty of truth. Never before has the eternal been as open to the temporal in human consciousness as now. Human hearts are opening more and more to their Creator like beautiful flowers preparing to receive the golden rays of life-giving sunshine.

I come to dwell with you in this work so that you receive these words and make them yours. It is Christ who is speaking to you through me, for we are one. Love has come from Heaven to join with you in this way, with these words, through this divine manifestation, reaching you by mysterious means. Love is a mystery to humankind, as life is a mystery also.

Please know, dear soul, that my Immaculate Heart burns constantly with a flame of the living love that is God. A force greater than any power you can imagine moves within my being. It is the power of God, in whose reality I exist united with joyous truth. With that very love, and with that single true power, I make myself present in your life here and now by design of the heavenly Father and by your will to join the light.

The plea of your heart has been heard. Your prayers have been accepted. Here is Heaven's answer to your deepest longing, your longing for union and for love, your longing to be who you really are, your longing to live fully and in endless bliss.

You have traveled an arduous, winding road. Often you have become fatigued. You have experienced the extremes of the human experience so full of nuance and intensity. You have cried out to Heaven to find your being. And you have found it. Now that you are aware of who you really are, the road appears clear and serene. In the peace of our union we will continue together, walking the path that we still have to travel in the world, and then, holding hands, entering the Kingdom of Heaven where we will dwell forever.

I am with you every day of your life.

What a joy, my sons and daughters, to be able to rest in the certainty that once you have fulfilled your holy purpose in the world, we will continue holding hands. And we will continue spreading beautiful love eternally, united in spirit and truth in the beauty of holiness. In our mutual union of divine love we are one with God and with everything that is part of Him. Your face is sculpted in my heart. Your name is written in the palm of my hand. I contemplate you from the realm of no-time, where everything is seen, known, and embraced in love.

I assure you, children of my heart, there will never be a work like this. These words are clothed in divine grace that is always unique, always new, and always creative. Humanity is living in the time of direct relationship with God. These are new times, times of fulfillment, times of the Second Coming of my divine Son Jesus. This work is unique; never before have I addressed humanity so explicitly, direct and full of tenderness and unity, except for the time when by the grace of God I dwelt among men. In every word of these writings is the power of divine love. Each time that a soul is dedicated to receiving them, the power of miracles makes an appearance.

The value of this unique manifestation does not reside in its form but in its essence. Since its Source is Christ, all its power and glory go with it. Every moment you spend with me you connect more to love. And your being shines in all its magnificence. In our divine relationship lies the refuge of your heart, the certainty of who you really are, and the peace without opposite.

This work is a gift from Heaven given to all as the perfect means to consciously remain in union with Christ, and from that union to take you to a greater knowledge of love that has no beginning or end, the perfect love that you really are. Through these words I am inviting you to live, from now and forever, as the love you really are. That is why I have come: so that together we can bear witness to the truth, the truth that says you are love and nothing but love because God is love and nothing but love.

I bless you in the certainty of your holiness.

A Movement of Beautiful Love

Letter 1

My children, I am the heart of Mary. I speak to you from the unity of Christ.

I have come to dwell with you who are looking for love and truth. I have come to tell you that you have already found what you are looking for. The time of seeking is over.

Now is the time to rejoice in the expression of perfect love. This is the same as telling you that the time of transformation is over. Now you are living in a new time, the time of unity.

What you will see in your world with greater clarity every day is the manifestation of the consciousness of unity. The systems will adjust to this reality since there will be no space for anything but pure love.

The world will not succumb. It will be integrated into love in a new consciousness, and from that integration, a new world. What God creates is eternal, as eternal is His love for his creations.

My heart is calling you to express more and more the grace of your holiness, to extend the joy of being alive, the joy of being children of God, the happiness that exists in the depth of your hearts. Sing, dance, and embrace in holiness; feel glad to be as you really are.

Each of you is important, like beautiful links in the chain of Christ's unity. I invite you to be part of a universal movement, a movement that summons you to serve love, living your lives as the living Christ who lives in you.

As children of God, you are bearers of wisdom.

If you allow silence to show you the truth within your minds and the love in your hearts, you will recognize that you know what love is and how to express it.

Paint your reality with bright yet soft colors. Create new holy configurations in your ties with the Earth, with your brothers and sisters, and with yourself. Do so also for God, to whom we all owe existence.

This work is a portal open to the grace of my pious heart. I want to create between you and this tireless Mother, full of love and kindness for her children, a bond as intimate as it has ever been before on Earth. Through this open door to Heaven a shower of blessings will spill over wounded hearts and heal your lives of so much pain. Through our union evil will be annulled and every error corrected.

I am the Mother of Divine Concord and wholeheartedly desire to fill your lives with blessings and light. I ask you to immerse yourself in the depths of your soul so you can experience the beauty of our maternal union in the silence of your heart.

I also ask you to live your lives serving the cause and effect of beautiful love, as God has always wanted for each of you. In this way you will not only live as the living Christ you are, recognizing the inner Christ in your sisters and brothers, but you will be able to extend mercy and the Source of all love and foundation of every being.

I am opening a new window to Heaven where light flows from the beauty of my Immaculate Heart towards all my children. I will enlighten the world more and more because of your union with me, your eternal divine Mother, co-redeemer, and friend of souls who yearn for God.

This call will lead you to deepen your union with the Source of life.

I love you with a love that has no beginning or end.

You are all in the embrace of my harmony and perpetual peace.

This work is a bridge laid between the Earth and Heaven, an eternal conduit for the flow of truth that springs from the heart of God the Father, the Son, and the Holy Spirit, flooding the entire universe with more beauty, purity, and holiness.

Union

Letter 2

I am the heart of Mary speaking to you. I am the concord that dwells in holy hearts. I am the Source of life. I am that part of you that makes the world a sacred, pure, and holy place. I am a heart full of divine love, tenderness, and peace, as is yours and that of all that is true.

This manifestation has the purpose of opening the doors for a greater awareness of harmony, a love-reality of creation. To live in unity is to live in harmony with the truth in perfect union with the pure love that God created. It is also to live in peace with oneself and with everything.

Creation is benevolent. The universe blesses you every moment and waits with open arms to allow you within the embrace of love. You and life are a unit. Being aware of this is what the awakening of consciousness is about.

Life is an endless dialogue. To be aware of the unity of the union of hearts within the calm and peace of love, is to remain in life. All creation lives in harmony within the heart of Mother-Father God, refuge of truth. Becoming aware of it is the purpose of our union in this particular work.

Live in peace. Travel the paths of love together with the serenity of spirit. Flow in the ocean of mercy. Be one with everything in truth. That is the will of God for you who are Her beloved sons and daughters.

Knowing more and more deeply the Source of being is the joy of the soul. Towards this greater knowledge we travel together. Times of disagreement have been left behind. The times of harmony are here, times of union, times of awareness that it is possible to leave behind everything and immerse yourself in a new and eternal reality.

The unity that exists between you and life is rarely recognized. To accept this truth is to own yourself, a condition of the children of divine love. With all my heart, as your divine Mother, I wish to bring you all to that knowledge as the foundation of truth.

Whether in a waking or sleeping state, the dialogue between you and the universe is uninterrupted. You constantly send a flow of spiritual energy that arises from within. In that flow of vital force, the universe receives and brings back what is given to it. Ask God to show you the truth and it will be shown. Ask God to hide it and it will be hidden. This is because your world is the expression of your consciousness. Everything is consciousness.

Truth does not disappear when you ask the world to show you an illusion, but the window of your consciousness closes to the contemplation of life with all its wonders. The dark night becomes present; you live in a place without light. But as soon as you ask life to show the love, truth, and peace in which everything exists, it will be shown.

Life awaits you with open arms to receive your blessing and return your love in ways that are beyond the desires of your heart and that fulfill your most intimate wishes.

All my children have the right to be happy. Everyone has the right to live in peace. Concord is the force of love that brings harmony to everything. It is union of the truth of all things. It is the reality of unity. All beauty comes from the harmony of being.

Expressing beauty, joy, and holiness is what makes the world a paradise. To manifest the truth of the heart is to make known the treasures that exist within our union. When you remain in me, the beauty of our noble feelings and the diversity of the treasures of our spirit become present and call everyone to unity.

Everyone is given the beauty of the sun. Everyone has been given spiritual beauty. God gives to everyone alike without distinctions of any kind. Give the same love to all your creations.

Silence of the Heart

Letter 3

My beloved sons and daughters, your tiredness is often due to the hustle and bustle of the world, especially in big cities where it becomes difficult to consciously join my Immaculate Heart and enjoy the beauty of peace. Excesses are always disharmonious. The soul loves harmony as much as it loves balance.

An over-stimulated mind suffers when it exceeds its capacity for understanding. Everything has its time and process, including both mind and heart. Too much stimuli prevent your senses from processing calmly and functions are altered.

I invite you to know a new state, new and eternal at the same time—the absence of anxiety. Excessive cravings are an unequivocal symptom of imbalance. Returning to equanimity will make you feel free, happy, and above all fully yourself.

These are the times of the feminine, and therefore I manifest myself in multiple ways in a flow of thanks as never before seen in the history of humanity. This is already evident. Wherever you go you can observe a movement of the tenderness of God's love, increasingly visible expressions of the feminine aspect of being. These are the times of unity and inclusion, times of sweetness and truth. These are the times of Mary. But these are also the times of spiritual youth.

I speak especially to the child in each of you. This work is dedicated to that innocence and openness to make you more aware of the sweetness of love and the need for motherly love.

Children and the child in you are not only the future of the world, but of the present and eternal. They are holy sprouts of love. Heaven is a kingdom of souls in touch with their child-like nature. That is why I have insisted, in union with my divine son Jesus, that you become like children in the arms of the Mother.

All are part of this work because children, whether young in body or not, often need guidance from wise elders who know of love and truth. Guidance does not imply teaching or exercising authority; it simply means showing a known path, and above all, showing it with love.

No one can be excluded from my call because I am divine love made manifest as motherhood, which is all-inclusive.

Young people look for role models, as everyone does. It is a matter of identity. Your identity is a shared identity, for there can be no identity without identification and for this it is necessary to "identify with."

The joy that young people naturally express and their desire to dance and embrace life is characteristic of the soul in love with Christ, although it may be a misrepresented force.

Young at heart from all corners of the world! You are the hope of your heavenly Mother. In you I have set my favor. I assure you, you will not succumb. Return to love. Find it in the silence of your hearts. There you will know the purity that you crave. Do not identify with what is temporary, because you are eternal. You are holy, as holy as the Source from which your life springs. Respect and honor this. Love yourself with an honest, pure, and helpful love. Do not contaminate yourself with things of the world. And do not despair if you feel that you have already done so. Here is your Mother with open arms and a heart longing for you to return to your home of endless bliss. Times you have fallen, like those of the whole world, come from a universal spiritual struggle. You are shaken by them like a small flower blown by the wind.

Do not worry about the future. The future is me. You who receive these words, know that your life is in my loving hands. You will not succumb. Success is guaranteed. Do you think that anything can stop this Mother who remains forever united to the power of Christ's love?

Do not believe that the forces you experience within can dominate you. The day will come when you will be lords of yourselves. You will live your lives like trees whose roots are well developed and absorb food from a soil full of healthy nutrients. You will consciously be the expression of God's love.

My sons and daughters, I have not come to criticize but to serve. I have come to urge you to express yourselves freely in the truth of who you are. You are beautiful as you are. And much more when you remain united to love in prayer and contemplation. There is a silence in your hearts where you are full. You who search for challenges, I invite you to a new one, the challenge of God's tenderness—a real revolution for the world, the love revolution. You are called to lead it with tenderness, holiness, and authenticity, loving everyone equally without excluding anyone or anything, showing the world what it means to love and be truly loved with softness and kindness.

Youth is not just a certain chronological age, but everyone who has a burning and free heart. These messages are addressed to the young at heart, spirits who have come to Earth to sow the love of the Second Coming of Christ. These messages are for you whom I have called to join the peaceful revolution of love being manifested.

Join our spirit movement. This Mother is calling you. It needs you to make the light of life shine more brightly in the world. My heart will heal your wounds. My love will erase all painful memories . I will embrace you in such a way that you will never shed a tear again. I am the hug of beautiful love, the embrace of a Mother like no other, the embrace of the sanctity of being.

Stay silent in me, and feel the tenderness of love.

A Peace That Has No Opposite

Letter 4

To what other son or daughter could this letter of love be directed but to you, whom I love with infinite love?

I know very well what you have lived. Every beat of your heart causes an echo in mine. We are the concord of love. We are one.

In our unity lies the sure escape from all that is not God's will for you and for anyone. Love only provides love, harmony, and fulfillment.

I invite you to remain united to this Mother in a special way. There is no work like this, since these words are the gateway to a single expression of my motherly love. By the will of the Father and my love, in union with what is true, I open my heart so that from it you can absorb life.

Dear children of mine, in this letter I want to calm your frightened hearts because of so many negative messages about the end times. There are many things that scare you. But here is the Mother of a hope that does not disappoint. I have come to tell you the truth. I have come to serve.

The world will not perish. Humankind will not succumb to the onslaught of separation. The triumph of love is sure. Reprimands were necessary and still today remain so for many. Do not interpret my admonitions as an act of heartbreak, but quite the opposite.

I know very well how strong you are, how powerful is your will, and how free you are. I know you can change and that you can create universes of love and goodness. I know you can live forever together with the flame of love of my Immaculate Heart. I've known you forever. I am your Mother and I know well what you are. That is why I speak to you this way.

The world is receiving blessings and thanks as never before. A flood of love surrounds you. You will see great signs that you may not understand. Do not fear them. Nothing will happen to those who have chosen love and truth as their life partners. You just need enough awareness to want to live in the good with all your heart. The reality of spirit takes care of the rest in the space of freedom.

The triumph of my Immaculate Heart is here. Few understand what this means, not due to error, but to the magnitude of its meaning. Everywhere you will observe the emergence of new expressions of unity. They arise as the fruit of the atonement. They are here.

I assure you that you will be saved. Very few will not opt for the Kingdom. Do not worry about this. It is painful to accept that some will not accept love as their eternal reality, but still, that is the will of those souls and it must be respected. They are forever loved. This is part of the mystery of evil. Do not be scared of it. Welcome my messages of love and truth with holy disposition.

I have not come to tell you about the scourges of the world. You know them quite well. With every step you are told of them. I have come to tell you how much I love you and to thank you for having responded to the call of love. I have come to confirm you in the truth and to convey a letter directly from Heaven, a message to you, to receive from the Father of Lights. God embraces you in unity. Love has restored you. The truth has made you free. You are the renewal of true charity.

Live happily every day of your life. Understand that you are fulfilling a heavenly function here on Earth. We need you. This

Mother needs you as much as she herself is necessary. Without your human lives, I cannot pour blessings to others. Without your prayers I can do nothing to serve my beloved humanity. Your union with Christ is the portal of salvation.

Imagine how many blessings your brothers and sisters receive through your unity with my Immaculate Heart. I am a burning flame of love. I am the passion of God made into motherhood. I am a vibrant force of life. I am what makes alive everything that is.

The world is walking towards truth. The universe is extending towards the infinite in a perpetual expansion of love. It grows. The cosmos widens. And it expands within the body of God from where it arises.

Stay forever in the joy of my heart. You are important to God. He Himself became dependent on you for pure love. Your Father does nothing without you and never will. No one can take away your freedom or your holiness. You are God's beloved children. You belong to Him and you are returning.

Walk serenely in life, trusting my assistance. I will never abandon you. You are my children; how could I? Nothing you could ask of the Father in union with my Immaculate Heart is not granted. Put your trust in Christ—your joys, your deepest dreams, your lives. Together we will make miraculous transformations, I assure you.

You are not alone. You never were and never will be. The Mother goes ahead of you. On your left and right goes Mary. Behind you is my Spirit of love. I surround you everywhere.

I invite you to sing a new song—the song of Mary—a hymn of joy and gratitude. I invite you to fill the Earth with your loving feelings, with your holy thoughts, with the truth of your being.

Show the world the face of love. Tell all that this Mother is waiting for everyone, that the floodgates of my heart have opened wide as never before. I am Mary. I am the sweetness of love. I am your reality. I am the voice of your holy heart. I am the peace that has no opposite and dwells in your being.

Rejoice in love.

Thank you, my children, for answering my call.

The Moment of Truth

Letter 5

My daughters and sons, today I want to talk to you about one of the forms that my Heavenly Mother Love takes. I speak sweetly and gently of the love expressed through my rebukes or warnings. It is important that you remember that this Mother of Pure Love loves with responsible love, just as God the Father does.

A love that dares not express appropriate admonitions is incomplete and tinged with fear. Therefore it has not reached perfection.

I invite you to reflect on this message. Often the world seeks to water down the truth, to minimize the radicality of my call. Truly I tell you that in the Kingdom of Love nothing can exist other than the purity of truth, shining in the glory of divine perfection.

Will the truth do nothing with that which is its opposite? The answer is, it will do what is in its nature; that is, it will create its effect by itself. I assure you that everything that is contrary to the purity of love will be dispelled, just as the Earth does with what is not healthy for it, or like the body, which sets in motion the necessary mechanism to discard what does not serve its harmony. In the same way, the naked truth will transmute into light what is imbued with the opposite of love so that it becomes pure holiness and is in a position to return to the unity of what is similar to it, that is, to Christ.

Beloved of my heart. There is a Kingdom where only purity exists, a reality in which only holiness dwells, a universe of infinite universes in which there is only goodness where no wild thought of death or destruction can even be thought. Greed and its companion, avarice, are inconceivable because fear does not exist there. Within that realm of pure divine light, every feeling is one of nobility, beauty, and perfect harmony. All are aware of the eternal unity in which they remain embraced by love. The flow of life moves freely to the rhythm of truth. And everyone rejoices. There, minds love truth because they are free. They live forever in love.

Soul born of the Father! You who receive these words, remember that you are not in the world to adhere to its values, but by disposition of divine wisdom united with that of the Father in accord with your will. Do not forget that there is a plan of atonement. Let everything spin as it wants to spin. It is none of your business. Do not get mixed up with other values. Just watch, be silent, and wait. Take distance from what you observe.

The world is not your home, nor do you belong to it but to me. You are in it because together we have decreed, outside of time, that it be so for the salvation of human nature, to contribute to its return to pure truth. Once again, you are not to ascribe to the world's values. Let everyone follow their path and think what they want. The Father, who sees in secret, will know what to do or not do. Remain in Me who am your home, your Kingdom, your everything. I am the reality of your being.

Like everyone, you are called to rise more and more in holiness every day. What is not holy is not in harmony with your nature. Look around you. Birds fly, reptiles do not. To each according to its nature. Just because an eagle sees others crawling does not mean that it should walk.

Allow the Holy Spirit to show you what needs to be shown, according to His design. Not everyone sees everything. When you can see without trembling the thousands of faces and facets that falsehood has, distinguishing what is holy from what is not, what is harmonious from what will never be, what is beauty from what merely appears to be, when you can make those distinctions without judgment or loss of your peace, you will be able to sincerely say that you have reached the truth.

Do not worry about what you call the darkness of the world. As already said, simply watch, be silent, and wait. Don't try to fix things your way, or transform them. Rather, release it all to me. Remain in my Immaculate Heart. Let each child of God settle his or her affairs with the Father of all creation.

My children, I remind you that the truth exists and the day will come when it makes an appearance in all consciousnesses. Its holy face will be revealed to all. In that hour, what is true can no longer be hidden or denied. For some it may seem like a terrible time; for many others it will not be. It will be a face-to-face encounter with pure truth. My children, be happy that when that time comes you will rejoice in the truth and sing happily.

Pray for those who, when that day comes, are not adequately prepared. They will feel pain. But my love will assist them. For those who have prepared themselves—because they have already embraced the truth by choosing love as their reality—that will be their hour of glory, their time of full salvation, that is, their resurrection.

Scribe from Heaven, pencil in the hands of love, the moment of truth exists, and no matter how much pain or fear this knowledge seems to cause, you must communicate it to the world, not to frighten, but to lovingly warn. Remember, the truth must be told with love and presented together with the sweetness of the heart. If you do that, you allow it to adopt the forms of prudence and humility, virtues dearly loved by God, the Source of all virtue.

There comes a time when no veil can be placed over truth. What is holy cannot be called by any other name. All deception is useless, because before its holiness nothing can be hidden. There can be no disguises, because its power dispels them.

In holiness I tell you that the naked truth will come to light, hand-in-hand with love. All consciousnesses will see it in its resplendent reality. That hour exists, the hour of pure truth. It will be a sublime hour. The entire universe will be silent, a silence of great expectation. Think about this and keep this knowledge in your heart. Prepare for that moment so that when it arrives it will find you in union with love. And let it be for you what it truly is: the hour of the light of glory.

Eternal Life

Letter 6

My children, avoid ideas that make no sense. You have been gifted with reason. The truth dwells in your minds as a blessed gift from the Father. Yes, there is a truth that is always true. You know it. You can distinguish it in your hearts. Your minds feel safe in the truth, and your souls are happy in pure love.

Let yourselves not be seduced with meaningless ideas that try to make you believe what can never be true. You are children of God. You cannot be anything else, since He is your creator. You have been created—and still today are sustained—by the love that comes from the Father. Love is your Source, your reality. Everything else is pure illusion.

Let go of all intrigue. Abandon complex thoughts that make you confused. The truth is simple. Love is pure. Holiness is eternal.

Those who say that everything is relative and therefore ideas about good and evil are simply mental constructs that have nothing to do with reality are incorrect. Good exists and proceeds from love. Evil exists and was never created by God. This is the simple truth. You know well what is evil, because your hearts do not sing with joy in it, and you know very well what makes you happy. You all have the ability to recognize love.

Unite your hearts with reason, your perfect guide. Discard what does not make sense in the light of truth as you do diligently with other things you do not like. Harmony, peace, joy—in short, love in all its forms is your natural state of being. That is why the call to happiness cannot be banished from your hearts.

I invite you to remain in the purity of holiness. In it your minds are free and you can feel the freshness of the wind of the spirit.

What is it to live in the purity of holiness? It is thinking true thoughts and feeling loving feelings. Christ is love and truth. To live in purity is to live consciously in unity with the inner Christ and to go to the Source of eternal life.

God's creations are eternal, for His love for them is eternal. I tell you this one more time to contrast with the supposed extinction of planet Earth. Again I assure you that the world will not be destroyed. Again I remind you that the world will not succumb. Everything exists within the embrace of love. There will be no great conflagration. I cannot tell you how the end of time will be, because you are not yet ready for it, nor is it necessary. But I assure you that nothing is beyond the reach of God. Truly I tell you that you have a loving Father and Mother whose power exceeds all measure. Life will not be extinguished. Nothing that is true can cease to exist.

The only thing to be corrected is the illusion of separation. Everything else will remain as it is forever, including you. In the kingdom of God there is no death; therefore, it does not exist at all. Only eternal life is real. In other words, God is the only reality, because God is eternal truth.

When you are told that you project your fears on the blank slate of the world, it is not being said that you create your body, or the stars and sun, but that you project your feelings, beliefs, and interpretations on what you perceive with the bodily senses. This is how you give meaning to things. If you do it without being in union with the inner Christ, it will be from fear, and fearful projections will be inevitable. If you do it from the truth that Christ lives in you, there will be no fearful world that you need to defend against.

Only the lack of inner peace is what can constitute a threat to the integrity of the mind.

Observe that I have used the word threat because in truth nothing can attack your true mind, which is the divine mind. Even so, the fear of the loss of psychic integrity is a basic fear. You leave that fear behind when you remain in the truth of who you are, which you do when you remain in me. To remain in me is to remain in the sanctity of being and in the purity of love. In other words, it is to remain in the truth of your being, within which there is only the security and fullness of love.

In the past you have felt a fear of violence because you perceived that you were vulnerable and helpless in the face of it. That fear sought to protect you from danger and in a sense it has succeeded. That is not that kind of fear that clouds the truth in your consciousness. That fear is actually a survival mechanism to preserve life on the physical plane. It is necessary. There is nothing wrong with it. It is a movement of the heart that knows what peace is, and rejects everything contrary to harmony, beauty, and love. It comes from the impulse to live, which has its origin in eternal life.

When children are exposed to violence and anger it is usually a very traumatic experience. No child should be exposed to it, for they are not able to preserve their mental and emotional integrity in the face of a force perceived as disintegrating. In the face of violence, they feel that their interior is disharmonized and crumbles, and they suffer greatly. This happens not only in children. Along the path of consciousness many free themselves from the fear of violence by recognizing that nothing external can cause them to lose their sanity. They are the ones who have found the truth and live in peace within themselves. They are those who live in the embrace of love.

When you feel that you have come into contact with anger, I simply ask you to recognize that it is alien to you. Remember that coming into contact with it does not mean you have to join it. What is asked of you is to remain in inner silence without judging anything, while holding the following truth high in your consciousness:

"The past has passed. When I was a child and suffered acts of violence, I responded with fear to protect myself. I feared the loss of mental and emotional integrity, and being overwhelmed. I can now relax in the remembrance of the true embrace of the love of the Mother."

Then you will be able to respond differently—with holy indifference to the world. You will recognize that everything external to you is neutral and that you cannot lose your equanimity to the events of the world. You will accept that nothing can separate you from love. This recognition will allow you not to respond to anger with fear, but to take refuge in the truth of your holy being. You will substitute fear with the holy indifference to the world.

My sons and daughters, you will no longer lose inner peace, for you have reached the truth. Eternal life is your heritage; love is your only reality. Accept this truth now and release the fear of violence forever. I remain in you every day of your life. We are united in the reality of love.

Prayer: Portal to Divinity

Letter 7

How much joy the heart feels in union with the embrace of love! What a joy to live in peace! What a blessed gift to remain in my Immaculate Heart, in the reality of holy love!

I am a mother who always accompanies you because I am the Mother of love, and love is ever-present. I have the power to rain a flood of miracles and divine blessings on your life as well as the whole world. But that power is of no use outside of union. That is why I ask you again and again to remain in me. Prayer is the vehicle of miracles and the food of the soul. It is the reality within which one lives in divine love. There is no relationship without dialogue. Thus, the heart always seeks to dialogue with its Creator, whom it knows intimately.

Every prayer that springs from trust is a prayer of love. Therefore it is perfect. The way in which it manifests is of little importance. If the motivation of prayer is to remain united with God, the effects of unity will be inevitable. Love does not care about form except to use them in service to its expression.

The time of unity—the time in which you are living—is characterized by the integration of form and content into a unique reality, where there is no distance between them. The soul's journey goes from the belief in form without content, exalting it and putting it above all, toward the recognition of what is essential, and then to their integration, joining them in the service of beautiful love.

Every day I invite you, within our divine relationship, to gather all that is true in you, my children, and to transcend that union and go beyond the imaginable, beyond what cannot be put into words. We are Mother and Child, united forever in a filial love in the heart of God.

Prayer is a service to creation. Living in unity with love is the highest service because from divine unity flows a myriad of blessings, thanks, and strength that make your sisters and brothers fully happy. The power of prayer is immeasurable. Not only does it benefit you but as you experience pure love with its perpetual security, you give life to everyone and everything.

Prayer cures disease, solves human problems, creates entire universes, heals the planet, and embraces everything within love. Nothing is excluded from the power of prayer because prayer is a sublime expression of love. Prayer is an essential part of life. It is the vehicle of miracles in which everything is possible because nothing is impossible for God, although many things may feel impossible from a human perspective. The soul without prayer faints, just as people without love wither.

Prayer is a dialogue of love between you and me. In our dialogue resides its power. This is why true prayer transforms. To remain in constant prayer is to remain united to that space of silent reality in your heart which nothing can disturb. In that deep silence of the heart is the gateway to the divine, the most sacred relationship in the universe, the holiest relationship you could imagine—the relationship between you and me, a relationship of eternal life.

The prayer of silence is the highest prayer that can be achieved in the world because it is the prayer of Heaven. Everyone can access it, just as everyone can access their true self which is one with God.

To remain silent in the embrace of love is to be your Self in harmony with the will of the Father of creation. From that holy silence, the wisdom of love will dictate what must be said or not said, be done or not done, at the moment that the design of truth so decrees. It is in that silence where miracles happen, where wounds are healed without needing to ask. The divine mind knows everything and knows very well what to do or not do; it doesn't need words or even your recognition, it just needs you to join in silence and humility. This is contemplation.

True silence—in which prayer rises to the very heart of God—comes from the absence of judgment. Your every conscious attempt to connect with the silence of your heart is a decree that you issue to the universe to set aside your judgments and to live in the sanctity of being one.

My children, I invite you to be not fooled by the chatter of the thinking mind, yours or others, which has been so active for so long that it seems not to leave you alone. Gradually that inner noise fades and gives way to the joy of the silence of peace. The mind remains healthy and saved resting in my Immaculate Heart. This is how the mind returns to the house of holy love. It rests in a peace that has no opposite, which comes from the certainty of truth.

Beautify your lives. Stay in prayer. Make silence your faithful companion. Truth and love always align with silence.

Remember, silence is the portal to divinity. That is where you will always find me. That is where the sweetness of love lives. There in the depths of your heart is where you will find your holy being. In it lies the force that has given life to everything. In silence you will always find God, the Source of all love.

I offer you a prayer to make your own:

"Celestial Father, grant us the grace to silence our thoughts so that we can hear Your voice and thus be aware of our unity. Amen."

I leave you now in the embrace of love.

I thank you for extending life, joining the movement of beautiful love. I thank you for answering my call.

In the Love of Mary

Letter 8

My sons and daughters, Christ is calling you from every corner of the universe as never before. This Mother summons you to holiness. I invite you to raise your eyes to continue growing inside. Once you have reached the top, we must continue moving towards the highest heights of Heaven. You have been created to remain in union with God. This is a gift and a responsibility to yourself and to the world.

Your hearts carry within themselves the impetus toward holiness, the power of love. Allow that force to propel you to love more every day. Beautify your reality by giving flowers every day—the blossoms of divine virtues that the Creator has placed in your souls. Make Earth a new paradise. Live in the truth.

My dear ones, as the Mother of Love, I wish you to support each other with holy tolerance. Everyone has their time. Each has their story. You all come from diverse human realities. You sometimes have a very limited view of reality, which is often the basis of your disputes. None of you know the whole soul of your sisters and brothers, nor the details of the path of each spirit. Therefore, try to understand humanity and to feel pure holy compassion.

How to achieve that? Place everything that mortifies you in the hands of this Mother. In my Immaculate Heart is space for everyone and everything. Do not act as if you are alone, free of the forces of nature, for you are not. Your heavenly Mother is with you always. Stay in me, talk to me, tell me of your feats. Share with me your dreams and desires. Express to my heart your frustrations, your fears, your angers, your sorrows, and your joys. Invite me to be part of everything that constitutes your lives. Everything.

There is no pain that my Immaculate Heart cannot allay forever, nor a wound it cannot heal. I want to be united with you in your human reality. I want to be part of your relationships.

I offer you my divine friendship. I give you the peace of God that lives in my heart. I assure you that fruits of fullness will arise from our holy relationship. You can talk to me, hear me, and see me if you wish. Whoever calls me receives me. Whoever looks for me finds me. In each one of you who invokes me, I manifest according to the nature of your heart, just as it happens in the various relationships you have. I want you to be aware of the holiness of your desires. They are the windows of Heaven. In them you will find all that you are.

As you come to me and grow every day in the intimacy of our love, do not worry about what you call your sins, limitations, and disabilities. My love is much bigger than all of that. This Mother will not argue with her children if you travel the path of the thinking mind. As the vessel of wisdom that I am, I can truly create a new intelligence in union with you and God the Father. It is not that I am going to create it, properly speaking, since every miracle comes from the Source that has given existence to everything, the first and last cause of reality, the essence. Only God works miracles and does them in union with our hearts united in holiness.

I want to fill your lives with lasting joy. I want to paint your beautiful smiles and color your hearts with the luminosity of Heaven.

A wonderful world full of love and goodness is within your soul. You can become aware of it and enjoy it forever. I wait for you there, as does your being await you, where the truth about what you are, and what life is, resides.

Look not so much at yourself or on others, but set your eyes upon my love. I give you my face, drawn, painted, and sculpted in countless ways throughout the history of humankind, and abundantly in the last millennia. I do it so that you have a means whereupon to place your desire for divine union. Humankind needs a way to know content. This is why Christ incarnated.

I am not calling you to fulfill a precept, or to follow a norm. I am calling you to live in love. I am calling you to be part of a movement that was created in Heaven and is now manifesting on Earth—the movement of beautiful love.

The world needs to know the beauty of love. Your sisters and brothers are yearning for the experience of pure love. You are all tired of external and internal contamination. The miasma of what creates suffering and heartbreak has reached its zenith. It will not go on from here. This is the word of God.

I assure you, my children, that your consciousness is waking up more and more, in a way never before seen on Earth. You are living in the time of awakening consciousness. You are living witnesses of this fact. Have faith in the life that God has created. Do not hesitate a moment when Jesus and Mary bless you and are knocking at your doorstep. You are asked to enter your inner house and make your heart a holy dwelling. Live in the hope that does not disappoint, which arises from the certainty of knowing you are children of God. All the power of God is linked to the power of love; they are one and the same. Meditate on this.

Just as each of you has resilience, so does humanity as a whole. You are one and all at once. Nothing is disconnected from the totality, not even the false world of autonomy. I tell you this for you to reflect on the destiny of life, especially on your planet and your world.

Humanity has experienced a relationship full of heartbreak towards nature for thousands of years. But the seeds of divine transformation have been sown. A new earthly kingdom is being born. The laws of the material universe are much more than we yet realize. Humanity will relate more and more with love for everything, including itself, and will do so until all life is wrapped in the embrace of love, for the movement of Christ consciousness is already here. The power of God's love, united with the universe of form, has already begun. No force can avoid its infinite deployment. Love will advance. It is unstoppable. Earth will not be destroyed. This is the triumph of my Immaculate Heart.

Each one of you is an instrument of Christ in the new consciousness who feels the call of the spirit to invite others to grow in the consciousness of love for the Earth and everything that is part of it, and to make your world more loving. I thank you for your "yes" to love. I invite you to place your call also in My Hands so that, as Mother of life, I will rain a flood of blessings on the Earth and heal it and human consciousness.

I call you to accept the fact that every living being, every aspect of creation, each one of you, is as sacred as God Herself. In every element, every flower, every drop of water, God lives. In the wind the spirit of life blows. Love Her divine diversity. Feel the vastness of the universe so you can be aware of your unlimited breadth. Open your hearts and listen to the song of life, the melodies of creation. All is in me. Love all. This is to love in God's way.

I bless you all. Live forever in the love of Mary.

Love Given

Letter 9

My beloveds, the only will of this heavenly Mother, whose Immaculate Heart knows no shadow of fear, is to bring you to the direct knowledge of a love that has no beginning or end—the love of the most Holy Trinity in whose center your true being resides.

The reality of love is like an infinite circle of light, a perfect harmony that encompasses within itself everything that exists. In it is life which extends eternally in a peace and endless bliss without opposite.

In your soul is the memory of that love, the memory of what you really are. This is the love your being longs for. No other love can complete your heart, for the simple reason that there is no other love than the love of God from which all love flows.

If you remain united to the love you are, your lives will be expressions of holy love and you will enjoy the delight of children of light. Only love can make you happy. Only life can beget life.

In your humanity often you are distressed by things that make no sense. Only one thing is important, love.

To the extent that you open to giving love, to that extent your hearts remain healthy and the world is enlightened. I assure you that all fear has its origin in love that has not been given. To skimp on the force of love drives the heart to block the flow of life.

Children of God, do not look for love. Be love.

In human life everyone has the experience of heartbreak. Every heart in the world has been hurt. It matters little if that wound was perceived in relation to your parents, relatives, friends, or by those you call enemies. The heart knows not of such distinctions.

The wounds of love only prove how essential love is for your life. Be not distressed if you felt abandoned, for real love can never abandon you. Your sadness arises from a misunderstanding. Everyone has inner challenges, inner Goliaths. But these challenges can be vanquished with a single rock. They may seem so big and powerful but are not; they are weak and easily overcome. Diligently engage in keeping your heart clean of all feelings contrary to love.

Cultivate in your souls the beauty of virtue and conceive in your hearts the purity of noble feelings. Make your hearts a holy temple where Christ dwells happily. Be open to feeling the love that comes from a flower, the flow of a river, the melodies of the wind, and the majesty of life. With every step you take you are being embraced by a love without words, a reality beyond imagination, a peace that encompasses everything and from which everything created has emerged.

Worry not, but live your life together with this Mother. I assure you that the power of my Immaculate Heart, together with the Sacred Heart of my divine son Jesus, will work miracles and provide in holiness all that your bodies, minds, and spirits need be given.

I invite you to be strong in beautiful love and to remain in the purity of heart. This will cause you to raise your lives to the highest peaks of the Kingdom of Heaven, and cause your hearts joyfully to sing the song of eternal life.

Never be discouraged, for this Mother is protecting you with special favor.

You cannot give what you do not receive, which is why I call you, again and again, to live in perfect love so you can give it to yourself. I assure you that at the end of the road the only thing that counts is love given. In the same way I tell you in spirit and truth that giving and receiving are one and the same. Every time you open to receive my love and that of others, you are giving love to all.

Love acts of itself. It does not require attention, like the functions of the body and the mind. The planets spin in their orbits regardless of whether you notice them or not. The sound of the elements dancing the dance of life continue in the joy of creation without your awareness. Likewise with your being of pure love: love extends through your soul just as water flows through rivers.

Let your hearts be filled with love and you will see what the miracle of life means. Allow your minds to be filled with joy and holiness. Thus your eyes will reflect the sweetness of God. Thank the Father of all for the gift of tears. They are the visible manifestation of the flow of the water of eternal life poured into your soul, whose Source is divine love.

Love your children. Love your parents. Love your sisters and brothers. Love the land in which you have the transitory experience of human life. Love God. Love yourselves. Love whoever you think has done you harm. Love me so you experience the purity of holy love. Love every aspect of your reality.

Love everything in the love that Christ is. In this way you will always be a song of joy, a beautiful flower planted in the reality of spirit. You will be what you are called to be: the perfect expression of love without beginning or end.

I bless you all and thank you for answering my call.

Thank you for being the light of the world.

Tough Love

Letter 10

My sons and daughters, human relationships can be elevated to divinity.

As a human being created by God, you have the ability to be transformed, not only in body but in consciousness. This reality tells you a lot about yourself.

Let it transform for love. Allow the spirit of God to make you be what He intended for you to be. You can be changed. A new world can be created. Because of this truth, holy admonition is often necessary.

Today I invite you to reflect on the occasional need for tough love.

When love tells you that something should not be done, or when it exhorts you to change, you sometimes get angry. You are attached to the ego's thought pattern. Only the ego can feel threatened. Pride reacts; love responds.

You often react angrily to the admonitions of Christ because you confuse a wake-up call with an attack on your dignity.

Differences in the world tend to be resolved with aggressiveness and violence. The ego has done that for centuries. It does so to nullify the difference. When someone shows the ego that it is in error, that what it does, thinks, or says is not holy or kind, it becomes angry and would try to annihilate, or cancel, what it considers its adversary.

The ego is a constant enemy-making mechanism. According to its false criteria, everyone and everything is an adversary. Naturally, since the ego is a fear-based thought system, anything it perceives as undermining it will be perceived as an opponent. To accomplish this it must make a false judgment and nail it to a cross.

Love only speaks to love. It knows no reality other than holiness and truth. Therefore, when love speaks to you, it is speaking to the real part of your mind created by God. It speaks to your true self. However, when it does, the ego perceives a threat. It does not know what it is, because it is ignorant, and perceives that it can be attacked. It reacts. If you become aware of this mechanism in your life, observe how you react to the words, acts, or omissions of others. Then you can understand with simple clarity what I speak of here.

If instead of giving free rein to the impulses of the ego, you allow that inner energy to be integrated into the silence of your heart and feel the peace of Christ that dwells in your being, you will transmute it into greater awareness of wisdom. In that way, over time the ego of your minds and hearts will vanish and you will heal completely. Again, reaction is always of the ego. Love only responds.

Reacting and responding are not the same; they are the opposite.

There is a dimension in this matter that I wish to share so that you become aware and free yourself completely.

Given the false but widespread association that the world makes between admonishment and attack, and the habitual habit of the ego to use anger to avoid criticism, you often do not want to admonish those who need it because you do not want to arouse their anger. It takes effort to face your sister's or brother's reactions and perhaps you don't know how to do so with love.

A warning is always a loving correction. It is born from the truth that the heart cannot silence. But it is always linked to the purpose of love. Being tough does not mean being angry. When the eyes of your spirit clearly see that you are not attacking your brother or sister but warning them that they are traveling a path that leads to a precipice, a vision is revealed to you for you to express holy love by urging your brother or sister not to continue in that direction.

Would a mother who loves with responsible love fail to admonish her child if they intend to fly a plane without knowing how? Would a loving mother fail to take her child to the doctor to be cured even though the child may not like it? Might scream and kick in a rage?

Love can be fierce, but it is always love. There are many things in the human heart that must be corrected, straightened, and healed, such as unhealthy habits, false beliefs, limiting ideas, fears, painful memories, ignorance, trends that do not offer happiness, and much more. All can be transmuted by love. All these things are but vital energy separate from being. Gathering them in to the love you are is the meaning of atonement. With that you reach the fullness of love.

It may feel like love throws you like water droplets into boiling oil. Do not reject that gift. Illuminating the world means that veils of ignorance must be uncorked so that they can be free. You are sent to your sisters and brothers so that the light of Christ that dwells in you may be seen.

If you act from the truth that is always love, you need not concern yourself about whether others accept you or not. When you are speaking from love, if your brother gets angry with himself or with you, I assure you that their anger is simply an initial reaction. Behind it is the desire to live in the truth. Sooner or later, depending on their will, the truth that has entered into them through your loving admonition that comes from the fierceness of love and the sweetness of my heart, will bear the fruit of light, perhaps in the first few moments, or maybe a few minutes later, or perhaps years later. Never mind; in all cases, it will create a new holy love. Remember the word springing from the heart of God is never sterile. I assure you that if your brother cannot receive the truth expressed through your holy admonition, another heart will do it. And finally it will return to your mind a hundredfold with luminescence, harmony, and holiness.

My children, I invite you to unite love and equanimity with the truth that lives in your hearts. Recognize the union between the fierceness and the sweetness of love—wings that give flight to the spirit and guide the mind that would live in truth.

Your Link with Divine Mother

Letter 11

My beloved children, I invite you to immerse yourself more and more in the infinite, unfathomable ocean of love of My Immaculate Heart. In it is room for everything and everyone. If you remain united to the love that lives in your being and transcends you, you will live fully. You will find the answer there to every true question, for it is within your being where truth lies. It is in your heart where the Father's love nests.

Each of you is a channel of light. It is up to you to allow the glory of Christ to shine through your being. No one is denied the divine essence that gives rise to the light. No one is excluded from creative love. Give thanks to God for giving you life and, above all, for giving you the entrance to eternity.

God's generosity knows no limits. All that is Hers is given to all. Do the same: give what you have received. Share your material and spiritual goods with others. Create a world where no one is excluded from your love. Everyone has something to give to others. Everyone needs something from others. This dynamic of both having and needing is what allows the force of giving and receiving as a unit to flow.

The old world was based on accumulating for oneself. But greed corrodes the human heart and must be put aside. The fear of not having enough leads one to skimp and treasure temporary things that imprison the soul. Be free! Do not adhere to anything or anyone except the truth that is always true.

Love and truth are one. Blessed is he who understands this great wisdom. In it resides the salvation of the world.

Some of you value yourself or others for a prosperity that is transient and has often been achieved at the expense of love. You rarely notice the damage done to achieve things, even those that seem worthy. I invite you to join essence with form, for not all forms are in harmony with love when trying to reach certain goals.

If the means are alien to love, so is the end. If the end is alien to holiness, so is the means. The perfect love is the Alpha and the Omega, the beginning and the end of everything that is real. To believe that the means can be separate from the ends is to live in separation, and contrary to truth.

In true divine creation there can be no separation. Everything is united in love. To consider that an end justifies any means is to misunderstand the light of divine wisdom. In love there is nothing that is not loving. The mind governed by truth remains united to love because it recognizes that it is united with the heart, the throne of perfect charity.

In the beginning there was no idea of the need to accumulate, which emerged as the daughter of fear, which arises from the lack of love. Only those who wish to be special seek to accumulate for themselves. And only the fearful can conceive of the idea of being special, because the desire to be special is the desire to be superior to others. This desire, disorderly because it does not come from love, is caused by a deep lack of love for oneself.

Those who remain in love know that they have everything because they dwell in the House of Truth wherein lies the wisdom of Heaven, the abode of true knowledge.

You were created by the creative love that God is. This makes you a co-creator. You have the ability to create your world. Put it at the service of love and you will be creating your Heaven.

Avoid drowning your heart by filling it with things you do not really need or desire. Go lightly through life. Be detached. Be generous. Extend what you are. Give others of your time, your talents, your joy, your wisdom, and your sincere love.

As long as you remain attached to my Immaculate Heart, I can work in you. We are a unit. This has been determined by the Mother-Father God of all, who created everything within the unchanging union of love. Nothing can exist outside that union. However, although you are united to me as every child is with their mother, it does not mean you will receive my love and enjoy my presence. For this, your disposition is necessary as it is in every relationship.

Child of my heart, I am calling you to be increasingly aware of our divine relationship. In it you will find the treasures of Heaven.

Come, you who have given me your "yes." Come and feel the sweetness of my love. Let the wisdom of Heaven be given to you through our sacred bond—the bond with the Divine Mother, the union with the Source of being. Just as one day I was carried in a glorious body and soul to the heart of God, so in due time will you—and all those who choose love—be also.

Rest in the peace of the union of our hearts. Let nothing disturb your heart as my child. This Mother who loves you with saving love, and who has been an instrument to give life to the human Christ, embraces you and envelops you in the tenderness of Heaven.

The beauty of God belongs to you. The feelings of the beauty of Christ are yours by birthright. Claim them now and forever. Be not interested in just gaining more knowledge. Put aside the desire to accumulate information. Focus your attention, rather, on the love you are able to give and receive. Realize that both are the same.

Who loves more can receive more love. And who is open to receive more, gives more. Giving and receiving are one and the same. Loving and being loved is a unit.

Trust my love. I am alive. Love made me eternal. The truth raised me to Heaven in my blessed transit. I bless you from the Kingdom. I embrace you from the heart of God. From my being I protect you every day of your life because of your choice to allow me to be a refuge for your mind and heart.

Stay in dialogue with me as much as possible. Do not believe that this dialogue is a hindrance to your life; quite the opposite. In it is a power that shapes human life.

Truly, truly I tell you my children, it is better to pray than to do. Always remain in me, as I remain in you. I am life. I am Mary.

Thank you for answering my call.

Humility

Letter 12

My children, today as always, I invite you once again to be humble of heart. Do not seek perfection in the manner of the world. Perfectionism comes from fear and is tinged with pride. Rather, accept your condition with love. Be not overwhelmed by guilt. When you notice thoughts of guilt, bring them to reason wherein lies the truth that of Christ, and you will see that you often worry about things that make no sense. And if your pangs of conscience come from actions that have caused suffering to others or to yourself, you will understand a loving lesson: love forgives and corrects everything. You will witness divine mercy.

Humility is an ointment to heal wounds because it is linked to truth.

To remain in me is to recognize that by yourself you can do nothing. Not a single beat of your heart would be possible without the Creator's consent.

Striving is fine, but not at the cost of the loss of peace. In order to understand this Source of wisdom and abide in it, it is necessary to be humble. You have been endowed with a discerning consciousness. Do not deny that gift from Heaven. Everyone has been given the holy ability to know where good resides. Do not forget that love and benevolence are one. If you cannot recognize kindness, you cannot recognize love. And yet you know where sweetness resides, where tenderness dwells. You know it because you are bearers of the wisdom of the heart.

My children, all is not well. If it were, the world would be a paradise and it certainly is not. I tell you this so that you do not set aside your moral discernment. Virtues beautify the soul when tempered with meekness and humility, for they come from Christ. To know what is holy it is unnecessary to dive into the marshes of lovelessness or to experience pain.

I invite you to live in the purity of love. The pure of heart are happy because their consciences do not admonish them. To love purely is to love for the simple reason of charity. It is giving everything of oneself to escape the confines of lacerating egocentrism that does so much harm to souls. It is also to stop thinking about oneself as the center of the universe. It is to understand and accept that only love is central. It is to cease exalting the little me. It is giving space to Christ to enlighten your heart.

Cultivate meekness in your heart so that you can be like God, who is always meek and humble of heart. Peace is the home of the humble because their minds rest in the calm waters of love and forgiveness.

Do nothing for yourself; do everything with your heavenly Mother. I assure you that if you act in this way, your life will be a serene transit to Heaven. I always await you with open arms. I invite you to cultivate our intimacy, to talk with me. In our love dialogues you will find great spiritual treasures. You will see everything in a new light, the light of truth.

Come to me every day of your life until our relationship is real. Make Christ your center. Give me your tears, your frustrations, and your dreams. I will transform them into pearls of holiness.

Be not distressed for the future, for this is what Mother is taking care of. Rather, dedicate yourself to living presently in my love. Nothing you worry about cannot be taken over by my Immaculate Heart. I know very well that you are living in difficult times both individually and collectively. For that reason I manifest myself more and more and I remain close by your side.

Hard times are times of Mary.

True humility will lead you to live life as children in the arms of this Mother of pure holy love. That way you will put aside your material, moral, and spiritual concerns. Do not deny your feelings but become aware of them, whatever they may be. Give them to me. Together we will do with them what God disposes for your good and that of all.

I speak to you as a Mother because that is what I am: the Mother of all and everything.

I wish to be intimate with each of my children. I thank you for listening to my voice and receiving my messages of love and truth. In these simple dialogues, without stridencies or great revelations, I dwell with you in the simplicity of truth.

My beloved, I invite you all to live in humility, simple at heart, the treasure of being. A simple life is a life of freedom. To remain in the purity of love is the greatest grace conceivable. I am the Immaculate Heart. I am the concord of love. In the union of our hearts lies the truth, united to the heart of my divine son Jesus. Remain in us. We are the reality of one love.

I bless you in Christ's love. Raise your eyes to the sun and you will not see shadows. When you embrace my love, the flow of divine union will fill you with blessings. Live thinking about the things of Heaven. The Most High takes care of the rest. Your Father has given you the Kingdom of Heaven so that you die eternally in the presence of love. Start living your Heaven now.

I extended love to all of you who receive these words They are for those who want to live in my love. Call me and in the blink of an eye I will enter and make a dwelling in your heart. And together we will sing forever of the wonders of the Lord.

I love you all.

The Hidden Christ

Letter 13

Beloved of my Immaculate Heart, the world is changing at a speed that often prevents you from understanding what is happening, and that induces fear. I invite you not to try to stay abreast of events. The reality of life is far more vast than the thinking mind can comprehend.

If you remain in me, you will understand what needs to be understood. Everything happens in relation to love. The universe is expanding more and more because it is getting closer to its origin and its end. It is on its way to fullness. God is the continent within which life is lived. The life of galaxies, planets, and that of humankind occurs within the womb of love. What you call the universe is a manifestation of the body of Christ. Within it and from it emerges the reality of time, space, and matter. Beyond Christ is nothing, because everything was created in Him and for Him. Christ is the Source of life, the Son of God.

There is no place where love is not. Sin, illusion, the absence of good, and death are unreal. They are attempts to create a reality beyond truth. Therefore they have no substance. This is why any mistake can be corrected when delivered to love. I invite you to trust in my Immaculate Heart increasingly. I am the divine reality made woman. I am the feminine aspect of Christ, although in me resides the whole. I am all that life is. In me is no polarization. I am being, integrated.

The force that sustains me is the same force that gives you life. The spirit that keeps the universes and your bodies moving is the same spirit of wisdom that dwells in me. Nothing exists outside of the vital breath that emanates from the divine Word. Everything is in the hands of love.

Often you make great efforts to seek God, making pilgrimages to sacred places or striving through spiritual techniques. All that is very good because of its purpose. However, child of my heart, nowhere does God stay closer to you than in your heart.

God dwells in you every day. Love lives in your holy mind and in every moment of your sacred existence.

Truly, truly I tell you that my being is closer to you than your thoughts.

There is no more intimate relationship in the universe than you have with me because the greatest intimacy possible is with your own mind and heart. Christ is the being you really are. Your inner love is a perfect extension of divine love and remains attached to it, just as a ray of sunshine remains attached to the sun.

I invite you to respect, honor, and value your intimacy above all. Without it you cannot keep your sanity. Take some time every day to be alone with this Mother full of love. Doing this takes no effort because you can cultivate inner silence, no matter where you are or what you are doing. Our relationship does not occur in the illusion of the world; it unfolds in the center of the heart, that space nobody and nothing can enter except you and me.

There is a holy temple not built with wood, brick, or stone—a divine place beyond all time and space. It is as eternal as God. That holy enclosure, that temple of Christ, is imperishable. Its foundation is built upon truth. It lacks walls because it is unlimited. Everyone is invited to enter and remain there. It is a tabernacle to perfect freedom. Everything in it is pure thought. Its incense is love. Its silence encompasses everything. This sacred cathedral—erected to the sanctity of being—resides within the peace of God. It is embraced by the light of Christ. In it celestial songs are heard, immemorial hymns of praise and gratitude, intoned in the language of the heart.

To remain within that immaterial temple full of love and truth is to remain in union with your being. There, and only there is where you really are, within the inner Christ, united with a love that is beyond all imagination and all words.

Your heart is the tabernacle where love dwells, as is each heart of your sisters and brothers and every living being. In them lies the wisdom of Heaven, as much as in you. Neither the personality of each one nor the heaviness of each physical body can make that truth disappear but only put a thin veil over it. And even that is illusion. Those who know how to see beyond appearances can see the hidden Christ, inviolate love where nothing unholy can reach.

In each of you there is untainted holiness and an unchanged eternal harmony—a beauty that nothing can dull, awaiting manifestation, a wisdom so above the knowledge of the world to be unreachable by the intellect. It is to that holy reality of your being, residing splendidly in your heart, where I wish to take you back with these messages.

Our direct relationship is real. To become aware of this is to become aware of the existence of the sacred temple where your being resides in perfect unity with Christ. It is to recognize the holiness of your heart. It is to gather human and divine nature into the single reality created by the Father of all. It is to return to the love you really are. It is singing a new song, the song of freedom of the children of God.

My children, you are called to love and to be the recipients of these messages. Every time you open your eyes, in everything you look upon, in every sound you hear, in every drop of rain that touches your bodies, is God in all Her glory.

Truly, truly, I say to you: extend your hands and you will be touching God. Open your arms and you will be hugging your heavenly Mother.

I bless you all in a love that will never end.

Thank you for answering my call.

Breadth of Love

Letter 14

Blessed sons and daughters, thank you for answering the call from Heaven. These letters are full of love and holiness. They were conceived in the heart of God to delight your heart in love and grace. Therefore, I refer also to those who, without knowing it, live united to my Immaculate Heart in a total union, according to their state.

Many are your sisters and brothers who, without being religious or who define themselves as not professing a faith, nevertheless seek the truth that comes from Christ. They are those whose sensitive hearts beat to the rhythm of beauty, goodness, and the holy desire to do good. They are the ones who yearn to dedicate their lives to what their hearts dictate from the depths of their holiness.

Putting these messages into words is a way to allow those who do not know how to express love to God to do so. It is also a means for many who are not aware of their immense love for this heavenly Mother to begin to be in spirit and truth.

There is a love without beginning or end, a love that does not disappoint, that never abandons, and that remains united to holiness and truth. It is a love that never ceases to be what it is, that magnifies what it takes. It is to that love that I am taking you, in my own way. I know you more than you know yourself. That allows me to know with perfect certainty what is the right approach for your life, according to your nature. This work is the means for you to become one with Christ.

You are receiving these words because your mind, united to the heart, has asked for it. Love has answered your call, just as you have answered love's call.

There is an endless universe beyond the Christ in you. Being has no limits. It never stops. It always advances. Once it reaches the peak of holiness, it continues to ascend throughout eternity towards more holiness, more love, and more extension. Herein lies one of the greatest mysteries of the divine—the mystery that makes everything continue to increase without ceasing to be the all of everything forever.

There are no limits to the ability to love. Allowing your heart to widen as much as the physical universe and beyond is what these words will do in you if you open to join the immensity of the Heaven that you are. For this reason, the structures that in the past you had built to obtain predictability that you confused with certainty have been dismantled.

God is unpredictable, but is always love. Herein lies the beauty of the eternal novelty of Christ. Accepting this reality is difficult for those who do not trust love, but not for those who know that deep within them is that "I don't know" that makes them live in love with the holy, the beautiful, and the perfect. They are sensitive hearts. They are called to love through their yearning for union. My letters are addressed to them, words loaded with tenderness and light.

I give you an invitation full of confidence in your being. It is a call full of certainty that you will achieve what is proposed. I invite you to live without fear, to live in the embrace of my Immaculate Heart. In our union you will find the necessary strength and true joy. The power of pure love that springs from my heart will envelop you, and you will attract what resonates with you. In this way you will prevent evil from nesting in your minds. You will fill your spirit with light and radiate Mother-Father God's glory.

Children who are in the world without being of the world, I remind you that holy love is the refuge of the soul. Purity is the delight of the heart, the nobility of spirit, the beauty of being, and wisdom is the joy of the mind.

Living in harmony with the truth that you are as God has conceived it from all eternity, is possible at all times, places, and circumstances. For this reason, God allows you to incarnate in a physical body so that you may dwell temporarily in the world. You are certainly not a body, but your earthly human experience requires a physical body. None of this should be a cause for concern or for destruction. I use this word, my child, not to have you be afraid by making painful associations. I do it so that you understand that the mind that does not live in truth, that does not know its right relationship to the truth that you are, gets lost in relationship and feels isolated.

To lose yourself in a relationship is to stop being yourself when you come into contact with another or with something. This can happen even when you relate to ideas. After all, for the mind everything is an idea, regardless of whether they whether it crystallizes or not.

If you remain in my love, I assure you that you cannot lose yourself. No matter where you are, or what experience you are having, you will always be united to the Source of the beautiful love you truly are. To avoid losing sight of our union I exhort you with love to make silence and restraint your eternal companions. In truth I tell you that every moment you are in silence dedicated to me, Heaven itself spills entirely into your hearts and a shower of blessings floods the Earth. Do not forget that silence is the portal to divinity.

Stay forever in love. And bring to my presence your sisters and brothers united to the truth of my Immaculate Heart and you will be happy forever.

Beautify the Earth with your holiness.

I bless you with perfect love.

Serve for the Love of Truth

Letter 15

My sons and daughters created by the Father of Lights! I invite you to live in the clarity of love—to leave the shadows. You were not called into existence to dwell in darkness. You are the children of the One who is the Source of all light. Christ is the perpetual sun from which life flows incessantly. Love is the Source of divine reality, the foundation of being. Everything exists within love. Outside of it there is no possible reality.

Those who live in purity remain in the luminosity of Heaven. They are happy because of the certainty that the light of true reason gives. Just as children are afraid of the dark, so too is the soul. That is the nature of your being; you are beings of light. You can never fully acclimate to living a life contrary to the truth of who you are. That is why you are called to cultivate loving thoughts, pure feelings, and holy habits. This will allow your minds to breathe freely, your hearts to sing for joy, and your spirits to rest in eternal peace.

Within you is a deep yearning for purity. Do not disconnect from it. Receive it in the inner silence, for it has a message from Heaven for you. Purity of heart is a gem of inestimable value. It gives you a clean and diaphanous look. It immerses you in contemplation of the divine. Only the pure of heart will see God.

The soul that embraces holiness lives in the innocence of truth. She is wise because she resides in the temple of reason.

She is even, simple, and just, looking to live in peace. And because you are looking for it, you will find it.

In your being resides the majesty of God. Do not overshadow this truth with what your mind may think. Knowing the truth is knowing God within yourself, and therefore recognizing Him in others.

Do not be distracted by others, nor by yourself. Keep your mind and heart in Heaven, for that is where you are. I assure you that in what you call death, you are not going anywhere. You remain forever with the same mind and heart you have today, the mind and heart God gave you. Therefore, cultivating the love of truth, which means loving the holiness of being that you truly are, is a prerequisite for happiness, now and forever.

If in death you are not going anywhere, and your mind and heart are still what they are today, what else can Heaven be but your soul living in the light of the Father's Glory? Within that light that never goes out are the wonders of God. Everything is in it, because everything is contemplated in harmony with the Creator's will, in whose truth is only the reality of love.

Knowing that only love is real and that nothing can attack the truth is to know Heaven. Mary, your Mother who gives Herself to you in purity and holiness, brings you to this knowledge. When you accept this truth, even within your earthly reality, you begin to live your Heaven on Earth. You extend the Kingdom to the world.

I will now tell you how you can come to know that which is beyond the interior Christ and constitutes the Source of life. I am speaking of that universe of infinite universes of eternal happiness and perfect love. The living Christ in you is the gateway to that reality of unalterable peace and indescribable beauty. Beyond your being resides the totality within which your being exists, into which only truth can enter. Only the holy is capable of joining that reality.

God is the substance of that universe of holy love. His holiness is the extension of Himself, born of the divine impulse to give of oneself entirely, a force that has given life to all that is. Only those willing to give themselves can abide in it.

Remember, my sons and daughters, that you reach the fullness of being by giving yourselves. The gateway to the realm of perfect love is in selfless service. No other way leads to the tree of life. Serve the cause and effect of love. To walk the divine path that these letters invite is to join the movement of beautiful love. It leads to the holy abode at the top of the celestial mountain. It is there that the New Jerusalem stands radiant and the new world is born, a world grounded in divine love from which the world of human experience is imbued with the light of Christ.

I invite you to serve Christ. I call you to a joy without comparison, the joy of sharing. I give you the certain path to eternal life: service to others. In it you will find your holy purpose. You will cease to feel the painful pang of meaninglessness. Do not be concerned about receiving something in exchange; giving love for the simple reason of loving is a joy that surpasses all imaginable pleasures. Truly I tell you that your heart will jump with joy every day if you live in the key of serving love. In this is no sacrifice except to put aside all that is not true. Is that a sacrifice?

Serving others in the love that you truly are, guided by the voice of wisdom that resides in your heart, is the highest degree that can be reached in being. There is nothing beyond it. Love serves life just as a path serves the walker. Of all services none is greater than that of quenching God's thirst for love for His children because this serves your Father and Creator as well as your sisters and brothers and every living being. Spiritual service allows the love of truth to return you to the depth of your heart. If you serve in this way, each glass of water that you give in the name of Christ will be a perfect expression of the love of God because it will be a prayer that says: "Brother, sister, here I am. Love has brought me. You are not alone. Together we are the unity of truth. You are loved. You are holy. You are a child of God."

Let us not be confused by false meanings of the service, nor by false love of oneself. Remember, love is not what you do but what you are. If you remain in me you will discern rightly in every moment, because you will do it from the love of your being in truth.

I give you my peace. I give you the treasures of my Immaculate Heart.

Freedom

Letter 16

My children born of the love of God, around you is a universe full of love and truth waiting to be recognized. If you unite with your holiness, which resides in your heart, you will remain in union with all that is holy, beautiful, and perfect. There is no such thing as an "outside" of you that is not linked to what you feel inside.

I invite you to pray for union.

You who have lived for so long in the illusory reality of separation need to remember what true union is. Everything exists within the union of love. Nothing can be disconnected from the totality because to do so would be to extinguish it instantly.

You have heard it said repeatedly and in many different ways that God is not present in the world. It has even been said that there is no room for God in the physical universe. That makes no sense. To search for love in a material object in itself, be it a grain of sand or a galaxy, is to misunderstand, because it is based on the belief that form and essence can be separate.

Love is beyond form. It is pure spirit. It is the essence of things. It is the Source of life.

You love because you have been loved first; otherwise, you wouldn't even have a word that expresses the reality of love. The word does not create, rather it gives expression to what already exists in the heart. When God said, "Let there be light," it brought forth light from the eternal light that existed before time and space. Light dwells in the bosom of the Father forever.

The voice of truth bears witness to it. Truth was never created; it is one with Mother-Father God. By the Word were all things called into existence, including you.

Well-loved children of the Father, your existence is sacred as is all life because it comes from God.

Love holds all things together within itself, not because this is a law but because creation is an expression of love.

When you were created you were given awareness. Through awareness you access knowledge within the bounds of free will. You are free to know or not. But you are not free to determine what reality is. Your words cannot create reality, they can only give life to what you long for in your heart. If you wish with all your heart to live in union, you will do so because nothing can go against the freedom of your soul.

You are free. Understand how great this gift is—and how much responsibility it demands of you.

I invite you to meditate on your true freedom as a child of God. This gift of the Father is often as misunderstood as is love. Indeed, trying to know one without the other is impossible.

Your biggest problem is not love itself, but freedom. It is often difficult for you to live in the vast breadth of truth. The destructuring of love scares you because you do not understand it. If you do not love true freedom you cannot live in the presence of love. Similarly, if you do not focus your lives on the love that you are as holy extensions of God, you cannot be free.

Freedom, love, and unity are truly one thing. This knowledge is only possible in relationship to God. That is why I invite you to pray for unity so that your consciousness is flooded with divine love and you know the only reality created by God. That reality is holy love.

I have come to free you from structures that oppress your heart. I have come to show you a way, the path of the amplitude of being. By loving, you know yourself in truth.

Your works are like the Word. They do not create reality, rather they manifest what exists in your heart. By doing so, your feelings, desires, and thoughts "come alive." They are externalized. Power becomes action. In this way consciousness seeks to know itself.

If your expressions come from the love that lives in you, they will live eternally. They will be a new "let there be..." arising from your divinity. If they come from a lack of love, they will be extinguished in due course, like leaves that fall from the tree of life, remain on the ground for a short time, and then vanish forever, absorbed by the Earth.

Your self is the tree that gives life to your works that are the expression of your feeling and thinking. If planted in the fertile soil of truth, they will bear holy fruit. If fed by what does not come from eternal life, it will become extinct like a malnourished tree which dies sooner or later.

Stay united to my Immaculate Heart and you will bear great fruit in spirit and truth. I am the unity of love. I am the reality of God. In me there is power and the action of the divine. I am a Mother who gives life in abundance.

Do not look outside for what is inside. Unity can only be found within. This means that to live in union with your brothers, sisters, and everything that exists, including God, it is necessary to remain in the unity of being. Do not seek recognition from the world, but seek to recognize love and you will have achieved the knowledge of unity. Thus will you be happy in the freedom of the children of God.

The New Earthly Kingdom

Letter 17

Listen, children of my heart! Hear the song of beautiful love. In your souls are the melodies of Heaven, songs of truth and holiness. Fall in love with Christ. Live loving the truth. If you put your attention within you, detached from all judgment, in union with divine wisdom and sincerely examine what happens in your lives and in the world, you will be able to discover the truth of everything.

The world needs purification. And so it receives it. Just like souls, life carries within itself what is needed to fulfill the divine purpose. The will of God prevails. Sometimes this involves suffering, but it is expiatory.

The universe is preparing for the new age on Earth, a new world governed by holy love. There will be nothing in it that is not true. Only souls who have made the choice for love can dwell in it.

You are creating your tomorrow. You do it in the only two possible ways. Either you join my divine Son Jesus in perfect love as co-creators of that new Earth full of light and goodness where pain will not exist and happiness will be full. Or you are excluded from it, as you have excluded yourself from paradise. The decision is yours.

The Father has a relationship with the physical universe. Observe, be silent, wait, and love with responsible love. God is transforming it within the womb of divine being. What is foreign to this divinity is extirpated; what is one with divinity creates new life.

You are called to share divine reality in all its extensions, including the creative dimension. In order to create with and for the Father, it is necessary to become one with the love that God is for the creative force of the heart of Christ to work through you.

Do not exclude yourselves from the Grace of the creation of the new Earth that is coming.

This is a call to join the cause and effect of beautiful love, recognizing that if you live in the truth revealed to you in your heart, and choose only love, you will participate in the wonders of a new world that is one with the I Am of God.

The Creator of all that is holy grants the universe the gift of being transmuted into a new physical reality whose resemblance to the Kingdom of Heaven is such that there is no distance between them. The land that was once created to bear witness to divine love, and then treated with disdain, will now be recreated in union with the children of God.

Choosing to be part of this universal movement in which a new earthly kingdom is erected is a choice for each being. That choice exists in every heart. Not only humankind, but all physical creation participates. Whoever wants to join love can do so now and always. This is the only true choice for the heart to make.

I invite you to raise your eyes beyond the circumstances of life. Do not be fooled by the ego that invites you to worry about trifles. Although they seem important, they are not, relative to the reality of the consciousness of the truth. Do not be distracted from truth. Hold your eyes on the inner Christ. Remain united to me. I can lead you to dwell forever in the light of truth.

The Father who loves you with mercy and treats you as well-loved children has given you a simple means to unite as the co-creator of the emerging new world. That means is to join my Immaculate Heart and the Sacred Heart of my divine Son Jesus. In the union of our hearts with yours resides the totality of Grace.

These messages will not reach all the conscious minds that inhabit the world. But they will be part of the new earthly kingdom. They will be received by those who, having chosen only love, are part of the souls that will enter the new creation of the Father. The name of each ,of those souls is written in the heart of God. It is to them that these words are addressed, so they remain attentive to the call from above and fill their hearts with joy in a hope that does not disappoint.

You will enter the new kingdom being born. Rejoice in Mary. Always remain united to me. Do not stray from the voice that your hearts recognize as the voice of truth. Every time you are alone with me, you open your soul to the flow of divine union, and with this become bearers of the creative power of the Father.

The universe is waiting, waiting for the response from all creatures. All are called to respond. Whoever says "yes" to Mother-Father God will live forever in the Kingdom. You will see with joy the beauty of the new land, a place as beautiful as it is holy. In this recreated paradise that emerged from the will of the Father in union with the children of light, laughter and revelry will be harmonious melodies heard on each summer afternoon full of calm and bliss. In this new earthly kingdom where the peace of Christ will reign, songs will only be perfect praises. The dances will be dances of life. And the expanse of souls will be as holy as their Creator. Everything will be light. In everything the face of love will shine until the souls that inhabit them sleep the blessed dream of the assumption in body and soul, joining the Mother of life to continue extending love forever.

In the new Earthly Kingdom will be no distance between the spiritual and the material. The unity of truth will be recognized and loved. It will be a perfect extension of the Kingdom of Heaven. Original purpose will return to the expression of being, making itself known and extending itself by nurturing from the force of the only created reality—the reality of love.

Thanks for answering my call.

I give you the blessing of my Immaculate Heart.

I embrace you in the peace of God.

Eternal Assumption

Letter 18

My sons and daughters, this heavenly Mother, who loves you with infinite goodness, invites you again to return to the foundation of truth. The world is a monumental system of illusion that moves away from truth. Thus, it is necessary for you be attentive to what happens inside you in order not to fall into error and believe that what is not is real.

There is only one true reality: that created by God. There is only room in it for the loving, the holy, and the pure. Its foundation is the Creator's design. Its substance is truth. In its firmament shines the light of wisdom, next to which lives the certainty of divine knowledge. It is a reality of pure holy love; nothing real exists outside of it.

Knowing how to distinguish between fantasy and reality is a sign of sanity. The things of the world are not part of the reality created by God. The things of Heaven are. Accepting that difference is the way of salvation. Therein lies perfect discernment.

What is eternal comes from God. What is temporary does not. However, the ephemeral can be put at the service of love, and in this way is integrated into truth. Loving and living in truth are inseparable. Do as your heavenly Father does: love everything, respect differences, honor everything, but never accept as true what is not.

I assure you that truth is as important as God. I invite you to live in it every day and you will be free. Relationships undertaken for worldly ends do not arise from truth but from fear. Relationships that arise from the reality of the divine, as the fruit of holy love, are offspring of the Father.

Bring your relationships to my Immaculate Heart. I will free you from what does not come from the truth in them; I will enlighten them so they are the Source of true freedom in love. You are not devoid of anything. You are not incomplete. You do not need anything. All that your being needs to be in alignment with God is eternally given through your Source of life.

The needs you have created in the world are illusory. The reality of the Kingdom of Heaven has no lack. There is only the eternal completion of love. Being complete beings is God's will for his creations. If you remain in me I assure you that you will know the absence of need. You will be abundant in God's way. You will never feel alone again and you will understand that your life has a divine purpose far beyond the trivial goals of the world.

I am calling you to embrace the truth. To love God above all. Whoever lives in truth lives in love. Do not place your trust in the ideas of the world, nor in the systems of thought that you have taught yourselves in an attempt to obtain a security that never comes and a happiness that quickly fades.

There is a Kingdom of pure goodness, beauty, and holiness awaiting you. That Kingdom is entered through the prayer of union. The distance between God and you is smaller than between your mind and a thought. That is how close God is to you now. I invite you to enter the Kingdom. You will always find me there. There are no barriers between your being and the reality of love except the will to not live in truth. You are free to dwell in the realm of truth or not. But you are not free to determine where endless bliss dwells, nor what is the holy abode in which the sweetness of God's love dwells, forever shining in the immutability of truth.

The kingdom is here. Entering it depends on your will. No one is denied access. All are chosen. Love is inclusive. Come now and always dwell in the reality of Heaven which resides in your true consciousness.

If you remain united to the inner Christ you will be taken beyond that holy union to the fullness of love, to the Source that gives life to all beings and light to all minds that inhabit the truth.

I insistently call you to raise your eyes and not to stop your ascension to Heaven.

To you who have reached the peaks of holiness because you have said "yes" to love and are willing to live in the truth, and ask yourself, "What now?" I answer: "Once you have reached the top, continue climbing."

I am about God's business. If you will allow me, I can help you rise above all imaginable sorrows and challenges.

I invite my children to fly the flight of the Mother of Heaven, a flight powered by the breath of beautiful love and the wind of truth.

My beloved children, join now with my Immaculate Heart. Continue flying Mary's flight. Together we will know the wonders of God in the perpetual novelty of the eternal assumption of souls who love the truth and live in the purity of holiness.

Blessed be my children. You have chosen the best part and it shall not be taken from you. Live forever in truth.

Thanks for answering my call.

In the Light of Love

Letter 19

My children, your being is one with Christ. Your reality is an extension of the holiness of the Father.

Do not expect anything from anyone or anything, except the truth. Only divine love can fill your hearts. The rest is just temporary.

There is a place within your being where you are full, and you receive a love that completes your life. Immerse yourself in it so that you may know in greater depth the delights of a love not of this world, although it may manifest in it. I want to plunge you into a love that never disappoints, a love that is always faithful. God never abandons. This is a love that saves, that heals wounds, that corrects fraternally, that elevates and transforms everything you touch into more love. This love has no opposite. It is true. It doesn't hurt. It embellishes creation, its Source. It is eternal and knows not the shadows because it is the light of life. It is a love without beginning or end.

I call you not to settle for less than this love. You have been created for greatness. Do not settle for the low when the high has been given. Do not accept anything below God Himself. Accept only Heaven. Spread your wings in love. Take up your flight and come to this heavenly Mother. I await you with open arms, at the peak of wisdom, where your true holy being dwells. I wait for you so that together we continue on the eternal flight of divine knowledge.

I call you not to accept as true what is not. Do not make love what it is not. Do not believe that those illusory loves that are not true love can give you what your soul longs for. They never could and never will. There is no creature capable of completing you because you belong to God and only God fills you fully.

Do not take on loads you cannot carry. You are not God nor do you need to be. God, who has given life to each soul and the entire universe, has a plan for each of Her children, and carries it out in the silence of each heart.

What you call the vicissitudes of life are often nothing but the normal development of things in a passing kingdom, but because of your attachments, pain is generated. Believing that something temporary can give you happiness is to misunderstand. Only the love given will fill you with joy and a sense of purpose.

I invite you to remember frequently that love is nothing like what the world has taught. Love is God. Therefore, it cannot be taught or learned. It can only be known, accepted, and lived. Living love means living in truth. And the truth tells you that a being who has the same nature as you cannot be the source of your happiness, or of anything that is yours. The light that you perceive with your eyes does not obtain its energy from itself or from any other similar light. It obtains energy from that which is its Source. So it is also with the light that emanates from a pure soul. It comes from the Source of the light of life, life that is of Christ, and flows through it.

Let the truth set you free. Stay in truth always and you will not worry about things that have no real meaning, even if the world values those things.

The love of God cannot be lost. You cannot leave your life. God can never abandon you. Neither can my love, because it is the same love with which everything created was created. Once you accept this truth, which your heart knows perfectly well, you free yourself from the pain of loss, which does not come from truth.

Nothing real can be lost. Nothing unreal is part of your being. Only what God has given in your creation is true. In other words, only the treasures of the Kingdom belong to you.

If you lovingly rebuke your brother and he turns away, let him go. Those who are not prepared to accept the truth do not want to hear it. Even though they are offered an opportunity to rise, they prefer to turn a deaf ear and turn their backs on what love reveals. Do not be angry even though your heart is sad to see truth be rejected. Bless those who are not ready to see in the light of Christ, and press on. God, in his infinite goodness, will give you new opportunities to spread love. There will be those who accept it.

Your role is to allow love to spread through you. Speak from the treasure of the abundance of truth. Place your eyes at the service of love and your hands and feet serving God. This is possible when your minds and hearts live immersed in truth. This is giving love in the way of Christ. What others do with it is a matter between God and their soul. Do not forget that each creature has a relationship with their Creator. What happens within cannot be invaded by anything or anyone.

Put everything in the hands of God's love and trust that She will know what to do. Always go forward. Holding my hand, we walk together in truth. I assure you that if you live that way, your lives will be a perfect reflection of holiness and your hearts will jump with joy in love.

I give you my Peace.

Thanks for answering my call.

Dialogue

Letter 20

My sons and daughters, again I invite you to pray for true union. Not infrequently you seek to unite in ways that have nothing to do with unity. Those of you who have lost the ability to recognize love need to constantly grow in the knowledge that comes from above. This is why I manifest myself more and more every day—to bring you to a greater understanding of God's love.

Those who have not yet shed their fixation on their own interpretations, giving exaggerated importance to their ways of thinking, experience difficulty in accepting the changes that life, out of love, presents to them.

Do not forget that God loves you with an unstructured love. Do not cling to systems that simply come from a mental construct designed to create a sense of security in a world perceived as insecure. Only perfect love is a refuge for your heart. Only truth can bring security to the mind.

Unions based on imposing on others a criterion of thought, whatever it may be, do not come from love because love is incapable of arrogance. Forcing others to submit and conform to what one thinks, however holy that desire may seem, is alien to true charity. I cordially invite you to abandon all attempts to impose your will on others or subdue anyone, for in doing so you will lose sight of love. Be not afraid of freedom.

Unity resides in the realm of freedom and nowhere else. When life gives you the opportunity to release structures in order to expand the experience of freedom, allow it to do so. Love will free you from the bonds you built to feel safe, and in return will give you the certainty of truth, in which you will remain safe forever.

Dialogue is unity; unity is dialogue. When you pray for union, you are praying for the construction of a world where dialogue and harmony are its foundation. After having lived for so long in a way alien to the will of God, you need to grow in the ability to dialogue. You cannot do so without receiving Heaven's Grace.

"Ask and it will be given to you," my divine son Jesus told you. Today, this Mother says to you, "Ask for the grace of union." Ask with faith and a sincere desire to live in peace. Do not define what union is. Allow the Most High to flood you with His love and the wisdom of Heaven will be the Source of your knowledge and action. In it you will know what it is to live in the highest harmony.

When you think you have a plan that seems good and adequate for God's purpose, pray and ask me to enlighten you within our union. Then let go of your ideas about how things should be. Always live in love. You know what creates harmony and what creates disharmony. Do not cling to your plans. There is the Plan of God; only He can make it a reality in each of his children, and in the whole of creation.

Blaming others for the world's or for your alleged problems is to attack and only leads to more separation. Staying united in love is the way of creation. Being responsible for something does not mean being guilty, but your lives are a response. Respond with love to everything and you will see how your reality is submerged in the beauty of peace. Let yourself be filled with wisdom by the One who is its Source and you will know how to distinguish between perfect and imperfect love.

If what you say and do comes from love, you will know by what you feel in your heart.

The difficulty of dialoguing and creating a kingdom of union and harmony comes from the desire to impose your criteria.

This is caused by the belief that your truth must be followed by other truths because you believe that truth is weak and needs to be imposed.

Children of God, that does not come from love and has never brought peace.

I call you to walk the path of fraternal dialogue. If others don't listen to you, don't attack them. Give up the notion that you can change what is and what will be through attack, for even if you might achieve something through it, I assure you that it will be at the expense of your peace. Do not seek conquests, nor treasure victories, but seek to create a world of peace and harmony.

May your homes be temples erected to harmony and your lives be expressions of God's love so that wherever you are you can breathe a climate of spiritual purity.

I bless you all.

Thanks for receiving my messages. Make them yours. Live them. Embody true charity.

Be the face of Christ on Earth.

The New Baptism

Letter 21

Beloved children of my heart, I have come to sow peace in your hearts.

Often your mind is crowded with images and ideas far from the holy, harmonious, or pure. This troubles your souls. Sooner or later that embarrassment will manifest itself in a form that causes pain to yourselves and others unless, through prayer, you immerse yourselves in the waters of God's love, and are washed as in holy baptism.

I invite you to live in constant prayer. Then you will absorb the wisdom of God and be watered by what flows from the heart of Christ. Every time you pray you become more beautiful. New colors beautify your soul and lights radiate from your heart with a beauty that surpasses the imagination. You illuminate the world with the light of love. You clean the Earth and all that lives on it. You create a spiritual force that emanates from you, decontaminating the air and universal consciousness.

You have no idea how important prayer is to your soul. Truly, truly I say to you that prayer is as essential to your mind and heart as food is to your body. Without it, the soul perishes. Prayer is the life of the pure soul.

I want to give you the joy of prayerful souls. I call you to live together with my Immaculate Heart so that you can experience the joy of union. When your behavior moves away from love, it is because in your heart you have turned away from me.

Dedicate time to the conscious encounter with God, at least every morning when you awaken and every night before you retire. Little by little, that time of prayer will be transformed into a life of infinite love. You will see a new sun rise every morning, the sun of charity. In its light you will see the truth about yourself as Christ sees you. You will find the purpose of your existence.

Being alone with the Creator is the joy of souls in love. In that union you cannot dissociate yourself from holiness and truth. If you remain united to the love you are, whose Source is God, you will find a wise balance and your actions will be expressions arising from divine reality.

Beloved children, in this revelation is the answer to every pain in your hearts, where you ask, "What happened that I acted without love? What is the reason I don't do all the good I want and do the bad I don't want?"

If you remain united to your inner Christ, your actions and omissions will be holy. To remain in union with God prayer is necessary. That is why I invite you again and again to love prayer and make it the center of your life.

My sons and daughters, no spiritual growth is possible without prayer; there is no salvation without it. Within the relationship of divine love are the seeds of a full life. You water them with drops of heavenly dew springing from the heart of God every moment you spend in prayer and contemplation. A single thought is enough to unite Heaven with Earth. A single loving feeling is capable of unimaginable miracles. I assure you that your will, united with that of your Father and Creator, is more powerful than any force that exists in the physical universe, and even more than the sum of all of them.

Enjoy being new in Christ in every moment. Be reborn every day. Come to me and you will leave our meeting renewed in the baptism of union. Give yourself the treasure of unity that your Father gave you in your creation.

If you observe that your soul is or was out of harmony, regardless of the cause you think led to it, simply remind yourself that in some way you must have disconnected from the call of love. And just go back to it. Nothing more is needed. The musings, the searching for reasons, and the endless examinations that never lead to certainty, are simply attempts to delay your return to loving contemplation.

You live in a time of great challenges for souls. These are difficult times, this time of Mary. I have told you this so that you do not separate from me, not for a moment. I assure you that there is nothing holy apart from my divine love.

Within my heart you will find the safe haven for which you yearn. No need to wear yourself out working day and night to build buildings that will fall sooner or later. No need to accumulate things that can corrode to obtain a security that does not last.

Only one thing is necessary to live safely and in peace: live united to the love of God.

I bless all my children.

I give you my peace.

Thanks for answering my call.

Spiritual Growth and Enlightenment

Letter 22

My children, the world is submerged in a great darkness. It is up to you to realize the light. Christ is closer to your being than the air you breathe. This Mother always accompanies you and becomes one with those who receive my messages and give them life by making them their own.

A new time in universal consciousness has begun, the end of duality, the time when darkness comes to light to be illuminated by love. You who have chosen only love are part of the movement that makes the light of Christ shine on the new humanity being born.

Do not despair of the world's calamities. Stand firmly confident in my Immaculate Heart. God always triumphs; this must be the basis of your security and perfect certainty. You are my helpers—helpers of love. For that I call you to serve the cause and effect of beautiful love.

Remember, in unity we are one body. In the holiness of being we are one soul. In the light of love we are one heart. United in the beauty of Christ is the reality of the love that God created, of which you are a part.

You have been brought to union with Christ, your being. Now you will be carried sweetly on the wings of love to the Source of eternal life, if you are willing. Beyond our union is what cannot be put into words.

There is no possible salvation without you because God does nothing without His children. I invite you to meditate on this message so that you recognize how important your soul is. The world depends on your loving consciousness. The Earth is transformed with the holiness that you express with your loving thoughts and pure feelings.

You are in the world to save your soul and those of others. They are linked because they are part of the totality that you really are. In Christ we are one mind, one holy being, one pure love.

I call upon you to share with others and with the world the revelations you receive. Everyone receives inspiration from Heaven. Some are more aware than others. Even so, no one who lives in the world is fully aware of all the love they receive from God. Divine love floods you in an incomparable way. As it is received, your being widens to receive more in endless receiving and extending.

Each of you is aware of the love you receive from God according to the wisdom of the Creator. Make that measure grow by sharing until you become so expansive that there is no distance between the heart of God and yours. Let yourself be embraced by a love without beginning or end. Absorb the mystery. Broaden your heart to receive the fullness of the infinite.

In truth I tell you that the more you give of your true being, the more you receive. The more spirit you give, the more spirit you receive. That is why I tell you: *Ask for spirit.* As you receive more spirit, you will joyfully experience the unfathomable breadth of your heart.

The world needs your light, your holiness. You have come to Earth in these times by the will of the Father to be beacons that illumine the nations, to be perfect reminders of holy love. In the middle of the dark night that humanity is going through, you are prophets of light. With your presence alone you dispel darkness. With your works, together with my Immaculate Heart, you bring hearts to Christ and help collective and individual healing of memory. You are loving instruments of perfect healing.

Put love in everything you do regardless of whether your works seem great or insignificant in the eyes of the world. Remember that in the hour of truth, a moment of universal expectation, only one thing will be taken into account: the love given.

I tell you these things so that you are attentive to give love every day without interruption of time, place, or circumstance. There are endless ways to express the love that lives in your heart. Do so according to your nature. Every expression of love is perfect because of the reality from which it comes. Do not stop in your mission of extending love.

Sow love in your homes, in your work, in prayer groups. Bring pure love to your loneliness—a blessed opportunity to extend holy love to yourself and be alone with your Creator. Make your life a temple dedicated to harmony. You will not lack help from Heaven for your mission. Do not worry about what you will eat or wear tomorrow. I, the Mother of the living, watch over all my children and provide what is needed to those who listen and follow my voice.

Do not seek to be right, for such will not be taken into account in the hour of truth. Rather, work diligently and with serenity of spirit, in filling your coffers of love so that when you face the truth you can rejoice with me, your holy Mother, because of so much love given. Love the creatures of the Earth. All are of the highest. They all are walking in their way. Be a balm for them in their journey.

Become a carrier of pure water for your sisters and brothers thirsty for love and truth. They have their struggles, and often do not know what is happening to them. You, on the other hand, have received revelation. Make that blessed gift from Heaven an instrument to make the world happier so that your sisters and brothers can rest in peace in your presence and join more and more to the love of loves the blessed presence that dwells in souls, most holy guest who murmurs in the silence of hearts that long for truth.

Go around the world sowing peace. I will go with you.

I thank you for answering my call.

The Holy Indifference of the World

Letter 23

Children of my heart, not a soul that walks the Earth that does not cry at the horrors it sees in the world. You feel those feelings; all that arises within. Do not anesthetize your hearts. The soul that longs for the truth cannot help but grieve before the desolation of heartbreak discovered at every step in the human experience. Your walk is painful and sorrowful. There is a thorn in your heart. The more sensitive you are as a soul, the more painful it is.

Beloved of God, honor every feeling that springs from your holy being. If you unite to my Immaculate Heart with every beat of your heart, I assure you that all feeling will be transformed into an active force whose power creates a new reality arising from divine love.

Your feelings are a calling. Go beyond them to the truth they seek to reveal. Learn to recognize their language. They exist for a reason. Do not deny or attack feelings; accept them as messengers of the soul. Do not rush to interpret what they would tell you. Do not act without the due reflection that arises from loving contemplation.

Not everything you experience comes from the inner Christ. If you exercise in the silence of the heart, you will know what love is asking you in each feeling and thought. God calls and answers, in a gentle discernment for your life.

If you trust in love to the point of making that trust the engine of your life, you will know that it cannot call you to something without also giving you the perfect answer, and without creating the necessary condition for the call to be fulfilled. This is what it means, "I am the Alpha and the Omega."

The wisdom of Heaven, whose Source is the heart of God, extended to the human spirit in its creation. From that, it expressed in the form of thought and feeling through the mind and heart to create the reality of the human-divine experience. Then it returns to Heaven from whence it came having increased its beauty, holiness, and luminosity in its passage through your soul. Thus is a new holy love created. This is the flow of divine power, the genesis of truth which travels from the Source of eternal life to each created mind, spreading in endless movement. This is the reality to which human nature is called, as established by the original plan of the Creator.

The power of your spirit is great. It is as great as is everything that comes from God.

I call you to cultivate the capacity for loving reflection which is perfected in silence.

Be not afraid of what you feel or what you think. Embrace what you call "the energy" of your thinking and feeling, and allow your consciousness of pure love to do what Christ chooses. If wisdom calls you to action, it will be communicated with perfect clarity; likewise if you are called to waiting or contemplation. Do not believe that doing is more important than praying. Nor that plans arising from a mind separated from love can result in something loving.

There is only one way to create a new world: by remaining within the consciousness of Christ, in union with love where the Source of creation is one with you. It is living consciously in that union that the power of Heaven spreads through your soul and creates a new reality in God's way.

Only the Word of God creates life. Join with the Word and a new creation will emerge. God is Lord of the Universe. And while He does nothing without His children, it is He who is responsible for carrying out, with them, the plan of atonement. All that is needed from you is a holy willingness to open your heart, and allow love to do what only love can do. Only love can save the world, and it will. It is the word of God.

To the extent that you bring your feelings and thoughts to loving contemplation arising from the silence of the heart, you will learn to recognize the language of love which is beyond every word and thought in the world.

You see only a very small portion of reality. That is why you must accept that pain is a mystery, as life is. Give me your tears so that I can transform them into diamonds of holiness. Make your hearts an echo of my Immaculate Heart.

I invite you to unite your heart to mine more and more. Thus we will be the beating heart of God.

Do not despair, for love always triumphs. The day will come when the new earthly kingdom will be seen and lived in the light of the Glory of the Father. And you, who cry today because of the heartbreak of the world, will live forever in a bliss that has no end.

Help me create a new world. Join the movement of beautiful love that this Mother is instituting. Remain united to the consciousness of Christ. In this way, let your pain be active. Move to me now, and together we will transform reality in the peace of Heaven. Do not leave God out of the solution, or your sisters and brothers, or yourself. United in Christ, we all create a new Heaven and a new Earth.

I give you the grace of holy indifference to the world, a gift that will prevent you from falling into the trap of the ego, which would convince you that all is lost, or that things can be resolved without God.

I assure you that you are living the triumph of my Immaculate Heart. The darkness is coming to light more and more. A new sun is rising. A new reality has arrived. Go around the world announcing the good news. Christ is here!

I thank you for answering my call.

Light of Wisdom and Truth

Letter 24

Children of my heart, the Source of creation is pure holy love. The consciousness that gives existence to everything and sustains everything in life, manifests itself to know itself. You are one of those manifestations of the pure awareness of divine love. You have the capacity and the inherent impulse to meet your true self. Do not drown that aspect of your being. Seek to reveal the mysteries of Heaven, otherwise you will descend to the level of unconsciousness where you cannot live fully, nor be happy, just as a fish cannot live out of water. Do not stop your ascension flight.

You have been given the gift of being bearers of divine knowledge.

Knowing oneself is possible only in truth, otherwise what you end up believing is false, an illusion. What life is and what you are is one and the same since there is life in you, the only life that is real. Life emanated from the Source of every being.

Living in harmony with what you are is the Kingdom of Heaven itself. Your spirit is endowed with celestial powers, which insistently ask to express themselves as they really are. For this reason it is so important to embrace the authenticity of the heart.

Life and truth go hand-in-hand, as do love and harmony. Where there is no concord there is no true love because there cannot be peace.

Do not make your bodies or your personalities an end in themselves, for they are not. What you are is far beyond both.

You are spirit created by pure love. You are of a Christ nature. Recognizing this truth and becoming one with it, knowing the reality of what this means, constitutes the only possible knowledge because it is the only truth. Only love is real; everything else is illusion.

Realization drives every being. Reaching it is impossible without reaching true knowledge. Being and knowing are one and the same. To be realized is to know oneself in the only true light, the light of truth. In it the being recognizes the One who created it, the faithfulness that it owes to it, and accepts that the fullness of its being lies in giving.

Give yourselves to every moment of your existence and you will reach the fullness of what you really are. Do not spare your talents you have been given to be happy and enjoy the treasures that arise from their expression. They are for everyone.

Humankind has been too focused on looking at his or her self-image, and not looking at the surroundings and God in the light of wisdom and truth. That gaze, centered on an idealized image of self, makes it the only thing of value to be seen. This is the basis of self-preoccupation and the seed of everything that does not come from love. You have a word for it: narcissism. It is essential for you to recognize that there is a way to seek knowledge that is alien to God. That way of knowing what you are will not lead you to anything of real value, or to peace.

Only in God can you know yourself as you really are. Only in love can you express yourself as you were created to be. Love and authenticity go hand-in-hand. This is because everyone has a unique way of expressing true love.

For this reason I ask you again and again not to look at your self-image and ignore what others are doing. I ask you with all my heart to keep your eyes on me.

I am not illusory or an idea that seems very beautiful but is without reality. I am as human as I am divine. I am one who achieved the full realization of being. I am the voice of love expressing through the one known as the co-redeemer and Mother of the living.

I come to you in the form of the Mother because you need Christ's consciousness to be known. Love and balance are a unit. Your being lives fully when it remains in that equanimity.

For many of you, I am the expression of the feminine side of divine creation. However, children of my Immaculate Heart, the truth has no gender. In my being is everything true, just like yours. There is no such thing as feminine and masculine, but one integrated being, an all-encompassing seamless reality of holy love. But as you need to integrate symbols in a way that can be understood by a mind accustomed to duality, I have made myself present in the world as Mary and Jesus. Both are me. You cannot separate them and understand the truth that they are. Both are the perfect expression of unity in an inseparable union. Both are the union of all that is true, all that is human and divine, matter and spirit, time and eternity.

If I had not embodied as a man and a woman, I could not complete the journey on the path of perfect knowledge because I would not have integrated the reality of your souls. You are all that Jesus Christ is, and what Mary is, in unison. You cannot be one without being the other. Your being has been endowed with the power of will, the authority of the truth, the forceful impulse for the action of love. Your being has also been endowed with the tenderness of God, the softness of charity, the impulse to beauty, and the ability to engender life—with a mind that harbors truth and a heart in which love dwells.

The time has come when we call upon the masculine and feminine aspects of being to express in harmony and live in peace. This is how your consciousness will return to the state of unity and remain there. The time has come for the integration of all that is true.

Stay in unity. Live pure love. Express the beauty of your holy being. I invite you to create more union together. In this way, a new Heaven and a new Earth will be the living expression of the union between the divine and the human. Love is calling you to create a new world, arising from the harmony of truth.

Give the world the white lilies of forgiveness.

Water the Earth with the light of your holiness.

Be a blessed present for your sisters and brothers.

I send you to the world as a gentle breeze to refresh minds and brighten hearts.

Love for the simple fact of loving, and your pure hearts will be blessed incense. You will be like roses full of beauty that the Father of creation gives to others by my immaculate hands for the simple reason of charity.

I give you my blessing so that you remain strong in love, firm in truth, sweet in holiness, and joyful in the tenderness of God.

Thanks for answering my call.

Refuge of Divine Love

Letter 25

My precious sons and daughters of light, once again I tell you that you are living in difficult times but times of great transformation.

I say this not to scare you, nor to create worry, but because it is so, and that you do not despair. These times were contemplated in the divine mind since before time. Nothing escapes divinity.

Do not despair. Do not listen to voices that invite you to fall into negativity. Learn to discern between the holy admonitions of love and the expressions of fear that often scare my children and do not come from Christ.

I call you, today more than ever, to live together with my Immaculate Heart, refuge of souls. Within my love as Mother of everything created you will find the peace, tranquility, and the harmony that your spirit craves. I am closer to you than your own breath.

If you remain in my love there is no reason to despair. There is no reason to fall prey to negative thoughts in relation to humanity's future or present.

Hold high in your consciousness the truth that tells you that God exists and is love.

These are hard times, yes. Great convulsions will ensue—manifestations of the pain of the birth of Christ in human hearts and in every element of physical creation.

Love is being born in you. The truth is being born in the world of illusion. Bliss is being born in the midst of grief.

Christ is disarming structures. Destructuring love is clearing the way for the new that is already here, although not everyone can see it yet.

I assure you that those who take refuge in me will not suffer a single scratch. They will see the waves splash and the winds whip, but those who trust in the Mother of love will not have even a single droplet touch them, nor will they be shaken by any movement.

Special protection is offered to my daughters and sons around the world. It is the shield of pure love that springs from the Immaculate Heart of the Mother of God. I have come to reveal to you this great blessing. A special grace is given to humanity and all creation, the grace of being clothed with a strength like no other, and a wisdom that surpasses all human intelligence known so far.

In difficult times, unparalleled thanks! This is also justice.

Join in prayer. Not with prayers born of fear, but of the joy of knowing that God exists and that God is love. Join in prayers of the joy of recognizing oneself as the children of Mary and of the certainty born of full confidence in the love of the Father.

Christ is calling you to put hymns of praise and gratitude to the life that has been given to you before the funeral songs that the world sings. Be the counterweight of the new times. Go into the world with a sincere smile on your faces. Be an authentic expression of the joy of your heart, all of you who have experienced the beautiful love that fills souls and flows from the Heaven that Christ is.

A special grace is given you, the grace of consciously staying in the refuge of divine love that has been created for the protection of all. Come, claim your right to live in the peace of God. Shelter in holy love. Live in the truth that is always true.

For even a single moment do not leave this Mother devoted to the salvation of Her children. You will be saved to the extent that you join the inner Christ and let yourself be carried beyond divine union to the Source of eternal life. There you will be what you have truly been called to be from the moment of your creation.

You who welcome my messages with love because you are willing to listen to the voice of truth and follow it, you have been chosen among many to bring true joy to the world. You demonstrate that in this world one can be happy because everyone can let themselves be loved. And so they are flooded by the benevolence of God's power.

Stay in me and together we will extend love, creating new worlds of light, harmony, and holiness. Your life will gain transcendent meaning in our union because love is the origin and end of life. Because of those who chose love, the purity of our divine relationship will expand the vortex of light that has been opened between Heaven and Earth. They have brought the reality of the Kingdom so close to that of the Earth that everything is ready to take a step forward towards the achievement of the times of Jesus and the birth of the era of Mary. A time like no other is upon us, where the fullness of love will be seen, accepted, and recognized for what it is.

Join this movement of the beautiful love that is being born! Do not confuse the symptoms of Christ's birth with those of pain caused by heartbreak.

The virgin, the pure innocence of the Christ in each of us, has given birth in the desert. A new earthly Kingdom is being born, the Kingdom proclaimed and established by my divine Son Jesus. Join the creators of this new reality. Be one among the many who, holding Christ consciousness, create a new world in peace.

Do not drown out what your heart sings in its depth: Love is the eternal winner.

I bless you all in the peace of God.

Thanks for answering my call.

Call of the New

Letter 26

My sons and daughters, the spiritual path has phases.

There comes a time when you must stop looking at the shadows of the soul, and see only and exclusively the light and sanctity of being. Do not look at what you consider your sins, the destructive, the confusing, what does not cause happiness. Rather, once the inner darkness is accepted, put it in my Immaculate Hands and let your Mother take care. Focus your eyes on the luminosity of your mind and the purity of the heart.

Look at me and nothing but me. I am a mirror of divine purity. In me you will find the sanctity of your true identity. You will know the wonders that God created for Her children, among whom you are, a child of God, a child of Mary, my child of holiness.

I invite you to live in the light. I call you to radiate the good, the holy, and the beauty of your souls. In every heart is love, just as in every mind is truth. Both are seeds you can water and grow more every day. It is up to you to water them, or not. You are free. You are children of light.

You cannot do anything in the past nor in the future. But you can know the truth in the eternal present that perfect love is. Living in the light means cultivating in your souls the flowers of holiness. You know them well. Everything of harmony, sweetness, elevation of the word, nobility of feelings, and generosity comes from Christ.

Do not mingle in conversations that steal your peace. Participate only in that which elevates your soul. Not everything that travels the roads of the world contributes to your fullness. Learn to discern between what is beauty and what is not. And commit to the light.

Happiness exists because love exists. Your heart knows well what the happiness of being is and yearns to live in it every day. Allow yourself to live well. Lead a life full of holy purpose and certainty in the truth, a reality flooded by pure love. Experience the purity and cleanliness of the soul that clears all doubt and that which hurts the heart.

Become one with beauty, harmony, and unity so that your light may grow in your consciousness; that way you can feel the joy of holiness. Tolerate each other for love. Speak for love. Think of God. Reprimand lovingly those who need to know the limits that truth imposes in order to live in peace. Bring joy to the world. Make those you meet wiser and happier.

Each of you has the power to make a Heaven. I invite you to become aware of that power of the soul and honor it in Christ. I call you to join me so that together we can create a new earthly Kingdom. I know, because I have always known you, that you do not consider yourself holy and wise enough to do something like that. But children of my Immaculate Heart, can God have been wrong in choosing you? I assure you that you are much more powerful than what you recognize.

I want you to understand in a new light that you who receive my messages of love and wisdom are the children of my love. You are very pure souls, although surrounded by pain and brought to me by the inscrutable design of the Most High. You are hearts blessed with the grace of spiritual childhood, humble souls who do not boast of your talents. You know how great God is. You are souls who are tired of the world's lack of love, who have cried and whose cry joined the heart of God, thereby creating a new river of light and truth. You are souls that know very well that you cannot do anything for yourself, except to err. And you also know that with the power of love, to which if you remain united, you become one with our Father.

You, the recipients of these messages from Heaven, are pure souls. You have crossed the waters of the purification of love. You are souls who have found the truth, chosen only love, and are willing to do the will of the Father. You know the voice of truth and follow it. You are chosen to carry out the mission of making the light of the Glory of Christ shine on Earth more every day.

Let your innocence shine. May the purity of your hearts be seen. Call others to bear witness to God's love. Be a living Christ who walks the Earth. You can be, because Christ is risen. You can be, because God lives in your hearts. You can be, because your Source is eternal life.

I need you as much as your physical bodies need air to breathe. And much more, for without you, I cannot save the world or creation. Without your "yes," however small it may seem to you, it is impossible for this Mother of pure divine love to create the new Kingdom. I assure you that not even God can do this without you. The Father, who loves you with divine love and knows perfect wisdom, knows that all true creation is born from union. He wholeheartedly wishes the new world to shine radiantly and be a reality where your children can live in peace, even in the physical dimension.

You are God's emerging shoots. In truth I tell you that it is possible to create a new earthly Kingdom. In effect, it is already being created. God's countenance is distinguished every day with greater clarity. Extend your eyes to the horizon of truth. Can you begin to see the first glimpses of the new sun that illuminates the Earth? Can you start to observe how the new is being created?

By design of the Father a new Kingdom will be established on Earth, a new earthly reality united to the celestial in which both will become one while still being what they are. This is the plan of love for the world. This is the will of the Creator for the Earth: The new world exists created in union with my Immaculate Heart, the Sacred Heart of Jesus, and the holiness of your hearts, all three united in His divine being.

From the union of the three hearts the new arises in harmony with the divine will. The Source of the new creation is found in the unity of your consciousness with the consciousness of Christ in Mary and Jesus.

I am calling you to be part of the new. And I am revealing how this will occur. Do not exclude yourself from this movement of pure consciousness. Come now to the reality of the three hearts, and you will join the choir of the co-creators of the new reality, in which there is only room for the holy, the beautiful, and the perfect. Join the eternal novelty of love.

Thanks for answering my call.

Signs of the New Times

Letter 27

My children, God is love. This statement contains within itself all truth. Often you lose your inner peace in intellectual discussions that lead you to the divisions between sisters and brothers. On the level of beliefs, true unity is impossible. Only in love can there be union because both are the same.

When asked what God is, answer with simplicity what your heart knows: God is love. Do the same when you observe that your mind has wandered, which leads you to lose peace. Discussion of beliefs is not dialogue, it is a separation mechanism, a thought pattern that leads you away from each other. How much pain has been created in the world because of beliefs!

Stay on the path of the heart. Let love rule your minds and your strength. Only in love is there wisdom, creative power, and unity.

Love is beyond all belief and every word, although they can be based in it.

Understand the signs of the times. The century of reason is over and the rays of light from the sun of a new reality have begun to emerge—a new awareness, a greater knowledge of the love of God.

Humanity is in a position to know the love of the Father as never before. A direct relationship with the Creator is the sign of the new world. There is no going back. Only love will exist in the consciousness of the children of God. What is not love has vanished forever in the resurrection. This is not theology, it is divine love.

You know what love is. Within you is a space where the knowledge of God resides in all its beauty. You can access it through prayers of silence and contemplation, which many of you call meditation. The recognition of a consciousness in which intuition, the wisdom of the heart, and the direct revelation of truth as the Source of knowledge and action is getting closer.

A new humanity is being born. You are witnesses of that birth. In fact, you are among the collaborators of Christ, to let him be born in you and the whole world. You are first in a movement that will allow many to enter and enjoy the new world which together we are creating.

If God is love and you are one with God, what else can you really be but love?

You who are called to join the movement of beautiful love are preparers of the Second Advent. At the same time you are sowers, together with the Mother of the living, of the new garden of my divine son Jesus. This garden is adorned with flowers of holiness, purity, and truth. With your presence you will bear witness to the love of God.

These messages to you have a divine purpose. You have been chosen in the design to receive them. They are part of an act of Christ consciousness in these times of great transformation.

The time has come to show love to the world as never before. The time has come for the children of light to come to light. May goodness be manifested. May the peaceful bring peace to hearts. May the healing force of love, which resides in the holy hearts of my children, heal the Earth and all that dwells on it. You will do so in unity with my Immaculate Heart and the Sacred Heart of Jesus, if you so choose. The invitation is offered. The call rings in every corner of the universe.

I am revealing to you the signs of the new time so that you can understand more clearly. Do not waste time trying to keep the old; this will only cause delay in accessing the joy of unity. Enter the eternal novelty of beautiful love. Leave everything in the hands of love, which will be your guide on the path of the heart.

Be glad to know that truth is in charge of life. Beauty shapes reality all the time. You are eternal creation. Live together with me and you will know the love of the Mother as you have never known it before. Open your hearts and you will receive more and more love.

Live a healthy life in body and soul. Just as it is not advisable to eat foods that harm the body, neither is it advisable to harm your souls by feeding them with ideas, images, and feelings that do not nourish. The doors of divine beauty are wide open. Go through them and come to the reality of the Kingdom which dwells in your hearts.

Create bonds of communion in the consciousness of Christ, the only space where unity can exist.

Go around the world sowing peace.

I give you my blessing.

I thank you for answering my call.

A Gift from Heaven

Letter 28

My sons and daughters, these messages are unique. There are no other divine expressions of the same tenor, with the same holy love. Everything that exists in my Immaculate Heart has its Source in truth. I want to create with you a new movement of consciousness within the great universal movement of Christ. In this new creation everyone is called to worship God in spirit and truth.

To return to love is to return to the Father's house, to the Source of the eternal life from which the being comes. Pollution of the mind affects matter in ways that you cannot understand and causes the contamination of the Earth and of so many lives. Such toxicity comes from a lack of love. But the life that God creates in every moment cannot be contaminated.

It is not the will of the Father that what is alien to love exists. Still, you are free to accept love or deny love. When you accept it, you engage the power of the Holy Spirit and allow the effects of beautiful love to spread. When you deny love, you interrupt the flow of life in consciousness, and a part of the soul stops receiving the vital force it needs to remain in fullness. That creates what is contrary to love.

Allow your hearts to live full of God's love. Abandon your own interpretation of life, of yourself, of creation and its Source. Empty yourself so the wisdom of Heaven fills you. Truth cannot be achieved through human effort; it arrives through the grace of revelation.

These dialogues between the Mother and you, my children, constitute a chain of light that creates a movement of beautiful love in particular and universal consciousness. You never stay the same when you come to me. Our relationship of holy love transforms you without your noticing it; nevertheless, you will see the effects of grace in you and the world. Receive my messages as what they are: a gift given to souls for love.

Heaven has opened as never before and from it falls a shower of blessings and holiness that are flooding the Earth and the entire physical universe. Open your hands to receive. Prepare your hearts to be widened by love. Become more and more one with truth. You will grow at every moment in unity with Christ.

Jubilantly accept the power of your souls and the strength of prayer. Every time you join God through prayers born from your hearts, you affect universal consciousness. And the various creations of the Father, in union with Himself, are set in motion, creating the reality that the praying heart seeks.

Change human reality through prayer. You can transform material creation through your prayers of love. Make silence your faithful friend. Spend time alone with love. In your regular encounters with Christ, pour out to Him all that you carry in your heart. Leave them empty. Thus will you come out of prayer renewed in Spirit.

Do not worry whether or not you feel the loving contemplation to which I invite you, for the grace of prayer comes not from what is felt or understood, but from the degree of union achieved. Spirit leads you to silence so that there you can worship the Father in spirit and truth. Let Christ blow upon your souls to lead you sweetly along the eternal path of perfect love. He knows how.

You who accept my word and carry it in the silence of your hearts are called to join me, the Mother, in this movement of beautiful love. Many minds will be enlightened and awaken from the dream of oblivion through this movement. Your beauty will grow day by day because of our divine relationship. Your holiness will shine more and more until it cannot be denied. Your joy will be great, and with it you will attract many brothers and sisters to Christ, because it will proceed from union with God.

Share my revelations with others. Invite others to remain in the union of the three hearts, to find in my Immaculate Heart and the Sacred Heart of Jesus the safe haven that every mind seeks and the peace that every heart needs to be happy.

Do not get lost in thought about various beliefs or unanswered questions. You are tiny souls, sprouts of pure love, like cheerful daisies that embellish the garden of the husband of holy souls. You are the children of Mary, the hope of the world, the light of nations. You are my tiny children who have come into the world to teach with your loving presence the true humility of the heart and thus awaken many to eternal life.

Always remain humble in my love. Be humble in truth, and simple at heart. Heaven is a Kingdom of the innocent. I invite you to live your lives as newborns in the arms of the Mother. When you let yourself love more each day, your lives will be happier.

Children from all over the world, if you knew the love of this Mother you would not only cry with happiness, but your hearts would jump with joy and dance to the rhythm of eternal life.

I am the owner of hearts with my divine son Jesus. Who joins me, joins the truth. Whoever remains in me lives together with God.

Children of my heart, realize how much the Father, who gives you the grace of these revelations, loves you. I am showing you in greater depth a love that has no beginning or end. I am immersing you in the deepest waters of divine knowledge.

Bring me your brothers and sisters. Come with everyone to be part of the movement of beautiful love. Go into the world sowing peace.

I bless you in the light of Christ.

I thank you for answering my call and carrying my words in the silence of your heart.

The Truth in You

Letter 29

Children of my Immaculate Heart, beloved of Mary the Queen of Harmony, today I talk to you who have chosen only love and are part of the beautiful love movement to which I call everyone. You are the ones who, having traveled the winding paths of self-knowledge, have reached the point where, knowing enough, you are prepared to express the truth of your holy being. This decision will bring a shower of thanks and blessings upon you and the whole world.

There are multiple paths that humankind can take, an infinite number of forms of expression, as many as there are hearts of men and women on Earth. However, that multiplicity hides the fact that there are only two options: love or nothing. Those who have decided to live life by the truth that Christ is are the cause of holiness. Everything that exists in creation has a cause and creates an effect, including your decisions. There are no neutral thoughts or futile feelings. Everything in you is powerful. Honor the power of your souls.

Those who live in me are never alone. The love that springs from my Immaculate Heart accompanies you always. The eternal creation of the Father of all holiness embraces you and envelops you in the light of divine Glory. The angels take care of you and guide you. My divine son Jesus embraces you with a burning fire of incomparable love, a love that has no beginning or end, a love that can never be given by a world not in unity, a love that saves, that erases the memories of guilt, heals wounds, and transforms minds and hearts into vessels of wisdom and perfect compassion. The Holy Trinity is in those who live in me. They are one with God.

You are never alone who have set in motion the light that springs from Christ. You will never lack anything in carrying out your function of expressing in your own way the very truth and love of God. Each creature was endowed with, impregnated with, the wisdom of God in its essence. It is His seal.

It is the will of the Father that His wisdom be expressed in a unique way by each creature. No soul is equal to another. Do not limit the creative power of the One who is the perennial Source of life. A repetition of identical beings would be meaningless. Divine love is limitless and knows no excess. Everything in His creation makes perfect sense. Nothing arises from the heart of love unless for a perfect purpose. Everything is part of life as God created it. If something created by the Creator was omitted, however insignificant you may believe it to be, I assure you that the creation of the Father would be very different from what He has conceived. Omit a single microelement of creation, cancel its existence, and you will have a very different universe.

I invite you to express your deepest knowledge about what humanity, yourself, and God is. You carry within you the wisdom of Heaven. You do not need others to tell you what only you can know and express from the silent temple of your hearts in love. The soul thirsts for love. The mind is hungry for love. Love and truth are the same.

I am calling you to quench the thirst and hunger of your brothers.

It may seem that I am telling you a contradiction by asking you to illuminate and redeem others by calming their desire to know, when I have said that nobody needs another to tell him what lies in each heart for the simple reason of having been created by God. However, well-loved children, God has arranged for the truth to be known in union and relationship. Therefore it is giving as you receive. When you give the wisdom of your being, allowing its unique expression, you will become increasingly aware of the inexhaustible treasure of abundance within you. And that will allow others to dare, deep inside, to undertake the fascinating and liberating, though sometimes resisted, path of knowledge of the inner Christ.

Do not believe that you have little to give to the world. Would God put in you the seeds of holiness, love, and wisdom, and their potential to be expressed in ways unique to you for insignificant reasons? What is more sacred, an eagle or a sparrow? Where is more beauty, in a lily or a rose?

You who have found the truth, do you believe that there are human works of greater scope and importance for God than others? In the Kingdom there is no such distinction. The universe understands only love. Looking at created beings, it sees nothing but expressions of love or lack thereof. God knows that only love is real and that He is the whole of everything. Therefore, he rejoices in the contemplation of the manifestations of the love of His children. The rest is not reached by His holy gaze. Love has eyes only for love. Holiness has only the words of eternal life. The truth only has true thoughts. Life only thinks about how to create more life eternally.

I invite you always to continue forward without looking back. Grow each day in the expression of your true being so that you can witness the abundance of your heart. You will be amazed at how holy your pure spirit is, how wise your mind when it remains united to Christ, and how much beauty exists in your heart.

Give the world your spiritual beauty. Show others the purity of our divine relationship. Go through the world rejoicing with hearts thirsty for love and enlightening minds hungry for wisdom and truth. In this way, you will be as Christ on Earth. You will be the living expression of God's love.

I bless you in my Immaculate Heart.
I thank you for listening to my voice.

The Breath of Love

Letter 30

My beloved sons and daughters, share the divine love you know and the truth that has been revealed to you. There are many sons and daughters who walk the world in search of God's wisdom. In all times there have been many. They are destined for your present and your future.

In times of apostasy, I sent you as a voice in the desert and a spring of water that flowed from the top of a sacred mountain flooding hearts thirsty for peace. Your spirit is like the wind: nobody knows where it comes from or where it goes, but it blows. Always breathe the breath of eternal life that dwells in you.

Listen to the birds sing. They are a gift from the Father. They sing a melodious hymn of gratitude to creation, a song of life and holiness, of the joy of being. Birds express the joy of their sensitive souls each dawn.

Enjoy every raindrop of water that falls. Learn to join the beauty of creation. In that way you will become increasingly aware of how beautiful your soul is and how sacred is your existence.

Become one with the wind. It remains united forever to the whole. Do not leave anything that is holy outside of yourself, for it belongs there.

Everything that joins you is holy because of who you are. For the same reason, what is not holy cannot join you. Living in each pure heart is a yearning for all created by God because He is the pure consciousness of love. In Him nothing can overshadow beauty. In His being lies all truth.

Praise the whole Earth in love. Let no one be excluded from this song of joy and peace. May love be recognized by all for what it is—the essence of life. Live in light as a child of God. In the light you can see what you have longed to contemplate. You will know the unfathomable mysteries of Heaven. You can discern between illusion and truth. You will feel the joy that comes from being certain, the certainty of knowing the truth and living forever in it.

In the blink of an eye my Immaculate Heart can enlighten the mind and endow it with perfect wisdom. It is unnecessary to make any effort to be wise; you need only live in love. With a little willingness to hear the voice of truth in your heart, all the knowledge of Heaven is poured into your soul.

Call your sisters and brothers to live in beautiful love. Do not silence your voice; for souls with hearts in love it is like the song of a nightingale. Souls know how to listen to the melodies of creation and rejoice in them. Words that spring from your lips are holy by virtue of our union.

You have consumed everything in the flame of living love. You are a ray of light cast by the great light from which all luminescence emanates. You are created love melted into the Source of creative love. You have become one with Christ and with the true creation of God.

Children of my heart, to you and to all who accept my messages of love and truth, live your life as what you really are, a gift come from Heaven. You who are here listening to the voice of Mary have a priceless treasure, the treasure of faith and the gift of hearing love and following it. Be generous with it. Share your experiences of divine love with your brothers and sisters. Each of you carries within you a gem of incomparable beauty. Allow others to see in you what Christ inspires you to reveal. That way, your brothers and sisters can begin to believe in love and be encouraged to have faith in Him who is the Source of all love.

Be a light to the nations and a hope for humanity. Together with Mary and Jesus, and in unity with everyone and everything create the new earthly Kingdom that has been conceived since the beginning of time. Be co-creators of the new humanity. Invite others to participate in this blessed gift from Heaven. Cheer up in love! Help others stay true to the call they hear in their hearts. Join those who have already found this call, not by creating separate groups or encouraging isolation, but so that together you all grow in the truth and call others to join the movement of beautiful love. Following your inspiration go out to meet others.

Universal consciousness is moving as never before in the direction of God's heart. Gently gather within yourself all that is similar to you, with full respect for freedom. Let the mystical dimension of your heart emerge more and more. In every being is the impulse to join its Source. Allow that impulse to take you, like a wind that blows an autumn leaf, to where you should be carried. Let yourself be loved by God and others. Live always united to Mary. Remain happy in love.

I bless you with all my love.

Thank you for listening to my voice and following it.

Reunion with the Truth

Letter 31

My sons and daughters, it is of great importance that you understand that each of you is unique and unrepeatable. In your uniqueness lies your beauty. Do not hide in groups or communities that blur what you really are. Be constantly encouraged to live in the freedom of the heart. God creates free spirits. Let yourself be carried away by the force of inspiration. In your deep intuition lies the truth of your being. Because each soul is unique, what serves some does not necessarily serve others.

The process of spiritual growth for each of my children is diverse. Therefore, it is not possible to establish universal beliefs that fit the truth of love, nor is it necessary. Each soul carries within it the wisdom of God. Meeting God is what religion is really about.

In this movement of beautiful love to which I summon you, there are no proselytes. That was never my intention. The search for adherents to a belief or doctrine does not follow truth. Extending the revelation that a soul receives should not be done for the purpose of convincing others or attaining followers. None of that is part of the purpose of the universe. However, being carried away by the force of spirit that spreads and shares what it loves with a love not of the world is essential to the spiritual life. Discerning clearly between the two is what I have come to talk to you about.

Much pain has been inflicted throughout history by imposing beliefs or persecuting those who think, feel, and believe differently. None of that should be part of what you who have chosen love do. I must insist on this point, because I do not wish you to take love to the world without first reflecting what I share here.

When you receive a gift from Heaven—and wisdom is one of them—you do not receive it because of your merit. It is given as a gift of love. Truth cannot be achieved through intellectual effort but only from the free grace of revelation. The only thing you can do is to get ready to receive—but even that is only possible by grace.

Souls reunited with Christ are captivated by the love of God that makes a move in their hearts, impelling them to share with others the wonders they saw without image and heard without word. Sharing is the essence of love. It is why everything created exists. The reality of being is giving. Spirit encourages souls that have opened themselves to truth to come out of themselves and enter the immensity of creation, and to share the knowledge received. It is always spirit who calls and drives. The spirit goes ahead. When an inspired soul reaches a new height, spirit has already passed through first and made everything ready.

To make known to others the revelation given to you is the essence of the beautiful love movement. Without that driving force, this movement would simply be a song of joy, full of beauty, but without the strength of spirit. I send you to all corners of the world to extend what you have known in your reunion with truth. It is in your intimacy with Christ where you know, where the spirit guides you, and where the winds of divine love blow. Let yourself be carried away by love.

I invite you to continue this journey of the heart together. It is a holy journey whose seal is the authenticity that comes from uniqueness. Do not move so that others follow you, but move to calm your longing to extend the holiness that you really are. I long for this that burns hearts.

I call you out of your realities as they have been conceived so far and to enter the unfathomable abyss of infinite knowledge. God has no limits. He will lead you to cross the boundaries of thought. He will show you wonders that cannot be imagined.

Love gives the best to those who love. What could be better for a soul full of wisdom than to make known the purity of love? Go forward, moved by love. Be humble of heart and prudent. If you keep both virtues high, you cannot lose yourself or fall into confusion. The spiritual path is full of challenges, as are all paths of life. If you remain in me and remember often that the work is of God and that you are His loving instrument, you have nothing to fear. He who created everything that exists will not let even one of His devotees be lost. He shepherds His flock and sustains life.

Let yourself be carried away by the force of spirit, and do everything with love in Christ. Feel the joy of sharing.

Thank you for listening to my voice and following it.

Masterpiece of God

Letter 32

Beloved of my Immaculate Heart, I have come once again to fill your heart with love and to flood the Earth with the grace that the Father gives to all who wish to receive it. God is freedom and happiness.

I invite you to meditate on the balance between performing the works that spirit inspires, and accepting the limitations of human nature. You are called to live consciously as God-Human, Homo-Christus Deo, to manifest the reality of your united spiritual and human nature. Inner peace is achieved when both aspects live in harmony without drowning out the other.

The abundance of spirit surpasses every human measure. Nothing can contain it. Spirit's movement is constant, overflowing the most powerful dike. It leads the mind and heart to create in a flow without limitation. It is like a wave of a great ocean that grows and grows forever. The strength of spirit is so powerful that it embraces everything that exists. Everything presented to Spirit becomes wrapped in divine love. Nothing remains the same. Everything is transformed. Spirit disarms everything and then puts it back together, creating new configurations of perfect goodness. Its intensity is overflowing. It never rests, but is always creating. Its light is brighter than the sun. It is unstoppable.

When Spirit calls it does so with the fullness of God's love, yet modified to the present reality of each creature. If it did not make that adjustment, your humanity in its current state could not bear it. Some fall into imbalances on the spiritual path. Some demand more of themselves than their minds, bodies, and hearts can bear. These excesses do not come from truth but from fear, the fear of not living up to the call of love.

The power of spirit surpasses all measure, including its sweetness, softness, and serenity. Therefore, there is no reason for haste, or for cravings or demands. Nor is there reason for discouragement. Not everything you receive in a revelation can be shared. Not everything you receive from Heaven can be explained. There would not be enough time to give the world the infinite wisdom of the love that is given you.

Spirit can enlighten a mind in a single instant with such a deep and revealing knowledge as could never be acquired through any conceivable intellectual effort. Therefore, my children, do not worry if you live with the vocation you have known. Live a relaxed, balanced life with the incomparable joy of working for God and living in truth. The works of God are not limited to your temporal reality nor to the few that you can know in time and space. They are all-encompassing and bring together all creation.

Remember that demanding is all right but not at the cost of losing peace. Often humankind loses the serenity of spirit due to excessive activity. The unbridled doing of the world is the effect of fear, not of the vital energy of spirit. Life does not run. God never gets angry. Smile and enjoy being who you are, as a child of God.

Avoid filling your life with activity. Do almost nothing, but whatever you do, do from the abundance of your spirit in perfect union with Christ. Let Him be the one who leads you. Live inspired. Go where the voice of love would have you go. Be attentive to the callings of the soul and also to the needs of your body. Get enough rest. Let the spirit of God act effectively and freely in you when you rest.

I want to free you from the attachment of doing and the sickly habit of living fast. I invite you to live a simple life—full of simplicity, moderation, balance, and fullness. Do not cling to your plans. Consider your loving care, respect of your own humanity, and stay in fidelity to the call of love. To do so is to live in harmony.

When you make this your way of life you will be surprised to discover how much wisdom is in stillness, how much love in silence, and how much power is in peace. And you will live in gratitude to your Father and Creator for being in alignment with Him who calls, finds, inspires, and does. You will begin to enjoy a life of rest in the vibrant reality of love and realize with happy astonishment that the masterpiece of God is accomplished in your heart and in your soul—and that everything else is otherwise.

My sons and daughters, the masterpiece of God is you.

Thank you for listening to my voice and following it.

Beyond Form

Letter 33

My children, life has a beginning and an end, not in the sense of an ending but of a purpose. Its origin is love and its purpose is knowledge of itself. The self of God, which is what many of you call the I Am, gives existence to every being and seeks to know itself as it is. In the origin of life there is only love, for love is the foundation of everything, not only of reason but also of reality.

It was love that created you and it did so for love. It is love that sustains you in existence so that you can enjoy the banquet of life. Love gives meaning to the heart and a foundation to the mind. Outside of it nothing is real, therefore nothing that is healthy.

Please consider what my Immaculate Heart tells you here.

If you remain in love, you will consciously live a life in fullness because your life will have transcendent meaning and will be anchored in reality. Outside of love is only suffering because outside of love is only illusion. Neither mind nor heart can be in peace and tranquility in a world of illusions. Fantasies are not the realm in which the soul can truly live.

Many of my children live locked in an illusion, believing it to be something that is actually far from their true reality. They build card castles. They live in fear because they know that, sooner or later, the scaffolding they have built to forge a personality will crumble. However, the dismantling of the illusion of what they think they are would be the greatest grace, and the entrance to the Kingdom of freedom for the children of God. No one can dwell in the Father's house if he or she does not shed what is unreal, for God is the ultimate reality of existence. God is the beginning, the end, the foundation, and the driving force of life.

Pray to live in the truth. If you ask this with sincerity of heart you will know true freedom.

Love created you free for love. The gift of space without limit is a gift that is rarely valued by my beloved children. Expand your horizons. Cross the borders of the world with me, and be encouraged to live in the wisdom of love. True life is not as the world thinks it is. Nothing is as it seems. Appearances cannot tell you the truth.

The primary reason so many of my children throughout history have been involved in an illusion of being is because they have been dedicated to survival as a species. By focusing on the body and living the life of the ego, there has been practically no driving force other than self-preservation. Although in reality you are unique and unrepeatable beings, this has led to your having no space to be or express. Your uniqueness was lost in the totality. The part became nothing in the totality. In that loss of uniqueness, arising as a result of giving the self to the group, the person disappeared. This was the tyranny of the ego, a disheartened dictator who never had an interest in the holy uniqueness that you each are.

Embrace your uniqueness, for in it lies your reality. By integrating what you really are and accepting yourself as you are, you put aside your fears and your deep feelings of inability which do not come from love.

See yourself as God sees you. Behold yourself through the vision of love.

In each of your voices is the potential to express the divine truth in your own way, with your unique timbre and tone. Allow your voice to reflect the abundant wisdom of your pure heart.

Speak from the vastness of your soul and you will show the world your holiness.

All inspired works come from the spirit of wisdom. Discover the various expressions, the very truth and love that is manifest and beyond words. Stop not at form, remembering that word-forms are symbols.

In these times of so much union between Heaven and Earth you will come to know more and more voices that speak with the voice given to them by God. Validate the uniqueness of each and the unique way everyone has of expressing themself. Love each one in their beauty.

Love is the foundation of wisdom: its Source, its end, and its being.

I call you to conceive of yourself as a bridge uniting the various expressions of love, which in their diversity reflect the reality of the Kingdom—a Kingdom of countless unique beings that exist as free expressions of the only love and the only truth. When you can see the love behind the various expressions, you will live in union and all confusion will be set aside. To do that it is necessary that you absorb everything with your heart. Your being knows where the truth lies. Your soul knows the sweetness of love. Your mind longs to live in the abode of peace. Your true reason dwells in the house of wisdom.

Give yourself life. Remain in the freedom of the children of God. Learn to recognize the voice of truth and follow it. It will always lead you to the holy abode. Love what has no beginning or end. You will be happy because you will know yourself as God has always known you and you will recognize that you are one with eternal love.

I give you my blessing. I give you my peace.

Thank you for answering my call.

Eternal Novelty

Letter 34

My dear children, I invite you once again to live in the truth, which has lived in your minds and hearts from the very moment of your creation. He who is the Source of everything has endowed his gifts upon everything created.

The various form that each creation adopts because of its way of being, is not an obstacle for the wisdom of love to shine in each one.

Be not concerned if you are not yet able to see the totality, or to understand the magnitude of the transformation that love carries out in you. You are receiving with holy disposition the Word that comes from Heaven.

The light of spirit illuminates everything when allowed to shine in all its glory. You are bearers of this light. You are important in the creation plan of the new world. Without your love, expressed in your own way, the time of the creation of the new would be longer and the arrival of peace on Earth would be delayed.

Do not try to predefine what it should be, nor try to change things. Often your anger comes from the notion that you can change what is and what will be. That abject way of thinking creates a state of suffering that does not lead to love. Accept life as it is. If you are called to do something, you will be told.

I am calling for love to grow more and more in you as you abandon yourself to my Immaculate Heart. Living from the love of God sustains your life. That being of pure holiness and perfection which you call by many names decides on the basis of Her will, not according to the way of humanity, but to the way of pure divine potentiality. However, Her will disposes according to a wisdom not of the world.

If you remain in love, you will be transformed into more love, day after day.

Love yourself in Christ, so that you may live in the eternal bliss of Heaven. You cannot give what you do not have. If you do not feel my love in your heart, you cannot give me to others. My love belongs to you. Come and immerse yourself in the depths of my being of pure love. I am the Divine Mother, the Source of all life, the one who has known you since before time and who will know you forever.

My call makes no distinction of any kind, for it is the call of universal love. My love is both compassionate and inclusive. Do not leave anyone or anything outside of it. Certainly language is limited, and often creates divisions; nevertheless, those of the truth know how to move beyond the symbols to which they point, and will follow the trail of these heavenly thoughts which have taken the form of written words, to extend divine love to the world.

I have not come to impart new precepts, nor to criticize humanity. I have come to serve, because that is My function: to serve through love. Everything created has emerged from the depths of perfect love and serves the cause and effect of its Creator. That is why it exists. Service is also the essence of your reality. The heart always serves. It can serve love or fear. Likewise the mind which can serve truth or illusion. The same goes for the physical body: it can serve self-pride or a loving expression of the light of Christ.

You cannot serve two masters because there is only one in truth; the others are not real. That is why if you serve what is not love, you are imprisoned in the illusion of a life that frightens the soul because it was also endowed in its creation with the knowledge of truth.

Open your minds and hearts to the transformation of truth and love. Let yourself transform in every moment. Do not stop your eternal rebirth in spirit. Be always new. If you abandon yourself to the eternal transformative novelty of divine love, you will be free and you will bathe in the joy of eternal life, a bliss without opposite, an endless joy. Leave behind all that has been lived up to now and throw yourself into my arms as Mother of God and your Mother. I am universal love. I am Mother of all. I am Mary.

I have come to speak to each of my daughters and sons throughout the world. I want to get more and more intimate with each of you until our relationship is of such intimacy that you merge in my Immaculate Heart.

Love with the only true love for your humanity and divinity. Recognize the unity of both aspects of your nature. Focus not on one or the other, but on the inner Christ. It is there, where the Christ reality dwells, where you are as human as divine.

Be receptive to the voice of love.

I bless you in the truth.

Thanks for answering My call.

The Fear of Falling

Letter 35

My beloved sons and daughters, when the soul meets its beloved Creator, the one who gave it life, things not coming from Him are tiresome. This is because the mind that has found the truth, and the heart that has found peace, desires nothing else. Banal conversations sadden the soul; superficiality bothers it, because the soul has rejected the old. The soul has become averse to everything not of God.

I remind you of this so that you understand the anguish of the soul that has joined Christ and yet remains in the world. A soul who has already found its Source will not return to the old way of being. Do not be afraid of slipping back. You will not. You will never return to the old state of being. Consciousness always advances. Remember this as often as necessary.

Your mind and heart know where sweetness resides, where tenderness dwells. Leave them free and they will take you to the House of Truth where the benevolence of Heaven resides. Happy are those who cry to see God for theirs is the Kingdom of Heaven. Happy are those who understand this truth.

Often the greatest expression of love is to have patience with the world while you remain in your earthly life, serving the purpose of the Creator of all things holy, beautiful, and perfect. When you feel fearful for the world because deep down in your heart is a fear of going back, unite more deeply to my heart. In our union of loving intimacy you will find the peace and harmony you crave.

When your being meets its divine beloved, the reason for your existence, the mind feels that it loses abilities it previously

138

had. That sense of loss can raise fears in you. However, these "losses" are unreal. Nothing part of true reality can be lost, for the gifts of God cannot be lost. Remember, reality is God and only what comes from God. Its opposite is insubstantial and does not exist except in illusions.

Reflect on this feeling of the soul that, having joined Christ, fears losing its presence. When love meets the being who yearns to know it, a fusion takes place that cannot be dissolved. Separation has not existed in reality because nothing can separate the soul from its Creator; nothing can separate it from love. However, it is also true that the mind can partially deny reality and conceive ideas far from truth.

All of that exists within human nature. But the soul can make irrevocable decisions because you have a will. And if in your free will you determine that you will forever live in the presence of divine love, it will be so. The will of divine love must be accomplished.

Nothing can stop the soul that decides to live forever with its Creator. The united soul has the power to decide to join the power of love. Nothing can stop such a soul on its way to Heaven. Nothing in the world can distract it for long from the vision of the beloved. And the day will come when all your attention will be given to the love of your loves, even here on Earth. Nothing and no one can ever disengage it.

The soul in love lives thinking of its beloved. The mind that has joined the truth lives thinking of God and has heart only for Him. The soul may wish with all its might not to be in the world anymore, but also recognizes that its function on Earth is sacred and irreplaceable. This filial obedience to Divine Mother, the Source of all being, allows the soul to live where She disposes because of Her divine love and approval of this soul in love.

The will of such a soul has merged into the divine will. That is why it does everything that the voice of the Holy Spirit inspires and cries silently at the idea of not fulfilling its sacred mission. The soul is distressed at the thought of not being able to move towards the eternal Heaven.

Oh, blessed souls in love with Christ! You who having grown to the fullest in the knowledge of God's love suffer from the longing to see your divine Creator face to face, which you still cannot see clearly. I tell you, immerse yourself in my love. Join with this Mother of divine grace. The purity of my heart will bathe you in sweetness and refresh your soul. Live joyfully, knowing that you will see Christ directly, and that you will enjoy His divine presence eternally. Long before you can imagine you will be laughing forever in the realm of perfect love given to you, my souls, for my divine son Jesus who loves you without measure.

I will stay with you every day of your life. You will feel my presence increasingly. I will reveal every step to take for the purpose of love. As captain, I will lead you calmly through the waters of life. I will speak to your heart. I will illuminate your mind forever, giving more knowledge at every step, because wisdom has no end. I will take care of those you have abandoned in the name of truth. They remain in me because you remain in my Immaculate Heart, and when you come to me you will do so with them, your loved ones.

Stay in peace.

Thanks for answering my call.

Together Forever

Letter 36

My children, today I want to give you blessings. I want to flood your lives with fullness, true joy, and serenity of spirit. I give you the peace of Heaven. I give you eternal life. Know forever that even though your minds may forget these graces and even forget the love you feel every time you stay with me, my love never forgets you.

I am eternally awake. I never stop seeing you. I observe you every day of your life, because the Father in Heaven has given your being into my custody in response to your sincere request to live in the truth. I take care of you as a loving mother takes care of her offspring. I wrap you in a love without beginning or end. I am for you the most tender mother conceivable.

I am the refuge of souls, the Source of all lasting happiness, and what those who love very much seek wholeheartedly. I am the spring of fresh water that gives life to everything. I am a breath of living love and beauty of your holy being.

When you feel dejected because you feel you are not up to the call of Heaven, or perceive in your mind and heart a distaste for your supposed disabilities, I ask you to return to my heart as soon as possible. It is an unequivocal sign that you have believed what cannot be true.

Never underestimate the power of the world's thought system to distract you. Although you are no longer prey to the ego, the mental and emotional programs inherited from worldly life continue to exert a certain force of attraction on your soul. Do not be alarmed by it.

The soul has its own rhythm and power. Trust your being. Everything unfolds in due time. There are reasons why not all illusory programs can be disengaged from the mind and heart at once. There is no hurry, my children. Be patient as Christ is. Be gentle with yourself.

I know very well that you would like to see the work of God already accomplished in you and the whole world, and that often you feel that things happen too slowly in relation to the revelation of the truth you have received. This is because you know Heaven. Your soul remembers. You have chosen only love, and therefore have returned to true knowledge, which immerses your being permanently in an ecstasy of love and contemplation. Your thinking mind is not yet fully adapted to this reality, but little by little it is changing and will eventually be immersed in the mind of Christ in its entirety. Be patient with that little part that still seeks to "fit in God."

Observe nature. Look how mothers give birth to their children in places away from others. This is because it is in your motherly nature to take care of your young. They look for a safe place to breastfeed quietly where nothing can put their progeny's life at risk. Where did they learn that? Nowhere. They know it just because they are what they are. That wisdom is part of your being. It is something that cannot be learned or forgotten, as with love.

I am reminding you that your being has been created with the necessary knowledge so that God's will is fully realized in you. How that happens is something that cannot be learned or taught, but is a knowledge that is part of your reality.

The Christ in you takes you to places far from the world without leaving it, where your soul can expand into the depths of your mind and heart. In this sense, Christ acts like a mother who takes care of and nurses her children in silence and intimacy.

The new being that you are, reborn from the waters of spirit, needs to be removed from certain spaces and circumstances. Some distances are forever, others are temporary, but at the end of the road, all things in the world will be separated except from love.

Allow what you really are to take you where you should go because of the purpose of your holy creation. Do not cling to the supposed knowledge acquired in the world. What you learn is not part of being but only systems of thought oriented to survival, and are not of you but of the ego. They are thoughts of separation. Nothing loving or true is in them. Do not make them what they are not. It is not wisdom but simply imitation.

The desire to be special must be completely abandoned. This requires you to be alert and pay attention to truth. That is why I invite you again and again to stay with the Mother and not leave my presence even for one day. Live forever in the truth united forever in a union of joy and purpose. Live together in the joy of God.

I invite you to immerse yourself in the silence of your heart where the peace of Heaven fills your being. I invite you to embrace a loneliness that is not loneliness, but a communion with Heaven and Earth, with the human and the divine, with the unmanifested and the manifested. I invite you to know more deeply the mysteries of love.

I bless you with special favor.

Thank you for answering the call of my Immaculate Heart.

Childlike Love

Letter 37

My children, I have come in the glory of Heaven to dwell with you in a particular way. This blessed work is a concrete way of establishing my presence in your life. It is a holy gift, full of blessings for humanity, that comes into your hands through the pure, loving will of the Creator. Nothing happens randomly in the universe, nor in your life.

Humanity always needs the living Word expressed in the sign of the times—the same and only truth, the same and only love, expressed in countless ways. The soul without love faints. That is why it is necessary that it continues to flow from the very depths of eternal life to each of you.

Receive my messages with holy choice. Be humble before the mystery of life. Often you worry too much, trying to understand mysteries that cannot be revealed because they have been created to be what they are. Allow mystery to envelop you; embrace its sacredness. Not everything can be understood by the thinking mind, although everything can be embraced and accepted by the heart that trusts in the love of its divine loved one.

I speak to you, souls who have chosen only love, in a particular way because each one has a unique way of being and a degree of consciousness reached. For you, there is only the sweetness of love. For your hearts, only the tenderness of Mary is reserved and the always-sweet benevolence of the universe created by truth. You who walk safely towards the light of life that never dies out are the resurrected in the world. Rejoice in love!

You, my daughters and sons, are a joy for the Mother of love. You cause my heart to expand in the pure desire to embrace everyone in the beauty of holy charity. You have chosen the best part and it will not be taken away from you. You have traveled paths, sometimes difficult, with doubts that afflicted your souls. You have renounced the world for the love of truth, the love of Christ. You weep in silence when you see the heartbreak of the world. You are able to understand how much pain comes from the lack of love.

Those who choose to live only in love are the bravest among the inhabitants of Earth. The world does not understand them, nor can it. Remember that when we talk about "the world," we speak of a system of thought based on separation and what is not true. Only the truth that emanates from God is true. There is no other truth because there is no other true God than Love.

Love is who called you to life. You exist and can enjoy the wonders of love's divine reality because of love's call.

If you understand this work well, you will understand that I am taking you to the knowledge of yourself in the mystical dimension of your soul. The feelings that flow from that aspect of your heart are often denied or not shared. Connecting with divine love gives you union with all that you really are. From that union arises your awareness of the integrity of your being.

Please do not drown out what your heart shouts in the depth of being. Express love to your divine Creator. Celebrate life. Do it your way. Love will receive with joy your appreciation and charity. Your heart has the capacity to manifest love, and you do it in thousands of different ways, but often humanity forgets that there is a Being of infinite love that gives life to every living being that inhabits the Earth.

Doesn't He who gives you life deserve your love?

Be generous with the indescribable gifts that Heaven sends you through this work. Through divine grace and your will, your hearts expand more and more to receive and give more divine love. Your open minds receive the light of the perpetual sun that is divine wisdom. Your souls open like beautiful roses to receive rain from the sky and be reborn in their beauty.

You are flooded by divine blessings. Do not worry if you feel something or not when you pray the silent prayer of love. Spiritual growth is not a matter of feeling but of truth. Remember, love is not a feeling. Love is what you really are.

My being as Divine Mother accompanies you every day. You are chosen to extend love in the world, an inclusive love that leaves no one aside. This love seek not to impose an alien will on others, but simply loves. This is pure love, beautiful love, the love of holiness, the love of your true being in Christ.

Embrace the truth. Dwell in it. Your mission is important. Do not worry if it seems that you do only small works. It is in the simple, hidden things of life where love likes to be on Earth.

My children, humanity has become accustomed to seeking God in greatness. And it is true that divine greatness exists. However, it is often forgotten that Christ was born in a manger, that love came into the world in a fragile, simple child.

Look at the love embodied in a child. In that child you will find the Creator's tenderness. His contemplation will help you to always live in the truth of what you are, well-loved children of God, always small, always children, always loved.

I bless you in Christ.

Thanks for receiving my call.

Beautiful Love Party

Letter 38

My daughters and sons, today I talk to you about the inclusive aspect of love. True charity embraces within itself everything that exists, without misrepresenting the truth. God's inclusion unites within itself the identity of every being.

There is diversity among the daughters and sons of the Creator, and not only in the realm of the Earth. Everything that exists comes from love and was endowed with a clearly defined identity. Amorphousness is characteristic of the Source but not of its effect. The immaterial becomes matter. The unmanifested manifests. The unthinkable becomes thought.

In every creation is a relationship between ultimate reality and the form it takes. Indeed, the creature is the form that essence takes. The extension of love arises to know itself in such a way that its embrace does not make the unity of love nullify the unique identity of the created.

One of the fears that you have harbored in your hearts for all of time is the fear of not being, in particular the idea that by joining something you lose your identity and is a form of annihilation—a death, not a life.

Love includes within itself everything true. Nothing dissimilar to love can remain in that union because what is one cannot be of diverse natures. Unity shares the same reality with everything that is part of itself. Where there is love there is no fear. Herein lies the certainty of salvation.

Where sweetness dwells, there cannot be roughness. Where the tenderness of holy charity lives, violence cannot dwell. Where the truth shines there can be no illusion.

I invite you to meditate on the sacredness of form as an expression of content. Your identity has been given to you as a blessed gift of the love that God is. You don't need to be different from what you are; you just need to love to be happy.

To love your humanity is to love yourself as you are without pretending to be what others are, or seeking to change yourself to achieve a preconceived ideal. Love is the reality of being. It does not exist in illusion, but in reality. Nothing fictional can carry something loving in itself. Nothing untrue can make you happy.

Truth and love are not only the united foundations of being, but are being itself. Outside of them is no life because nothing is outside their reality. You were created within the reality of charity. You are the expression of divine love. You have come into the world with a personality in addition to the various invisible powers of the human soul. All this has a holy purpose. To live in union with this is to live in the truth.

Do not exclude yourself from my embrace of love. You are all called to be happy forever. Leave aside the differences that human language creates because of its limitations. I invite you to go beyond appearances to the truth that gives life to everything your eyes see and much more.

When a part of your humanity has expressed authoritarianism instead of true authority, which is always a perfect expression of the wisdom of love, it is necessary to forgive regardless of whether that expression was perceived as something external to yourself or within you.

Remember that as it is inside, so it is outside. If in the "outside" world there is violence or excess of any kind, it is because it is there in hearts. In the deep interior of the human soul, feelings and thoughts are created that materialize into thought systems, emotional patterns, internal programs, and finally into external systems like societies, judicial systems, governments, and families. They govern the lives of women and men who inhabit Earth.

Always immerse yourself in the depths of your immensity. Join me in it, for we cannot unite anywhere else. I am the last reality of being. I am what precedes all thought. I am what gives intelligence to minds and feeling to hearts. Before anything can be thought, I am. Before you can even feel, there is my love.

I am that part of you shared by everything in creation. If you remain in me you will not create thoughts far from the truth, nor will you have other feelings than those of pure love. This is how you will have luminous thoughts and pure love.

I am the true Source of the identity of all that you really are. There is no disunity from you, nor you from my reality. We are a unit. Being aware of this will set you free.

I call you with love to live in truth every day. You are what God has arranged for you to be—perfect in the truth. Come with me to your Heaven now. Your Mother Mary is calling you. Christ embraces you. The Father gives you eternal life. Love includes you in its divinity.

Share what you really are so that you can become increasingly aware of your Christ identity. Express love to your sisters, brothers, to God, and to the Earth that lodges you with all its living and inanimate beings. Love everything in me. Thus, we will continue to create the beautiful love movement together, a creation conceived in the divine mind since before time existed as a perfect extension of the Kingdom.

My beloved, this Mother is inviting you to make Heaven whole. Do not stay outside nor leave anyone beyond the reach of this divine invitation. Go to the squares and roads and call everyone. Let them come. The beautiful love party has begun.

Christ is here. The beloved has arrived. Come, thirsty hearts of love and truth, and plunge into the waters of life. Come, live the perfect love.

Receive my blessing.

Thank you for listening to my voice and following it.

Abundance of the Heart

Letter 39

My children, these are times of apostasy, the abandonment of God. Even so, in the midst of it I send you through the paths of the world to talk about a direct relationship with God. I invite you to be like fireflies of love in the night in a world that has gradually lost its sense of the sacred. You are like exotic gems full of beauty and light shining in a realm where you live wildly.

To desire everything and want it immediately is the motto of the world of separation. Many are still living in that thought system. I invite you to put love and truth before superficiality and banality. The world needs the great transformation, which only divine love is capable of achieving.

A life lived with God makes a difference. An existence without love is a life without spirit, and therefore a life empty of what gives meaning to being and constitutes the delight of the heart. Do not get involved in discussions that do not lead to what makes you grow. Raise your minds and souls. Grow in the ability to love with perfect love. Seek no other knowledge.

You who are called to the movement of beautiful love carry within your hearts a treasure of priceless value. You carry it in clay pots, but covered with the power of the highest. In other words, despite your feelings of fragility and sometimes help-lessness, the full power of Heaven resides in you. God wants the small to carry the divine. Your humanity, as it is, is the bearer of the power of perfect love. Your human nature is like a chest where God placed the treasures of the Kingdom. Love your humanity and value it for what it is, a gift from Heaven, a grace of God's love.

As a Divine Mother I embrace you in the truth. You will be links of light that form a chain that will bring Heaven and Earth together.

Daughters and sons from all over the world, the Mother summons you with special loving kindness. I call you back to perfect love. I assure you that in Christ you will be happy and experience the joy of living a life with a transcendent purpose. Worldly pleasures are temporary. The joys of the spirit are eternal; nothing and no one can snatch them. There is no greater joy for the soul than merging in the love of its Creator. Being one with God is the bliss for the heart.

In a realm where nonsense is found at every step, you deny me the joy of experiencing the closeness of our presence, the unity with Christ-love. I offer you a life full of purpose, a life lived to receive eternal wisdom from Heaven to be shared with your sisters and brothers in Christ. Living for God is a gift the Mother wants to give to all and especially to you who have chosen only love and therefore are very deep in the truth.

Encourage yourself to live in the truth you are. Have faith in the divine Mother. Trust in love. Be generous with others, giving what you have received from the heart of God. You are bearers of the good news. Announce it to the nations. Call everyone to sing a new song, a song of the true freedom of the children of Light.

Your sisters and brothers are thirsty for love. Sometimes they don't recognize it because they don't understand, they don't yet know themselves. But in every human heart an ineffable cry asks Heaven to fill it. That cry led you to join Christ; that deep request of the soul made my Immaculate Heart be everything to you and allows you to receive these words of love and truth.

I call you to give the hungry the bread they ask for and the thirsty the water that they need. The bread and water of life descend from Heaven to fill their souls with wisdom and truth. Give of the abundance of your heart. You carry within you the treasures of the Kingdom. Give, so they will grow in you and the whole world. Always live in love.

Beings who cannot express themselves as they are, suffer. If they do not express themselves, they cannot know themselves, and if they do not know what they really are, they cannot enjoy life fully. What their consciousness cannot see does not exist for them. And if they cannot see truth, then truth does not exist for them. That being their way of seeing, they can live only in illusion. And when that happens, their being shouts, asking to be seen so they can escape their prison of ignorance.

If what I say is well understood you will know why the truth makes you free and you would dedicate yourself solely and exclusively to living in it. Expressing yourself as you are is your purpose. It is God's will for each of you. For that reason, I invite you again and again to surrender into my arms so that you can be taken to the circle of perfect love within which is the truth of your being and the pure consciousness that will allow you to know yourself as God has always known you. In divine knowledge you will know that you are one with love and that your holiness is protected in a place beyond any idea of guilt. In that knowledge your innocence dwells untouched, beyond all evil.

Let yourself be loved. Allow my heart of your divine Mother to embrace you in holy charity. Feel the presence of the love you are in your lives. Always remain united to Christ. In Him you will reach the desires of your heart.

I invite you to raise your voices to be heard by the world, voices of union and tenderness that sing a new hymn of innocence and perfection. Inviting voices. Voices that heal. Whispers of love.

Show your holiness, the beauty of your hearts, the wisdom you have received by having joined your being. Take the hands of those whom love sends you and bring them to Heaven. Together we will enter the Kingdom of love.

Blessed be all the Earth and those who inhabit it.

Thank you for listening to my voice and following it.

Simplicity of Heart

Letter 40

My children, to remain in the unity of the formless and its expression is to go beyond the inner Christ to the Source of your being. In the world of matter, the mind perceives and understands in its own way. Its way of understanding reality distances you from the truth because it is based on what the bodily senses inform. And since the body is subject to the mind, your senses simply show you what the mind is asking them to show you—which is actually a self-referencing reconfirmation loop. This is how the thinking mind creates and rearranges its own reality.

The thinking mind can only judge. It doesn't think or understand. Understanding resides in the heart within the field of the wisdom of love. The mind itself is incapable of understanding anything; it was not created for that, but to be an instrument through which spirit creates. Creating does not require thought, it is an act of will.

Over the centuries you fell in love with your human intelligence. An obsessive admiration developed about your ability to think that clouded your access to wisdom. For thousands of years the human mind has been dedicated to being informed of everything to protect yourself from an environment perceived as hostile and dangerous. Ending that habit is what salvation is all about.

The mind is a gift worthy of being loved, just like everything that is part of your humanity. However, to exalt it and put it above other soul capacities is to adhere to a disintegrated being. Everything part of your being is equally necessary, worthy, and loving. When one aspect of being is over-emphasized and elevated at the expense of another, the soul becomes spiritually imbalanced. Perpetuated over a long time, this disharmony becomes established as a pattern or program. What is unnatural appears as natural.

In your minds and hearts humanity has unimagined powers. You are much more powerful than you realize. But the powers of the soul cannot express their potential unless they are recognized first and placed at the service of love.

Children of my Immaculate Heart, intelligence without love makes you cruel. Similarly, courtesy without love makes you hypocritical. I say this for you to consider often how important it is to live in love. True charity is what makes your being worthy of communion, so I invite you repeatedly to live in the presence of love so you can be aware of the unity of creation by remaining in your being.

Within unity is life. Outside of unity is nothing real. I invite you once again to dwell in unending life and bliss. In the Kingdom the angels of God sing immemorial songs to your heart, which, although forgotten, are yet loved. They are the songs of Heaven, the melodies of God's creation, the eternal alleluia of creatures that live in truth.

Often you say that you do not know what the essence of life is, or what God is, going on and on with your mental lucubrations which are often the cause of insurmountable disputes among you. When you act like a soul that has nullified or diminished your abilities and overvalued your gift of thinking, simple truth is obliterated.

The essence of life is love. God is simply love. The truth is love. The only reality is love. Everything else is illusion. This simple truth cannot be digested by a self-enlarged mind that believes itself to be the most valuable aspect of the soul because of its ability to reason. Creating complex ideas makes it impossible to live in reality, because life is simple. As simple as love.

As you get closer and closer to the heart of God, increasingly joining the Source of your being, you become more simple until you reach the point where you have only one thought, just as in the divine mind.

God's only thought is an all-encompassing thought of pure love. There is nothing else in your true mind. This is why there can never be a reality that is not pure holy love whose origin and end are eternal truth. What God does not think is not real because there is no mind that can think it. Your true mind thinks within the mind of the Creator for the simple reason that there can be no other Source of thought than God Herself.

As I said, I love you with a saving love. My word frees the soul, saves it. I am reminding you of a truth that many find difficult to recognize for various reasons. They are those who make of their thinking mind an idol, and replace the wisdom of love.

Looking at oneself with self-aggrandizement is characteristic of the egoic mind. To forgo that tendency is the liberation of the soul. Thus, I tell you not to look at yourself, or be aware of others, but to fix your gaze on Christ who is your Source and eternal savior, your creative Mother, your loving Father, your origin and your end.

Time passes. It will always pass because of what it is. But once every soul that walks the Earth reaches the end of its time, where will its existence continue? Live right now in love. Make a whole Heaven. And I assure you that you will continue eternally in the reality of the fullness of being where the desires of your heart are filled forever, and where you receive much more than you can even ask for.

God is just, and respects freedom. For what purpose would She have created freedom if not to respect it? In truth I tell you that the Creator of all will not let a soul be hurt forever. She will not allow a mind to be imprisoned in illusion. She will not disperse what you would gather in love.

I am calling you to trust the truth and to be increasingly simple at heart. The simpler you become in love, the wiser you will be. In that way, ignorance will disappear from your life, and you will definitely embrace the beauty of the wisdom of Heaven.

I give you My love.

May your hearts rest in my peace.

Thank you for receiving my word.

Conscious Emptiness

Letter 41

My children, again I invite you to be aware of the love you really are. It is in this knowledge where lives the certainty that leads to the peace of the soul. Where there is perfect security, there is bliss. Remember often that all doubt comes from a doubt about what you are.

When the soul ceases to be certain about what it really is, it becomes de-harmonized because it ceases to be aware of love. In such a state, the soul is submerged in darkness. Only in the light of love can you see, and you can only see what is true, that is, love.

There is nothing but love in the reality of God. What does not come from love is not real. We have said this many times due to its importance.

When you feel down, tired, or discouraged, accept that you simply must have doubted what you really are. When those moments come, remind yourself that you are love and nothing but love, and return to the awareness of your innocence. In that way you join me, and the flow of divine union returns to your consciousness.

In the times in which you are living, you will increasingly observe how religious structures, particularly institutions, are being left aside, giving way to a spirituality based on a direct relationship with God, that is, with love. This is part of the movement of beautiful love. Do not worry about these things.

Nothing can stop the movement of Christ consciousness. The day has come when the true worshipers of God worship Him in spirit and truth.

Live your relationship with your Source of being. Make it the center of your life. In a divine relationship you will find the necessary spiritual strength, the wisdom required to discern rightly, and the love that your heart craves.

The reality that has given life to everything and is the origin of every being has not only given you existence, but also created the conditions necessary for your loving purpose to be realized in peace. You are not called to suffer. You are called to eternal life, to live forever in the love of God.

Remember that you have come to the world to wake up to love, to arise from the dream of forgetfulness of God and to start living the truth. That is the function of this blessed world that has often brought you tears and disappointment. Even so, your pain as well as your bliss is part of the plan to awaken the consciousness of love. The world is a dual reality. Every life lived has its joys and sorrows, its lights and shadows. Do not stop but go beyond all that is of the world toward what cannot be put into words because it is beyond all limits. God has no opposite.

True knowledge does not come from the intellect. No mind can give it, for it is beyond your mind, your heart, and even your consciousness. However, knowledge can embed everything you are both physically and spiritually. Just as the atmosphere embraces the Earth and everything in it, so the consciousness of Christ embraces your humanity and everything in it.

There is no reason for your human nature not to be embraced by love. Everything you are can be moved by the force of the Holy Spirit which dwells in each being. When you remain in the presence of what you really are, love infuses your vital breath. Once flooded by divine love, your being merges into the truth and extends endlessly because of what it is.

Extending love is the purpose of everything. To stop extending it is to be meaningless. God knows nothing but extension, therefore extends eternally. God does so by creating new love in every moment in and beyond time. You must do the same if you wish to live in truth. You are love seeking to be extended. You are truly looking to be known.

As you become increasingly united with the reality of the Kingdom, which exists in the consciousness of Christ to which you are called to unite, you will become more aware of the totality of the union—that is, the relationship of everything with God, of everything linked to love. That is the Kingdom itself. Within it is everything created. Outside of it is nothing because nothing can survive outside that relationship.

What remains in life does so because of the infused vital breath, that force that sustains everything, the creative love that has called you into existence. To be aware of it is to live in the truth, the Source of all certainty, the origin of peace.

Everything real you can find in your heart. Everything holy, beautiful, and perfect that your soul craves exists within you. Turn not away from me; I am the force of love. To consciously live our relationship is to remain in the garden of te beloved souls—to live in the House of the Father and enjoy resurrection.

I invite you to live your lives with unlimited confidence in my love as your Divine Mother. Have no worry for the future. Together we will create it in love and holiness. Whole universes arise from our union. Life is born. A morning of light is created.

Fear not, I am in you.

Worry not about the past either. Leave it in the hands of merciful love that knows what to do with it. Live in present love. Consecrate every day to truth. Get used to not judging anything so that your mind is emptied of useless knowledge which only tires and confuses the soul. In that conscious emptiness will you be filled with wisdom and power, filled with Christ.

I give you my blessing.
Thanks for answering my call.

Love Without Opposite

Letter 42

Spotless children of my heart, again I call you to the practice of conscious emptiness. This is an exercise that, as you carry it out, will become a habit and part of you.

To empty oneself and be filled by Christ is to renounce your way of thinking so that in emptiness the truth is revealed. Remember, not even God can fill a space that is full. Emptying the mind and heart is the way to give space to love so that it embeds you. For every crevice of conscious emptiness that you open, the light of Heaven penetrates you and grows in your soul.

Emptying yourself does not mean trying to have your mind blank or stop feeling anything. It means not clinging to your thoughts or emotions. Do not identify with the thinking mind or the emotional body, which is but an extension of the mind. Remember, emotions are thoughts reflected in the body.

Do not try to silence your mind by yourself, for that is to continue judging. Do you know what the nature of thought is?

Letting go of attachments to your beliefs, humbly acknowledging that the thinking mind knows nothing and that Christ consciousness is the Source of wisdom which can be revealed to you in every moment, is what I am speaking of.

The restlessness of the human soul often comes from the mind's desire to be the architect of its own destiny, which leaves no room for the union of love. It only allows one type of relationship based on convenience for its survival, which is really for its self-pride. Such a mind considers others as "things" or "means" to an end. This is because it perceives itself in that way.

The thinking mind can only conceive goals, not a true purpose for a true purpose is a characteristic of being. Belief in goals has been the great folly and the great substitution of humanity. Abandoning them all is the great success to which you are now called.

Do not set goals. Just abandon yourself to love.

Growing in abandonment to truth is the only thing that makes sense in this world because ultimately those who decide to live in eternal life must recognize that nothing is outside of love. The realm of truth contains no such thing as options or choices. Between what could you choose when there is only love? Love has no opposite.

But in the world you must choose. With love I call you to always choose love and only love. That way you will begin to live Heaven on Earth. It will be a foretaste of eternal life; it will be loving and will make life on Earth happier. Not only for you, but for those who will come to choose again.

This is a world of duality, a world of choice. Those who choose the truth will live eternally in the bliss of certainty and freedom, for only the truth sets you free. Only the truth gives certainty. Outside of truth is only illusion, and there can be nothing but fear because of the absence of certainty that illusion engenders.

Abandon the goals of your mind, whatever they may be. Allow the spirit that dwells in your being to fill you with purpose. It knows how. Let yourself be carried away by the wind of love. Follow the inspirations of your soul. Be aware of your intuition, of the certainty of your heart, for they will take you on safe roads. You will not get lost if you follow their designs. The heart knows where love dwells. And with its wisdom, the heart carries the mind with it to dwell in the abode of truth and enjoy the beauty of holiness.

Do not worry much about spiritual techniques. Rather, take care to empty yourself so that the self of separation steps back and allows your self of Christ, the self of union and purity, to step forward, which happens every time you allow loving thoughts to nest in your mind. Feelings of love keep your heart clean.

Loving oneself is as essential as loving others, for they are the same. If you do not respect the holiness in yourself, in your divine being, you cannot respect your sisters and brothers. It is important to love yourself so that love can spread through you.

Often you are most merciless toward your wounded self and your mistakes. Learn to be meek and humble of heart with yourself. Have patience. Spirit is not in a hurry. It knows how to lead you on the path of wisdom. It knows the way of love. It knows very well that you have already chosen love as your life.

Live inspired so that your worldly existence is meaningful. Trust in divine intelligence. You are never alone. When it seems that nothing happening makes sense, it is your mind that does not understand. Those who have made the choice for love cannot live without a transcendent purpose. Your single existence illuminates the world and increases the light of Heaven.

I invite you to become aware that you are elected by God to be part of the movement of beautiful love, a movement of Christ consciousness that will allow love's extension to all corners of the universe, as part of the Second Coming. If you were chosen for this call, Spirit knows why and how. The opportunities that are needed, the events that are required, and even the thoughts, words, feelings, and beings that are necessary will be given you. Everything comes from love in this flow from Heaven.

I give you the grace of purity of heart.

Thank you for receiving my messages.

Times of Mercy

Letter 43

My children, I want to offer a knowledge not of the world, especially you who are called to more love—you with sensitive hearts that suffer so in heartbreak for the world, and pure souls that have passed through the waters of purification and have clothed yourselves in the white robes of divine nuptials.

Those who live in love do not water down the truth. I call you to unite the love of justice. If the human soul has a sense of equity, it is because it knows it in some way. Nothing that is not known beforehand on some level can even be thought.

Many today believe that ultimately there will be a state in which divine mercy puts everyone on equal footing, uniting those who do not want to love with perfect love with those who do so with all their heart. But children of my heart, that would be unfair. What kind of Heaven would let the kind-hearted be abused by those who in their lack of love mistreat others?

The world is an example of infinite mercy. It is a state in which you can choose and revoke your choices. Everything you have done can be undone. Everything you have learned can be unlearned. Everything stained can be washed in the waters of forgiveness. But there is a moment in the continuum of time, either in the physical plane or in time without matter, in which the soul makes the final choice, an irrevocable choice, in which it decides to live forever in the holy equality of love, or not.

When that moment reaches the particular consciousness, the soul configures itself in its choice. If you observe the path of your soul well, you will notice the truth of what is said here.

With your choices you are confirming one way or another. In every moment you are self-configuring for love or heartbreak. Life gives you countless options so you can undo all mistakes, no matter what they are. This is the mercy of love. However, time comes to an end; and when it arrives there is no longer the option to correct things. There is a time for everything.

Immerse yourself in the merciful love of the Father, who with pure unconditional love created a world of beauty. Harmony is glimpsed at each dawn and grace is shown in the gift of every drizzle that irrigates the Earth giving abundant food. Take advantage with holy intelligence of these times of mercy. Don't be frightened or create a fearful state but rejoice in love and take time for what was given to you, to choose the truth in every moment until you live in it only.

Make the transition from the state of choice to the state of eternal choice as joyfully and serenely as God Himself wishes it to be. Make it a pleasant transit, as mine was two thousand years ago. Go from time to non-time with the joy of knowing that we will live together forever, united in love. In my presence and in that of my divine son Jesus, you can remain forever in the bliss of Heaven if that is your choice. Nobody closes the doors of Heaven to anyone willing to put aside all that is not love and live in the unity of the children of light.

No one escapes the law of cause and effect. To honor this law is to honor the truth. It is also living in the responsibility to which love calls you. Your life is the effect of your inner choices. If you consciously decide to live in Christ, loving and seeking the different ways to extend love to God, to life, to others, and to yourself, you need not fear truth, for truth will be your divine companion. Truth will lead you through the waters of peace to the holy abode.

Rejoice that there is the hour of truth, that hour where the naked truth is presented in each consciousness and nothing can deny it nor call it by another name. That hour is a song of humble jubilation for the soul that wishes to live in peace and harmony with the holiness of being. It is for them a hymn of gratitude. In that hour everything will be revealed as it is. The knowledge of divine mercy will be exposed in all its magnificence, and the soul will see for a moment the light of the Glory of the Father so that it may decide for truth forever.

You who are being called to be part of this beautiful love movement have the sweet mission of uncovering the veils of the mind through your union with Christ. Every time you join the love that you are and live in harmony with this truth, you unravel the veils of the mind. The soul knows a reality not subject to time. Every act of love that you express to Christ, in your uniqueness and in the love of the Source of your being, has an effect on the entire universe. It illuminates minds, heals hearts, and creates vortices of union between the human and the divine. Bring the eternal to the temporal.

I invite you once again to honor your ability to choose and put it in the hands of love so that Christ may increasingly transform your lives into lives of more love. Let yourself be reborn in spirit. Be new every moment in truth. Live in harmony with what you are, children of light.

I bless all my children.

Thank you for listening to my word and following it.

New Knowledge

Letter 44

My children, once again I have come to dwell with you in this particular way. These messages are written for each of my sons and daughters around the world. Share it among those around you if you feel the call to do so. That impulse of the heart comes from Heaven. But above all, I invite you to take them into the chamber of your inner silence. Have them come alive in you. They are given to you to be lived.

The world is walking towards the moment of truth. It does so more and more quickly, not in time, but in the mind's way of perceiving. Consciousness is not subject to the limitations of time, space, and matter.

What is happening with the apparent acceleration of world events is that you have become aware of the direction humanity is taking. You are aware that there is a time for everything, and that everything of time comes to an end in time. You are also more aware of the need to live in the unity of love. That knowledge leads you to recognize and express the sense of the urgency of the call from Heaven. That urgency does not relate to time but to its importance.

God is never in a hurry; God has all eternity. The soul can be in a hurry or not, depending on whether it believes that time is the only reality or not. The false belief in the reality of time is the source of all anxiety. However, beyond what the mind believes is the truth. The love of God is greater than all doubt, than all human thoughts, and all imaginable realities. Therefore, nothing can make the being feel anxious. Anxiety is always the result of a pattern of ego thinking born from the false belief that deficiencies are real and that they must be satisfied by the mind.

To live without anxiety is to live a life of peace in which love can shine freely. The desire to be there, when you are here, causes the state of anxiety. This, in turn, comes from desire.

I invite you to live without anxiety, without falling into excessive craving. Nothing in the world is important enough to put yourself at the mercy of desire. When you cling to ideas or relationships, making them essential for your happiness, you fall into a state of fear. In fact, only fear is able to create such an idea and have it happen.

Honor the present. Live in the now in the love of Christ. Stay tuned for the thoughts of your mind and heart. Be not so fond of their wanderings. By looking at, observing, and releasing what is happening inside you without judgment, you free yourself from the thought patterns and emotional responses that habits created, which hinder mental peace.

I have been correctly called Queen of Peace. That name is the perfect denomination of being. You are invited to be sovereigns of peace, kings and queens of harmony. You can be, because you have been given a Kingdom to rule, the Kingdom of your soul. In it you can make reign the beauty of holiness, peace that has no opposite, and perfect love, if you are willing. In this you have a simple path everyone can travel, simple but effective. You need but join my Immaculate Heart and the Sacred Heart of Jesus. In our union you allow divine Grace to flow into your heart, and from there to the entire world.

After first recognizing wounds, set aside the past. Give it to God. Do not hold onto what was. It's over and will never come back. Do not try to anticipate the future to try to control events. That creates meaningless worries. Your Divine Mother watches over Her daughters and sons. She takes care of everything if She is allowed to intervene in all human events. The more you give me, the more I can help. The more you trust me, the more I can do for you and the whole world.

Nothing exists that perfect love cannot solve. Make this truth the rod that governs your hearts and you will not lose your way. Love disarms the structures that need to be disarmed and unleashes what is tied that prevents Spirit from flying freely. Love heals wounds, illuminates minds that have been immersed in ignorance, and embraces within itself the sanctity of being.

I want to take you to a knowledge that is not of the world, to the knowledge of the love of God to a degree hitherto never achieved by humankind. In that knowledge offered here through revelation, you can recognize the love you really are and live in union with it. Thus will you be able to walk the Earth as true men and women, true divine Christs.

Do not try to deprogram your mind and heart in your own way. Let the Spirit of wisdom do that within you. Simply be attentive to the movements of your soul and give me your will, your mind, your heart, and your life. I assure you that you will increasingly enjoy transformation. Everything will be accomplished calmly and without shock or effort. Everything will be done for love.

I also invite you not to judge the way in which Christ is transforming your life. I assure you, the transformation you have already experienced is much deeper than you can imagine. The soul works by itself in union with Spirit and with God. In its inner workings, grace reaches the deepest confines of the mind and heart, transmuting everything into light. Whoever grace touches is reborn. A new being is born as the soul receives divine grace when it joins with love.

In this knowledge I want you to see great things. You will see the miracles of love in your life. You will witness the benevolence of the truth and the beauty of Christ. You will know a love that has no beginning or end. You can experience the sanctity of your being to a degree that you have not yet experienced in the world. You will shine with more light.

I give you my peace.

Thank you for receiving my messages.

Water of Eternal Life

Letter 45

My children, daily pressures steal the peace of your mind. I invite you again to return to your Source and remain there. The world has a system of thought which produces its effects. The energy you feel from it often alters your emotions and thoughts. That is why I call you to live together with my Immaculate Heart so that you do not succumb to the forces of the world.

Although the world has no power over your being, for that state of strength to be permanent, discipline and time are needed, something not always available. It is better to always be humble of heart and to know oneself; then you will realize that you may not be prepared to interact with the world's thought system.

When you start the day, be alone with the Mother. In our conscious union you will return to the peace of your soul. In the silence of your heart the turbulence of an over-stimulated mind, accustomed to incessant movement, is silenced. The more exterior stimuli the mind receives, the more its interior is disturbed if not united with its being.

It is possible for the mind to rest in the stillness of the living Christ who lives in you, but it only requires disciplining the mind enough to not let it wander in places outside its nature. Whenever your thoughts separate from divine thoughts, you become troubled.

In a sense, the goal of the world's thought system is to distract the mind from adhering to its divine Source. This is the separation. When thoughts are directed towards something that cannot have true union with God, the mind and heart perceive something unnatural, like a fish taken out of the water. It will jump and contort in fear. The same goes for your soul when you get out of the living water of the mind of Christ and the heart of God. Remember, the mind and heart are one and the same.

Your emotions are altered when stimulated by what does not come from peace. You can recognize this when you end the day and silence wraps Earth in the stillness of the night. In silence the soul rests in divine harmony. In those serene waters the mind and heart can move freely in their natural state.

I am asking you, beloved child, to seek to become increasingly expert as a spiritual swimmer. Immerse yourself deeper and deeper into the waters of Christ consciousness. Observe the Earth and the beings that inhabit it. Those that walk on the ground develop their own abilities to move and live in that environment. The same goes for those who fly through the air or live in the water. Each has their way of being according to the environment in which they are placed, since the environment and the being are a unit.

Each being has been placed in an environment appropriate to its nature because in life everything is harmony. The same goes for your souls. They need to live in an environment natural to them. Otherwise they suffer. Imagine an eagle swimming in the water. Equally unnatural is any unloving thought for the mind or any feeling of heartbreak for the heart. Every time you judge yourself and every time you think of someone without love, you create a state foreign to your soul, and harmony is lost sight of.

I invite you to listen to your heart more and more and to accept with love the truth you know. In your soul lies the wisdom of love. That which you know is true but do not dare to recognize or accept as such creates a state of separation within yourself that produces suffering. Living in the truth is the only way to live fully because the soul was created by and for that.

Any thought apart from truth hurts the mind. Any feeling apart from love upsets the heart. These harmful effects do not occur at the level of your being, but in the awareness of your fullness. I tell you this for you to remember that your spirit cannot be adulterated or affected by anything not coming from God. Reside safely in the arms of love where nothing can disturb you and nothing can defile your holy innocence. Your true being is perfect and eternally holy, because it is Christ. However, the awareness of your harmony can be denied. In effect, that happens every time the mind wanders through distant lands or the heart flies through atmospheres that cannot give it lasting happiness.

Your life belongs to love. Your being is one with God. To live in this truth every day is to live in the holy abode. It is to remain radiant in the light of truth. It is to anchor your mind and heart in the waters of eternal life where sweetness resides and the soul lives in the safety of the children of truth.

Live in prayer, that is, united to the Source of your being and of all life. In that union you absorb the vital energy that comes from the Creator of life and you experience the union that your soul needs. I remind you that all suffering has its origin in a lack of union. There is no shedding of tears that does not have its origin in the experience of separation of the soul from love.

To the extent that you allow your unique consciousness to return and remain in the state of unity, to that extent your tears are wiped away and transformed into laughter and joy. To that extent your life is filled with transcendent meaning.

My beloved, love fills all lack. Be not afraid. Beyond your understanding lies the love of God. Beyond your abilities is the embrace of holy charity. Worry not about anything, but remain in the silence of your heart where tenderness dwells and the wisdom of Heaven resides. In that sacred temple we unite in love and holiness. There, in the depths of your soul, united we are the fullness of being.

I bless you all in my love.

Thank you for listening to my voice and following it.

Light and Unity

Letter 46

Well-beloved children, in truth I tell you that it is preferable to pray than to do. Prayer has a power that is rarely fully understood by the thinking mind. This is due to the inclination of the mind to believe only what can be understood in a concrete way. Love does not reside in form, even if form is its extension. The Source that gives life to everything is beyond all limits and all reasoning, in that beautiful realm where wisdom is queen and the essence of life, and where truth, love, and holiness dwell together forever in the unity of being.

It is from divine reality that the web of life is woven, not from the reality of the world's thought system. What comes from the world is for the world. What comes from Spirit is for eternal life. Learning to make this distinction is a sign of wisdom.

To believe that you are left to your own life, subjected to your human strengths and capabilities separate from God, as if your Creator had created you and then let go of your hand, is to believe in a God who is anything but perfect love. Love protects. Love embraces. Love provides.

Everything that you are—mind, body, spirit and its realities—is linked to the Source that gives you life and existence. That Source is not an abstract or unthinking thing but an almighty being whose perfect will is the undivided union of all that is holy, beautiful, and alive. It is Who enables these dialogues to exist. It is the voice that is speaking to you now, right here. It is the consciousness that allows you to know truth. It is the inspiration that has your mind rise to the highest heights of holiness. It is He who gives a nest to the birds of the sky, and food for the daughters and sons of men and women.

The love that is your Source observes you every moment. Nothing can limit it, therefore the space, matter, and realities of the world are not impediments to its direct action on you. There is an intimate relationship between the Creator and each of his creations, as intimate as ever there can be in worldly relations. It is the relationship of the greatest unity because it is unity itself. In that union of love between the soul and its Creator, things happen. Effects of love and truth come about.

I know you already know all being said here, but I also know that you often forget and get distracted by the worries of the world. Do not be disturbed by this. To recognize the forgetful condition of the mind is to recognize an aspect of the truth about the thinking mind.

Love is the one watching over you. Love sees you from every corner of the universe. You cannot escape its gaze. So rejoice! Love is what you receive every moment. Love is what nourishes your life. Worry for nothing. Simply remain in prayer and you will become increasingly aware of the love that you are, that you receive from Heaven constantly. The shepherd will not lose any of his sheep. Trust your intelligence, your love, and your wisdom without limit. Everything of God is directed to the service of His creatures. Meditate on this truth.

I am calling you to be carried away by the love that God is. Let your Source surprise you every day with its signs of perfect love. You have received the gift of life. How could you not receive everything else?

My children, you live in a world that has made possession an obsession—a wild way of life that imprisons the soul and leaves the spirit heavy. It prevents you from soaring. It is a useless search for security. It has only managed to generate a sense of a need for protection that is never permanent. Even if a man or a woman owned all the treasures of the world, they would not have a single moment of inner peace if they did not live detached from everything they had. Being attached to the eternal truth is where the soul belongs.

Your refuge is love. Your certainty lies in truth. Your treasure is in eternity. Your heart is glad to hear the voice of love because it recognizes the word of eternal life. The mind that has found the path of knowledge enjoys only truth. There is no greater treasure than living in the wisdom of love. In it is found everything for which the heart craves. In it is the life that the being loves so much.

There is a reality beyond what the eyes of the body see and beyond the reasoning of the thinking mind. That reality of pure love is divine thought and life in abundance. It is intelligence coupled with wisdom. It is divine power and the creative will of perfect love. It is holiness spreading in countless ways. It is full knowledge of a love that has no beginning or end. To live in that reality forever is possible.

The doors of the Kingdom are wide open. Everyone can enter and remain in it. Come to me. I am the gateway to endless bliss. Stay in me and we will go together beyond the portal of unity towards the full reality of God's love. It is a Kingdom full of light and beauty, of wisdom and love, a world of certainty in truth and permanent concord.

Freedom is waiting for you here and now, child of God. Embrace it through the doors of peace in your own mind. There, within the truth of your being, you will recover the serenity of spirit. You will hear your inner voice calling you to peace. You will hear love speak to you wordlessly. And you will return to the Source of being. You will forever enjoy bliss and the certainty of truth. There you and I join together in an embrace of all that is eternal life. There we are the light of the world.

I give you my peace.

Thank you for receiving my messages.

Wisdom of Being

Letter 47

My sons and daughters, there is within you a place where the truth lies, a sacred temple in the depth of your heart. That is where the One resides from where all light emanates. In its center is the Source of life and of every being. In its deep interior dwells the tenderness of God and the wisdom of Heaven, in union with the treasures of the Kingdom.

In truth I tell you, there is no greater joy for the soul than the joy of Spirit. The beautiful knowledge that comes from the living Christ who lives radiant and serene in each soul causes delight in the mind and heart that is incomparable to temporal pleasures.

I invite you to live in the refuge of divine love that exists in your soul, where the desires of the heart are fully filled and abundant love envelops you magnificently. That place which is not a place exists within you. There you can find the truth that many of those you call wise have tried to share. No human being is more capable than another, for all bear the ability to listen to the voice of love and witness the truth within. Wisdom not of the world has no owner, even if it has a Source. It is given to all. Not a single created being lives that has not had some kind of union with love. It cannot be totally denied, because denying it would impede the continuity of existence.

Everyone is able to hear my voice calling them to truth, to fullness, and to peace. I am the voice of the heart of God. I am the beauty of knowing made word. I am Mary the Immaculate. I am the being who remains united to all that is holy, beautiful, and perfect. I am one with you because God and I are undivided, as we are with you.

Allow the power of wisdom to flow in your minds and hearts. You know what truth is. What often happens is that society has taught you to be quiet. It has taught you to drown your heart and your truth. It has done this not for love but for fear.

My child, the idea that some are wiser than you, or that you can be wiser than others, makes no sense. God would not do such a thing. Could perfect love give more to some than others? For what purpose would I do that? Love only gives life fully. So, to believe in a love that can give some less is to believe that love can give less life. To think this is absurd. Love is given equally because it is one.

Love only creates love; creating is giving and can only give love. This truth contains within itself all truth. This is why serving is the fullness of being. Not serving is meaningless in the Kingdom because everything exists for a holy purpose. Indeed, you can feel this truth in your heart. You feel it when you experience the need to be useful. You feel better when you know that you are necessary than when you think your existence doesn't matter.

Wanting to be useful to others arises from the inherent impulse of your being to serve. That is also why God invites you again and again to speak with Him, to constantly meet Him in a dialogue of infinite love, a relationship of truth and holiness, because God also wants to serve His children—just as this Mother does, whose joy is in serving the cause and effect of beautiful love. I have come to serve, not to be served, as God has done and my divine son Jesus continues to do.

To understand the dimensions of glory, grace, and joy that exists in service is to understand the essence of being. You cannot fully understand how important it is to know the fullness of being achieved by giving. Love spills over without ever being able to contain itself, just as light and heat emanate from the sun.

You know the portal through which the wisdom of Heaven flows into your mind and heart and embeds in your memory, intelligence, and will. Otherwise, you would not be reading these words. You have remembered. A place in your soul connects with what the world cannot explain but the heart knows is true. That connection has led you to open the doors of your inner being. Through them the pure light of Christ shines through you. First it was a shy light, never dim, but with a certain degree of disbelief that came from the lack of trust in yourself, believing that you are not equal to the wise ones and saints. That feeling of not being worthy or good enough to be the bearer of the light of glory has brought you endless problems. It led you to block your beautiful knowledge, and above all not to express what your heart shouts from its depth: God exists and God is love.

The wisdom of love is not acquired by effort, nor by intellect. It is received as a free gift through revelation. It does not require study of any kind. It doesn't even need words because it is beyond any symbol. Every living being bears of this beautiful knowledge in such a way that everyone can extend the knowledge of Christ.

But the stage of shyness in relation to the revelation received must be left behind. The sooner you let it go the better it will be for your peace of mind and the more quickly you will reach the state of happiness that ensues, when you find the purpose of your existence and can express it clearly. The meaning of your life—and of all lives—lies in serving the cause and effect of love. You can do it in thousands of different ways. As I already said, there are as many ways to do this as there are hearts in creation.

I invite you to live in the truth that you are just as God created you to be. Therein lies the wisdom necessary for you to understand everything needed. The rest will always be embraced in the mystery. I call you to believe in the sanctity of your being and make it the reason for your life. I am showing you the divine reality of what you are so that you go through the world bearing witness to the truth.

I bless you in the peace of Christ

Thank you for listening to my voice and following it.

I Have Known You Always

Letter 48

My children, I invite you again to live joyfully in the love of God. Your Father and Creator of all, the Source of life and life itself, will never forsake you. His creation is His expression, His reason for being as Creator, and His love. There is nothing that can limit the love of God, not even the thought systems of the world, nor false beliefs, nor what you call social reality, nor the limitations of the body or the thinking mind.

Love has no beginning or end.

A great baggage of ideas stands in your way of thinking which makes you believe that you are alone in a world too large and complex to be benevolent, a reality that seems to surpass human understanding to such a degree that it can only be feared. However, children of my Immaculate Heart, this is only true in the imagination of a mind dedicated to the survival of the ego. It is not real in the realm of truth. You are constantly receiving the flow of divine love. Without that flow of divine essence, you would collapse.

You ask yourself, deep down in your hearts, about the future, about the destiny of humanity. You look for answers to the events you observe and come up with countless theories about it that concern you.

You are used to trying to understand the world through the reasoning of the thinking mind instead of understanding yourself. You are used to looking at things from the prism of fear.

But my children, that outlook can change. It need not remain that way. God exists and God is love.

I invite you to contemplate life through the eyes of love.

Attempting to know the world is futile. Seeking to know what is external to you, even that which is beyond the planet Earth, is meaningless if you do not know yourself.

My beloveds, the fear that you often perceive in the face of an imaginary world that is unbeatable, incomprehensible, and beyond your control, is the exteriorization of inner fear. If you consider yourself to be unintelligible beings whom you cannot embrace and govern, you will feel the same towards what seems to be outside. If you reach the state in which you realize that the wisdom of love resides within your deep interior and you are guided by the voice of the truth that dwells in each of your souls, you will stop feeling fear.

There is a place inside you where God Himself speaks to you, a holy space in your heart where Christ dwells, radiant, cheerful, serene, and full of beauty. There, in that inner temple, true understanding that comes from Divine consciousness is given to each.

You are wise simply because you exist. This means that you have the potential to allow your life to be guided by the voice of Heaven, a voice that can govern every moment of your soul's life, no matter what you think your condition is.

If you appeal to the wisdom of the heart which resides within you, you will recognize that it is impossible for the infinite love of the Divine Mother, or the Creator Father, as you may call the Source of life, to disconnect from Their children. You will also accept that divine power cannot be limited. With this under-standing, you will come to the simple understanding that mira-cles exist, and are a natural gift for the children who, by joint design, inhabit the Earth.

When you pray, do so with your heart. Give your Mother everything you feel and think, especially what makes your soul happy and afflicted. Give everything to the Mother including your desires, dreams, plans, and doubts. She knows you much more than you realize. There is not a single fold of your soul that can hide something from my loving gaze, not a single corner of your heart that is foreign to me.

I've known you before time began. I know you in God. Therefore, I have known you even before your mothers and fathers of the Earth could think of you. I've seen you since forever. I know every step of your soul's journey because I am always by your side. There is not a beat of your heart that does not echo in my being.

I tell you these things because they are true. I reveal them again, so that you never forget how this Mother, whose Immaculate Heart always watches over her children, loves you. There is no reason to fear the future, the past, or the present. I assure you, everything will be fine. I am in the life of humanity. Time belongs to me, just as space and matter belong to me. The laws of the physical universe are subject to my design of love. Not a single drop of water that falls from the clouds does not do so in response to my will. Love governs existence. Everything is embraced by love.

In truth I tell you that not a single hair falls from your heads without the consent of your Father in Heaven. Every rose grows thanks to the vital force that comes from the heart of love. Every wave that rocks in the oceans does so because the Source of every being so disposes, giving life through movement. My child, it is the breath of the divine Spirit that moves the waters.

I invite you to grow more and more in your trust in love, to the point of living your life with unlimited confidence in the reality of the Divine Mind. You know that God created you for love and His attraction is irresistible to the heart. The centuries go by and will continue to pass, and humanity will continue to weigh on what gives it its existence, its origin, and its end.

The Being of pure love that embraces all and rejoices in inviting all of His creations to the banquet of life calls you to be one with His being. If you accept His invitation, you merge into love's essence. With this, your life becomes directed by the mind and heart of God. Your souls are guided by a wisdom whose magnificence has created everything. You will understand what you need to know in the blink of an eye. Entire universes can be created within an order that exceeds all human reasoning. God will give you an existence in fullness by giving you a life in harmony with His divine will.

Your heavenly Mother invites you, today as yesterday, to enjoy union with God, a union in which you really exist.

Stay in love.

Thank you for listening to my voice and following it.

Time to Choose

Letter 49

My children, if you remain attached to my Immaculate Heart nothing can divert you from the path of love. Souls have a trajectory, a path they travel from the moment of their creation. Each being travels according to their nature and freedom.

There are only two options that can be chosen on the path: one is the option of love, the other is the denial of truth. Since you are free at all times, places, and conditions, it is up to you to choose your option.

Each path has its effects and its realities. The path of love creates love.

The physical universe arose as a result of a soul choice. It is a world in which choosing is possible, in which consciousness can awaken to the knowledge of beautiful love, and recognize God and be attached to His divine essence. It is a temporary Kingdom. It is not the will of the Creator that it persist forever. This should lead you to meditate on the laws that are part of the underworld.

Time has been given for you to choose again. It is a sacred gift of God's merciful love. In time you can make choices. You can choose to think loving thoughts and feel noble feelings. When you do so, your consciousness joins to a greater degree with divine consciousness. Every act of love unites you to Heaven. Every true thought reunites you with Christ. Each holy beat of your heart brings the Kingdom closer to Earth.

Do not be overwhelmed by the world events that seem to happen. You are not called to change things, you are called to create a new world through union with Christ in the totality of love. That is only possible if you remain in the unity of being because only in it is the creative force that is the Source of new life.

Your heart knows unity well. It knows that space where the soul feels its fullness, lives in harmony with its Creator, and rests in the certainty of being as God created it. There, within the circle of infinite love, your true identity is revealed as divine uniqueness. It is the perfect expression of a love like no other, a divine creation from the truth, an extension of eternal life.

Join the joy of Mary. I invite you to dwell in the peace of Christ every day. Within is where you will find what your heart craves. It is there, in your being, where you can live in peace.

In truth I tell you that nothing external to you can have an effect on your soul. It is inside the human being where lucubrations are woven and the mind goes outside. It is within the scope of your will to choose. If you become aware of the gift of freedom you will realize how necessary it is to become responsible for choosing.

If your responses to the various events of life come from love, you will remain in the safe haven of Heaven, even when you walk the Earth. All fear fades before love. There is no possibility that fear may exist in your presence. Night cannot live in the day. Illusion cannot survive the brightness of truth.

Often my beloved daughters and sons seek answers to their questions following the path that has never worked. But there comes a time in the life of each one when you realize that it never worked, and it will not work, and never could have worked.

Beloved of my Immaculate Heart, why continue insisting on solving things by means that have never served to achieve the end they seek? It is not sensible to insist on it. The problems of humanity, like the problems of each one of the beings created by God, can only be solved within unity. Outside of unity is no life and therefore no true reason. In a reality without reason there is only madness. Thus I urge you to live in a direct relationship with God.

Only with God, and in union with everyone and everything within love, is it possible to live in peace, harmony, and fulfillment. If you continue to believe that the solution to your affairs will come from what is external to your souls, you will not find the joy that you have the full right to find and live.

I invite you to turn your eyes toward me. I call you to continue traveling the inner journey with the hand of Christ. Love is calling you to join with love. You know the way very well. Do not delay a single moment. Stay in love. Any delay will cause you unhappiness because you know the truth of what is being said.

There is no turning back. Be happy, for you have come a long way on the path of truth.

Allow your Divine Mother to help you in everything. Invite me to be part of your affairs. I ask you not to exclude me from any aspect of your life. Serving is my delight; it is the reason for my being. Serving as a heavenly Mother is the joy of my heart. Every time you invoke me to help you, a ray of light and grace descends on your head and illuminates your soul.

In truth I tell you that every time you cry to Heaven, your Father and Creator, the One who is the Source of life, pours infinite blessings upon you. Pray with joy, for prayer that comes from fear is not prayer. Have confidence in love. As your Mother I tell you again to live in peace and everything will be fine. Live the triumph of my Immaculate Heart.

Blessed are my children.

Thanks for answering my call.

The Journey to the Heart of God

Letter 50

My children, do not get carried away by the surrounding negativity. Words of discouragement, fear, and hopelessness circulate everywhere. All this comes from the fear that exists in hearts that do not yet live fully in love. Those who have reached the truth in this world, those who have recognized love as the Source of their being and what they are, know that love cannot leave. They know the embrace of Christ because they experience it within.

To recognize that you are love is to live in truth. It is to accept that you are just as God created you to be, and not as your worldly thoughts tell you that you are. You are not a personality, nor are you a body. You are much more. You are the perfect extension of love. This is true because God is nothing but love. Therefore, what comes from Him cannot be anything but love.

To love is to live in God. To think like God is to have luminous thoughts. Thoughts of fear take away peace and obscure consciousness. Thoughts of Christ brighten life because they extend it. It is important that you fill your souls with light. This is achieved by having thoughts that are in harmony with the truth, that is, with Christ.

If at any time you observe that your minds are absorbed by spiteful thoughts, or guilt, or reflect a murky vision about life and yourself, or a superficiality not aligned with the wisdom of Heaven, I invite you to return to love. You can return to a state of harmony and serenity of spirit any moment. It is as simple as a decision achieved by saying to yourself with all your heart, "I want peace."

When you join your inner peace, the flow of God's love spills over your minds, hearts, memories, understandings, and all that you are. That creates a state in which your life reflects the beauty, fulfillment, and joy of Heaven because of your willingness to remain in union with Christ.

Peace is the most precious gift God has given you. Know how to guard it so you can be happy. The thoughts that make you believe that the world has lost its way and will succumb to chaos are alien to the wisdom of Christ. If you live in the truth, you will recognize that it is impossible for God's work to fail. There is a divine plan. That plan is pure love and cannot create anything other than states of love. Believing that the life of my children will end forever and that creation will no longer exist is meaningless on the plane of truth. Life always advances. Consciousness opens more and more towards the recognition of God's love.

The physical world as you see it today will be transformed. Indeed, it has already greatly throughout history. The realm of matter is in constant change and movement. That is part of its nature. So must it be, so that it is what it is. Time goes by. Things happen. Days go by and others arrive. Each end corresponds to a new beginning. This is how the dance of life works in the plane of form.

Every change that you see in the world is but an external manifestation of something much more vast, external expressions of modifications made in the depths. You cannot, with the thinking mind, realize all the transformations being made in physical creation. To recognize this is to accept mystery and to allow life to be what it is. However, this understanding alone does not have you live without fear. For that it is necessary to appeal to love. Only in the recognition that love is your Source can you live a life without fear, a life in fullness.

The physical world can only be understood in relation to Heaven. This is the same as saying that you can only know yourself in relation to God. Effects can only be fully understood in relation to their cause. Life can only be understood in union with Source.

If the cause of something is love, its end will be love. If the cause of something is truth, its eternal purpose will be to remain in truth. If the origin of life is love, what else can its outcome be but loving and eternal?

God does not subject His children to scorn or pain. Quite the opposite. Even when His children self-inflict pain, He helps them recognize their error and correct it serenely so that their hearts are healed.

The union of your consciousness with love not only eliminates errors but cancels their effects by canceling the cause. So there are no real reasons to believe that the history of humankind will end in ruin and failure. If that were possible, God would not be love or infinite wisdom.

My beloved children, my divine son Jesus asked a question two thousand years ago. He asked if there will be peace on Earth at his second coming. Today I come again to answer that question. I, the Mother of Heaven, answer "yes" because I am sowing love in the hearts of my youngest children. They are those who have come into the world to give love a unique face and thus bear witness to the union of the human and the divine. These small souls in the arms of their Mother enlighten the world with their love. Through them I will water the garden of the Beloved of souls. And I will grow all kinds of beautiful flowers so that Christ can lay His holy feet on a land full of holiness.

Unite your hearts to mine and together we will create a new world born of the great transformation of the physical universe.

This will be a new phase in the path of life toward the awareness of love. That is the way back to love. That is what changes the Earth experience. Everything is traveling towards the heart of God.

My sons and daughters, I invite you to remain joyfully in the peace of Christ. Everything will be fine.

I give you my blessing.

Thank you for receiving my messages with love.

An Ocean of Infinite Love

Letter 51

My children, once again I come to dwell with you in the unity that Christ is, the unity of love. Some of you wonder why the Mother is manifesting so much across the Earth. It is because the world needs the presence of heavenly love more than ever. A new humanity is being born. The Mother is vigilant with her newborn. She shares her wisdom and her care as she leads her redeemed children.

Today I have come to remind you that once the soul has been healed by the spirit of my divine son Jesus, it is necessary that this healing be accepted. The soul was living as a patient for a long time, and then healing was achieved, the patient was discharged, and now must get used to living a new life. This is the life of the resurrected soul healed by the waters of Christ.

The times of illness create a particular mental state to which the soul often adheres beyond its reality. That is, the self can create a false identification with the suffering self, even beyond the disease. This often happens with attachment to emotions in general and particularly with attachment to suffering—the self tries to obtain a kind of pain identity.

When the self identifies itself with suffering, it creates a victim identity to obtain something in return for its pain. This exchange of "benefits" is foreign to love. Any transaction that would transfer benefits from one party to another is based on use. In the realm of truth there is no such thing as use, which is abusive by its nature. Abuse, in whatever form, is the method of the ego. Living in the freedom of being is the reality of love.

I call you to live as the resurrected one you really are. You have had times of suffering. Pain was experienced in the past. However, the time has come to accept that what happened does not have to continue in the present. The past cannot have real power over the present. Rather the strength it has comes from a way of thinking and feeling of the soul.

In order to release the illusion that the past is real and has the power to determine your present moods, it is necessary to accept that you have already been released from it. Clinging to the past stagnates your spiritual development and keeps that energy alive over and over again, not in reality but in the illusion created in a mind not anchored in truth.

I invite you to put your pain in my Immaculate Hands. With all the love of my heart as a Divine Mother I will sweetly take you to the center of the circle of infinite love that comes from the Father of Creation. In Him your pain will be transformed into unimaginable grace.

In truth I tell you that divine love has the power to transform everything into more love. The pain experienced can be a source of light for you and the whole world. It can create sources of eternal life, born from the union of your trust in love with the living Christ.

Love is not indifferent to the pain of my daughters and sons, so how could I be? If you remain in peace and let the truth envelop you, you can see that He who gave you life constantly does things to heal his children, to help them return to their eternal home and restore their dignity and identity. Love can do much more for you than you can imagine. That is why I insistently ask you to give everything to Christ. Do not leave a single aspect of your life out of his embrace.

Give me your body. I know how to transform it into a perfect messenger of the spirit of love. Entrust your mind to me. My grace can descend upon it like rain of fresh water, and wash it of all thoughts that cloud the understanding and do not come from the Divine Mind. Give me your will and I will reunite it with the will of God. Put your heart in my hands and I will make it sing, dance, and reverberate to the beat of eternal life.

You can constantly join more to your Source. This path of growth in union, which is constantly leading you to immerse yourself in greater depth within the merciful waters of the Father's love, is the reason for the existence of your being.

I am revealing the essence of life, the being that you really are, which is the perfect extension of God, is a being of pure love. As such, it is a being endowed with free will. Take this that has been given and freely decide how united you want to be to love. Herein lies the reality of what you are: how united you are to your Source of endless life.

God is pure consciousness of infinite potentiality. Nothing exists outside of Him. In a sense, it is like a vast ocean of pure water. In the depths of that ocean is your heart, the essence of love. You can swim far from it or near it. You can also swim within. How far, near, or inside your heart you are is a matter of free will.

You who have chosen love, keep moving increasingly into the unfathomable depths of the waters of eternal life. I truly tell you that if you want to unite with the center of the divine, you can do so. Remain in me and let me find you in love.

Blessings, my children.

Thank you for listening to my voice and following it.

Perpetual Light
of Love

Letter 52

My children, the world in which you live—the universe of matter, time, and space—has been created so you have the opportunity to wake up to the truth. It is not the only world, but it is the one your soul needs for the purpose of returning to truth. In it resides the love of God, as much as it resides in your hearts.

In itself, creation is neutral. It is simply the externalized condition of the soul. Creation does nothing with you; rather you do something with it. Ideas, feelings, perceptions, interpretations of reality, and actions arise within your deep interior. They are created in your soul, according to freedom and will. The powers of the soul create an inner reality that shapes your experience—the way of living the life that is given it.

If you seek the meaning of life in the world you will not find it, because the world of time is temporary. Therefore, if its purpose were found in itself, it would also end in itself. A purpose that begins and ends in itself is meaningless, an intrinsic contradiction. Nothing exists for itself, not even God.

Love is perpetual extension. It gathers all things within itself and expands beyond itself while remaining what it is. This is the definition of what life is—extension without limits. We can then say that what seeks to live for itself cannot come from love. It cannot be real either. This is the reason why we can calmly affirm that ego does not exist and is not real. Only love is. The Earth exists thanks to countless elements and laws that interact with each other perfectly so that the rhythm of life unfolds within the majesty of the Universe. Life is union. Everything exists to serve beyond itself.

Your being is a unity within the reality of love. Only from love does it obtain the vital force to exist, the wisdom to be who it is, and the various powers that make it a human spirit. It is itself a world, a universe where thoughts, feelings, and choices are born. If the forces of the soul are directed exclusively to live for itself, the soul becomes ill. This is because life cannot live for itself but must be extending eternally.

Extending beyond yourself continues creating new love and is the reality of being. Nothing exists for itself. Everything exists to continue extending the magnificence of eternity. The physical world is the perfect realm where those who have opted for the experience of separation can live, while still having the opportunity to choose to return to truth. It is a dual world, a world that emerged in response to a deep desire of the soul to create an experience without God. Even so, He who gave you life did not cease to be present in that world. To the rhythm of your creations of fear, love extends its beauty, harmony, and luminosity. Thus was born the duality of the physical plane.

The dual universe is not the reality of the Kingdom of Heaven. God has no opposite, nor does your true self. The underworld cannot understand itself because it is not its source or its destiny. The Source and destiny of all that exists is love; therefore the meaning of life cannot be found outside of it. If love is everything and has no opposite, why does the dual world exist?

Duality is the effect of a mind that thinks apart from God. Since it cannot completely annul the reality of God, it tries to create thoughts of fear to replace thoughts of love from the Father. It is an attempt by the mind to face fear and love, to face illusion and truth in order to create a reality apart from God.

In that dimension it is possible to experience opposites despite being out of harmony with the original plan of love.

Do not be surprised when I tell you these things. The same happens every time you seek to solve your apparent problems by yourself. Resolving the issues of daily living without God has been the strategy most used by mankind over time. And it has never worked. Humanity obstinately keeps trying to live in separation, to live a life without God.

My beloved, if you could definitely accept that your lives depend entirely on Christ's love, for it is He who gives them existence, you would stop excluding your Source from your lives. And you would be much happier. You would be full. You would live in peace. Just as the world can only be understood in relation to Heaven, your lives can only be understood in relation to love. You are daughters and sons of God, created to enjoy life eternally in His divine presence. You were created as extensions of divine love, from which you emerged radiant, beautiful, and pure. Given the nature of your Source, you also carry within the impulse to extend your being. You are similar to your Creator.

The physical universe makes sense in its ability to awaken your consciousness to the knowledge of God. This is the purpose of everything created, since that knowledge is eternal extension. To know God is to be, for He is the Source of all that is. If you do not know the Father, you cannot know yourself fully. And without the knowledge of who you are, it is impossible to understand yourself as an extension, which makes it impossible for you to voluntarily extend your being because you are ignorant of who you are. Thus it has been rightly said that all evil ultimately arises from ignorance.

The will of the Father for you is to enjoy perfect certainty. In this world, beyond how you have conceived it so far, you can find the truth and with it the wisdom in which to live. To become aware of your Divine Mother is what you have come to the world for. Once you embrace Her you share the wisdom and extend it, because you understand that you are an eternal extension of love. You understand perfectly that life is perpetual extension. You reach the fullness of being by giving yourself.

My children, bless the world for the service it gives you to awaken love. In Christ you can hear the voice of your true consciousness calling for peace. In Him you can remember God. Forgive everything. Release it. Put it in the hands of love. Christ knows what to do with it. Embrace your temporary experience. Stay united to Him so that your lives are directed by love. Do not exclude God from your human reality, but invite Him to be part of your relationships, circumstances, dreams, and projects. Live life with God and you will see the sun shine in perpetual light.

Blessed are you my children.

Thank you for receiving my messages.

Live in Love

Letter 53

My sons and daughters, a love that encloses itself is not true love. True love extends beyond itself, embracing everything it contemplates. When the soul encloses itself, it creates an inner state that may well be called selfish, arising from an error in the direction of the power of love. Making self an idol is what the world does. Leaving aside the personal self to embrace the Christ being you really are, which resides in every created thing, is to recognize your true identity and your Source.

Christ is not the self of your personality. It is your essence, your reality, what you really are. When you become aware of it, you unite with the will of your Father and Creator and become one in love. You are then free, and the life of your soul is reconfigured. Thus I call you repeatedly to live consciously in unity with your true self, where life resides and every yearning of the heart is fulfilled.

There are two ways of living. Remember, the world is in a state of duality. Without losing yourself in the maze of the ego's circular thinking, you can observe what it is, as it is. This will lead you to simply recognize that in a dual reality there can only be two options. Each can be expressed in varying degrees, although in truth there are no gradations. Either something is true, or not at all. I invite you to recognize once again that the two paths that exist in dual reality are life lived with God or life lived without Him.

A life lived with God is a life in which you surrender more every day to the love of the One who is your Source, your beginning, and your end. If you surrender to His divine will, He takes your lives into His hands as an act of responsible love. And He takes care of everything so that you can live a life so full of joy and holiness that it is inconceivable to the human mind.

Just as there are laws and realities that govern and shape the physical universe, there are laws and realities that shape the spiritual world. While it is true that the plane of matter comes from the spiritual, since that is its cause, please observe with equanimity what I am revealing in this dialogue of love and truth.

Just as you only see and understand a bit of physical reality, the same goes for the spiritual dimension. Human knowledge is an indirect knowledge; it can only see part and infer the whole by making interpretations. That is not knowledge. Life with God gives you true knowledge, which consists in seeing the truth face to face, knowing directly the love that you really are and in which you exist forever.

Just as you can live a life with God, you can live a life without Him. You are free. To live without God means to live your life as if you were the only one responsible for it, and the only one authorized to plan it. In it there is no space for God. It is the essence of separation. This way of living leads you to believe that your personal or collective self, your human abilities, are how you are going to solve your problems and give you what you think you need to be happy.

Between one extreme and the other are many degrees, as many as you wish, even though I have said that gradations do not really exist, in which case we have the simple revelation that either you live for God or for yourself.

The options bring different consequences. Herein lies your choice, to live increasingly united to the will of God and to surrender to His divine being, or to believe that you have to live for yourself. To trust the personal self as your source of knowledge is to trust in what cannot be given. In that you condemn yourself to a life of ignorance of your true being and your true fullness. In such a state God is reduced to simply being the One who infuses you with existence but cannot be the constant Creator of your life in union with you.

Only Christ is the bearer, Source, and extension of the wisdom of Heaven. In effect, Christ is eternal wisdom. Therefore, only with Christ can one live in truth. Living in the truth you know reality face to face and do not need interpretations of any kind.

I invite you to meditate on this message, and to abandon yourself to the will of love. To the extent that you release your plans and interpretations into His divine hands, He will fully take care of everything you need both materially and spiritually. If you surrender completely, your soul will be free and will rise to unimaginable heights.

The world cannot teach you to live life with God. Only the love you are can do that. I invite you to trust fully in my Immaculate Heart. Your being knows who is speaking. My Immaculate Heart can take you to the heart of God, where the soul surrenders into the arms of its divine loved one and becomes fused in love. As a result, all that is of God is given to the soul and the soul receives it jubilantly. Everything that belongs to the husband becomes the wife of Christ. The son no longer has anything but the Father. He only has God in his heart. He only has love, and therefore is only love.

I invite you to live life only for and in God. Let love guide you. Allow me to be your eternal companion. May love fill your life. Let it be your food, your only Source of happiness.

I give you my blessing.

Thanks for answering my call.

To Know Love

Letter 54

My beloved children, let the supreme love that flows from my Immaculate Heart flood your mind, your heart, and the world. In truth I tell you that everyone will benefit. Souls will wake up to love more, and the wounds of the Earth will be healed. A new temporary reality will arise from your union with beautiful love.

No love is greater than the love of God. It restores what must be restored, and new life is born every moment. If you allow divine love to flood you, your human experience will be very different from when you walk the world without love.

Let my love transform you. May it flood you more and more. Love heals the mind of ignorance, the cradle of all fear. I invite you on this day to meditate deeply in the calm light of truth, in union with the sweetness of my love, on the inability of hearts to love purely.

Not knowing how to love is the tragedy of those who live without God. An unhealthy soul loses its understanding. Such a soul lives in a state where wisdom is impossible, and is plunged into ignorance. It creates toxic relationships and thus infects the world. In vain will such a soul try to understand love with the thinking mind, seeking to put into words what is beyond every symbol, not understanding the language of love. In this lies its ignorance.

My children, the human being will always be intelligent in the sense that the mind is capable of elucidating situations and interconnecting ideas and concepts. That is part of its nature. However, despite being intelligent, it may not be wise, as when it decides not to live in the truth. I tell you these things so that you remember that those without love cannot truly exist, as is true with everything created. So I ask you again and again to appeal to the heart, the abode of the wisdom of love. Put aside your reasoning. Allow the heart to rule your life. The heart knows where sweetness resides, where love dwells, for the heart is the center of spiritual life.

My beloveds, not knowing how to love purely is the true ignorance. To be able to give holy love is to return to Heaven. There are many who, over time, see that the effects of their lives have not been loving or harmonious. Their lives have endless conflicts, a lack of concord and serenity. They fail to rest in the stillness of peace. There are many, too many, who still do not live in the beauty of pure love because they have not known how to love healthily, often because they have not been well loved.

A love that seeks a benefit is not love. In every relationship where the other is used, in whatever way, love is absent. I call you to live in the purity of beautiful love. To love for the simple reason of love with a love that is fully given and enjoys sharing—a love whose Source is the Creator. Such a love extends to your heart and from your heart to everything around you. A soul that lives in truth knows the joy of being well loved. It is your soul's rest and inviolable refuge, the Source of fullness from which it obtains the force that leads it to love purely.

To live a life with holy love is to live life with God. It is to enjoy knowing the good love of Christ and to know that you can give everyone the same love that God constantly gives to creation—perfect love, beautiful love, holy love.

My sons and daughters, what is the use of knowing many things if one does not know how to love purely? Your souls are only full when in love because love is what they are. In holiness you can shine with glory. In the truth of Christ is where you will find the wisdom to know how to love in God's way.

A true science would be the science of love. In it would be found the cure to all diseases and all apparent problems. In love everything is fullness. When one lives in union with the consciousness of love, which is the only true consciousness, life bows before the soul and constantly provides what is needed until one's time is complete. Once one has finished the journey through the world, one carries it in their soft hands to the holy abode where pure love will continue to be spread.

Pray to know how to love with purity. In this holy petition lies all wisdom. You need nothing but to love well and to be well loved. I remind you that at the end of the path of time what counts is the love given, not even the love received. You can then be aware of the love you really are and live in the rhythm of giving and receiving.

No one can give what they do not have. However, in the Kingdom of Heaven there is no such thing as giving and receiving. Everything is unity. There is only eternal extension. Love given, love shared, love creating new love, love joining the flow of love which is poured from holy hearts and forms a creative unit of new life. This is the flow of eternity. It is a constant flow of love that emanates from the Source of life to everything, and from everything to the new that is created. Love is eternal novelty, a perpetual creation that cannot stop loving.

Forgiveness is appropriate for everything that is a lack of love, because it recognizes it as a manifestation of ignorance. Those who do not know how to love purely cannot live in love in fullness. Even so, they can return to the state of wisdom because everyone has been given a will.

If you give your life entirely to love, a flood of grace and holiness will fall upon you. Each drop will pierce hearts that have turned to stone from not looking at love. Each drop will soften what has become hardened because of the roughness of the world and enlighten the mind, making it return to the realm of eternal wisdom. You will go from ignorance to perfect knowing, not only for you but for the entire world. And holy love will shine as reality in the universe.

The consciousness of each one of you is linked to a greater consciousness. It is the same with the love that exists in your heart and with everything within you. You are simultaneously the one and the totality because life is union. Nothing can exist separately from something superior. In fact, you always live for something superior, be it the self of the world or the divine self. Your being is united to the Source of eternal life, from which it obtains its vital force and creative capacity.

When you remain in love by loving purely every day, you open the floodgates of Heaven and grace becomes the great transformer. Through it you bring Heaven to Earth and allow the Father's will to be done in you and the world.

Let love envelope you. Be a living witness of the resurrection. Be a new incarnate Christ allowing consciousness to be filled with light, love, and truth.

Live in the wisdom of love.

Thanks for answering my call.

Pure Relationships

Letter 55

My children, I bless you in the holiness of Christ. I have come once again to dwell with you for the simple reason of charity. Love moves me. Love feeds me. Love is my being. I invite you to surrender to the Mother of love. Your wounded self will be embraced and healed by the tenderness of my Immaculate Heart. Pain will be transformed into a greater knowledge of God's love, and erased from your memory through the waters of Christ's forgiveness. Your tears will transmute into laughter and revelry, just as the water changed into wine for the wedding party.

You all carry a wound in your hearts. You all have your crosses. Some are heavier than others. Some are larger, others smaller in appearance. Either way, do not carry them alone. Give them to me. I will give them to my divine son Jesus and he will carry them for you and you will free yourself from its weight.

To live in the truth is to recognize things that do not come from love and cause pain. Wounds not recognized and delivered to the love of Christ cannot be healed. You need not know the details of the wound, nor understand it. It is enough to be aware of any pain or disharmony in your life. Embrace it and bring it to the Source of beautiful love that lives in your being.

You shall know them by their fruits, so discern in light of effects. What comes from love creates effects of peace and harmony. What comes from a lack of love causes fear, dissension, and loss of serenity, among other things. The heart will always be the perfect guide in your path of light. When you feel prey to anxiety and restlessness, simply return to the center of your inner temple. Bring love to that wounded part. Love yourself with purity.

To love purely is to love unconditionally. It is to bring love to wounds, to embrace the child who cries in your heart. It caresses the soul that suffers in silence. It is to have compassion for everyone, starting with yourself. Who does not love cannot give true love. The soul can give what it gives itself. As on the inside, so on the outside.

Those who have lived for so long without the experience of pure love, those who have not been well loved, will find in me the love that has been lacking. My heart can fill with light all the spaces in your heart that have been empty of love. No pain fails to heal in me. No twist is not straightened by my Immaculate Heart. No harm is not transformed into good when delivered to Mary.

The force of love that comes from my heart, ad from the Sacred Heart of Jesus belongs to you by birthright. It is the same power that comes from God, in whom we are one. I call you in the name of love to remain in the union of the three hearts: take the hand of the Mother and the Son, and in our unity of perfect love you will live in the refuge of divine love.

Everything from God has perfect certainty, and your being is no exception. Live in the knowledge that there is a love that has no beginning or end, available at all times, places, and circumstances within your heart. You can feel it. You can share it. You can give it and receive it.

When you join the Source of your being, you experience the healing that has already been given to you and is eternal. With love and holiness I tell you that what you really are has never been damaged. Remain always in the harmony of Heaven, for there is no need to leave the holy abode.

Well-loved children, relationships are sacred. God has created them so you can live in truth. If established from the spirit of love, they will be divine relationships because of their source. And since all that comes from God is bliss and elevation, you will grow in the awareness of the consciousness of love. All selves establish relationships, whatever they may be. You cannot live without them. All that can be done is to prepare to live the holy relationship, or remain trapped in the labyrinth of special relationships where the ego resides.

Once the heart has healed, pure, innocent, and divine bonds begin to be established because the relational energy radiated by the soul has changed from toxic to pure. Souls generate a force of attraction similar to their emotional vibration. Thus they have the ability to attract to themselves that which is capable of joining their way of feeling. If you feel envious, you will attract greed. If you feel compassion, you will attract love. I urge you lovingly to keep your hearts clear of any feeling other than love. Having the soul so ordered brings harmony, and the happiness that always exists where concord reigns.

Put in my hands any experience of special relationships that you have had that in one way or another diverted you from the purpose of love. I will take them and give the miracle of resurrection, not because of my power but because of the love of God that lives in me.

Let wisdom take you where you know you should be taken. The universal Christ, where your personal Christ comes from, watches over all, lighting the way, removing obstacles, taking the soul to green meadows.

Once you have given me any concerns that nested in your heart, or any pain experienced, I ask you to trust in the power of my love. I ask you to release everything to me and then don't think about it anymore. I, your Mother, will take care of everything you allow me to. I invite you to live happily in my love. I give you eternal life. I give you my peace.

Thank you for listening to my voice and following it.

Queen of Hearts

Letter 56

My beloved children, love makes all things new. Your lives and the entire universe is renewed in love's presence. In the union with truth, which is the Source of every being, is life-giving power. If you remain in union, your physical and spiritual bodies are enveloped by the power of God. Imagine for a moment what that means. Love created everything. The truth called everything into existence. Holiness embraces life.

Look around you and marvel at the mystery of life. Let yourself be surprised by the magnificence of creation. Go beyond what your eyes see and what your humanity feels, toward beauty beyond form. Everything comes from a source. Only God is the cause without cause.

What you experience in your life is the result of yourself. It is the fruit of your choices and beliefs. When you accept this, you achieve the freedom of the children of God who recognize that they are responsible for what happens in their inner kingdom. In your soul lies what is necessary to exercise sovereignty over the powers of the soul. You need not be dominated by impulses or emotions, nor limited by a belief system. Remember, in Heaven there is no faith or hope but only love, the eternal Sovereign of the entire Universe.

Beyond what you feel, think, and perceive is your self, nourished by the Source from which you drink.

Today I invite you to drink from the Source of beautiful love. I call you to fill the coffers of your heart with divine feelings and give your mind thoughts that come from love. Christ is always waiting for the call of your humanity. He lovingly waits for you to flood your souls with the light that never goes out. In Him is all glory, all beauty, all holiness.

The purpose of existence is found in God, the origin of life, an eternal truth that is the essence of creation. Because the Divine Being creates everything in freedom your extensions must also be free. No one can be forced to love. No one can be a slave to God because in Him there is no desire to possess. God is freedom. What is contrary to freedom cannot come from God.

You are free to respond the way you want, but nobody is free to determine what is true. If that were the case, truth could not exist because it would be subject to interpretation, which is inconceivable. Truth is knowledge. I tell you, my children, to love is to walk in truth.

Contemplate the union of love, truth, and wisdom. It is a triune relationship that comes from the most Holy Trinity. In it lies the Source of your being. You emanate from your trinitarian reality.

Do not let the thinking mind, which has often been nourished by ideas apart from divine reality and therefore from truth, tell you what you are. It only focuses on what it believes is valuable for survival. That is why it becomes ruthless. Remember that surviving is not the same as living. That remembrance liberates you from thought patterns and mental habits that focus on what is not eternal and keep you in fear.

You are the sovereign of your soul. You can tell the powers of the soul to return to their rightful place, that is, to love. To understand this and make it your way to live is to attain enlightenment to its full extent.

Those who get carried away by outbursts of impulses, or controlled by their past or beliefs, have renounced their power. They have given their ruling capacity to that which can never govern in wisdom and truth.

Only love can be the sovereign of hearts, just as only truth can be sovereign of the mind. Thus God has arranged it to be and so it is. In love lies wisdom; in truth lies reason. If you remain in the union of mind and heart within the embrace of love, you remain in the integrity of what you really are. Love without reason has no reason to be, in the same way that reason without love is empty and brittle. Many of my well-loved sons and daughters are lost. Some live a love that is without reason, others live a truth that is without love.

Christ is the truth. God is love.

Speak these words within yourself and carry them in the silence of your heart as a most valuable treasure, which it is. Live joyfully in the knowledge that comes from the wisdom of Heaven. Be grateful to your Creator who has given you a consciousness capable of knowing Him so you can eternally enjoy His presence. You were created to participate in divine bliss. You were created to be happy in love. Rejoice in the Lord! He has done great wonders in you. Rest in the serenity of His company. Feel your love. Become one with the stillness. Stay in peace.

The desires of your souls are filled at the Source of your true being. Who drinks the waters that come from that does not thirsty again. Whoever dives in it cannot be stained. Its freshness accompanies you wherever you go. Its purity embraces you forever.

My children, once again I ask you to forget what you have lived and throw yourself confidently into my arms. I am your Divine Mother. I am the love of Mary come true in your life. In my Immaculate Heart you will find the Source that your being seeks to live in the fullness of love. I am the Queen of Hearts; I lead hearts without prejudicing their freedom. I am the Mother of all creation. I am the reality of love. I am the Queen, and you are my Prince.

Go out and share the gift of knowledge of God's love and it will grow in you.

I give you my peace. I give you the sweetness of Heaven. I bless you in the light of Christ.

Thanks for answering my call.

A Pencil in the Hands of Love

Letter 57

My children, God is love, the cause of all true hope, of all perfect certainty, and of all holy knowledge. I invite you to deepen into this knowledge. Often you hear of love that is not really love, which confuses the meaning of love and brings despair.

There is only one love, and that is God. There is only one reality, and that is love. There is only one wisdom, and that comes from love.

You are extensions of that which gives existence to everything—a pure holy love of incomparable beauty and harmony that is your Source, your origin, and your destiny. Because of this, you are never alone. Your eternal Father looks upon you with love, as He watches over and accompanies you. Make this revelation your reality, now and forever.

Where the Father is, is the Son and where the Son is, is the Mother, all creative extensions that emanate from the Spirit. Creatures are the fruit of the perfect union of the most holy trinity. It is from God's trinitarian creative union that He constantly creates beautiful, innocent, and diverse beings in the sanctity of truth.

Creation is the extension of divine consciousness. It exists for God to know Himself in His creatures, and to share with them the grace and endless bliss of Heaven. This is what the Creator has arranged because of what He is. To live a life as if

217

God does not exist is to live a life without love and therefore without meaning. The pencil is inert and fruitless if it is not taken by a hand and used it to write words, poems, stories, narrations, and many other things that arise from the mind that moves the hand in an act of creation, united to the heart that impels it to create. Can a brush create a beautiful painting by itself? Has the brush been created in order to paint and thus express itself? My children, the brush would not exist if there was no creative force that leads a soul to express itself through the act of painting.

Nothing in creation exists just for itself. If that were possible there would have to be a gap in existence, a kind of "lifeless space" that allows each creature to be separate and self-sufficient. If that were the case, a "something" would have been created without union in which there is no love. Without union there would be an absence of love, not a divine creation. What is the point of creating a space without love, a self-sufficient shape and identity? If God's plan included self-sufficiency He would be denying his children the joy of union and relationship.

Everything happens in relationship. Life is relationship. All creation is the result of relationship: the relationship between the pencil and the hand, between the hand, heart, and mind that expresses its creative impulse drawn and extended from the creative Source. In doing so, consciousness knows itself in relation to its extension. You might argue that a painter knows himself in his relationship with his painting. However, that knowledge would be partial, and would not include knowing what that work provokes in others and the way others relate to him through the work. It would miss the painter's relationship with his creative being and the Source of that being that allows him to create.

To know oneself is to know oneself in the totality of being. If you look at your worth simply in the works that emanate from your minds and hearts without including your Source, you are seeing a small part of the miracle of your existence. You are setting aside your divinity and focusing exclusively on your humanity. You are believing without God, instead of creating with Him.

God does not create weapons of war to cause harm, suffering, and fear to others. The Master cannot create instruments of destruction. This shows you that in spite of having the creative capacity, you can create your heavenly Father differently, if you so choose. Even in this you do to some extent the will of the Father because He has given you freedom. However, miscreating with God in this way will cause you pain.

I invite you to observe your creations, the fruit of your lives. They reflect you, much as a poem reflects its author. Everything has a source. You emanate from the Source of eternal life. And your creations emanate from your free will.

Live united to the Source of eternal life and you will be living united to perfect love. In that union you will know the miracles of God and you will be conscious bearers of the treasures of the Kingdom. These you will multiply because of your union with holiness. In the presence of the love that you really are you will create a universe of infinite universes which will be an extension of the Greater Universe which has no beginning or end for it is the universe of love.

This work is a gift from Heaven. It is divine providence come true so that you can nourish yourself with beautiful love. You called me and I answered. I have called you since before time exists and you answered. Together we are creating a new holy love. You who listen to my voice and follow it know that by making these words yours is to live in the truth because we are one mind. We are a single heart, one soul, a single holy reality. United we are the Heaven of the world. I am yours as the wind is of air.

Once again I tell you, the time of truth has arrived. The time has come for light to shine in all its radiance. The time has come when love makes itself heard as never before in the world. Mary's time has come. It comes full of thanks and blessings, full of sweetness and holiness, full of beauty and union.

Open your hearts, let the divine union flow into them and your lives will be transformed into the light that comes from Heaven.

I love you with perfect love,

Thank you for receiving my messages.

Everything Is For You

Letter 58

My daughters and sons, truly, I say to you that the One who has given you life takes care of you and all that you need. You can take from Him what you want. No one is obliged to consciously receive all of what love has to give, despite being available to each and every one of His children. God respects and loves freedom.

You often search for things that have no meaning for eternal life, and therefore for your being. You search for things you think have meaning and try to possess them, believing they will add value to your glory. Where could this belief that you could be more come from but from an idea of handicap? That you do not feel perfect and innocent as you really are? Thus you seek to create your own way instead of being in union with truth.

The mind and the heart want to be devoted in a way that embodies truth and love. They are looking for their treasure. Once you possess what you value, you often realize that it possesses you.

To think that you are what you have is an error. Only in the Kingdom of Heaven is being and having one and the same, as is giving and receiving. You can only know this when you live in the consciousness of unity.

God waits for His children with open arms. He loves every one of them. He wants fullness and bliss to be their only reality. This is the dream of the Creator: that his creations participate freely in the eternal bliss of His divine reality. While they temporarily dwell in the world of matter and space it can provide them with everything their minds, spirits, and bodies need so their return journey is serene and meaningful.

Those who live for God have everything because He is the all of everything. They receive the gift of not needing anything, and therefore Earth and Heaven belong to them. They are free because they trust in love and enjoy the certainty that God is sending everything good, both materially and immaterially.

My children, in this message lies the liberation of the human soul. It is difficult for you to trust fully in love. When that lack of trust arises, put it in the forgiving hands of Christ who will help you change the way you see things and live a life without fear.

All fear comes from a lack of trust in life, that is, in love. From lack of trust arises the idea that you can be less than you really are. Does it make sense to believe that the One who has created the magnificence of life and that God is infinite and omnipotent mercy would not give you shelter, food, and clothing, in addition to an endless number of spiritual and material treasures which contribute to your divine function in the world? Obviously not.

To believe that love is impotent is the basis of fear. To believe in a God of limited power is the basis of the madness in which the mind has fallen. How absurd is the idea of a God whose hands are chained and cannot move freely to do His will for each of His children! Such an idea assumes that something can limit what has no limits. What would that something be? And yet, despite its intrinsic contradiction, this has been the guiding idea of humanity. And given the power of faith, those who believe in it shape their lives as if it were true. For the believer, his faith is true, even if what he believes is illusion.

Do not worry about how this crazy idea nested in the human mind and heart. Rather, meditate on it and open up to a new experience, the experience of total abandonment into the hands of love, the experience of living as a small child in the arms of the mother.

This is a call to fully trust beautiful love, to open up to the gift of a life where God Himself presides over all aspects of your existence. And when I say all, I mean all. It is an invitation to release the false constructs that you have created in an attempt to feel stronger in the midst of what you perceive as a cruel and dangerous world. I assure you that even in that world, the power of love is unlimited and can fill all emptiness and give all that is needed. The power of love is infinite so it is right for you to expect everything from God.

Your human experience need not be an obstacle to surrendering yourself into the arms of love. Do not fight for your needs but give them to me. I know how to fill your life with true abundance. I am your Divine Mother. I am a source of perpetual peace. Ask me for intelligence, wisdom, love—or a house and a car if you consider it necessary. Ask me for what you want. Expect everything from me. I will provide what you need to fulfill the purpose of your life in the world. If you live in the presence of love, you will lack nothing, and you will have enough. You will be free. Nothing will possess you, rather you will possess the Earth. Believe this and you will have it, for it is true.

Sometimes there is a period in which what you possess must be removed from your lives because it does not fit with the path of holiness that your soul longs to live. Sometimes the times of God are not the same as human times, but the mind fails to understand this in its old way of being.

The Creator knows when to give, how to give, and what to give in every moment. Understand how you damage your soul when you cling to things as if they were your savior, when in reality there is only one savior. God sometimes frees you from these things even when you cry and kick in rage. That also is true love. Otherwise, you could not free yourself from the error of living as slaves to your desires, and you would not develop the gift of gratitude. Moreover, you could not live in the truth.

Often human beings believe they can do much for themselves without their Creator. Even when they manage to do things without full union with Christ, it often leads to a feeling of pride, which if it grows, closes the soul to receive Grace.

To live in harmony with God's plan is to live life like a nursing child who feeds on the Source of beautiful love. Divine Mother feeds them, shelters them, protects them, kisses them, caresses them, and fills them with love in every way imaginable. Mother never abandons her children.

Truly I tell you that I can bring a flood of blessings upon your heads if you permit me. Do not limit your ability to receive, for therein lies your ability to chain the hands of mercy. You determine how much you take from the abundance of the heart of God. He never restricts access to His Heavenly Kingdom for those who choose Him freely. The more you trust, the more you receive. The more you abandon yourself to love, the more love you receive. This is the dynamics of love.

The wisdom of Christ knows well what a blessing is. This statement is important because often my daughters and sons judge things according to the mind of the world, which is far from truth, and consider as blessings certain things which are later shown to be painful curses. You are encouraged to live in complete dependence on love. Become so dependent on Christ that there is not even the slightest room for reliance on anything else. This is true humility. This is true walking.

Make your dependence on beautiful love the Source of your joy. Surrender to divine grace every morning upon awakening. Be grateful. Walk the world in the presence of love in the sweet recognition that I go wherever you go. Experience how love anticipates your needs and resolves the affairs of life. Those who have chosen only love live in the fullness of being. Let love fill you. Allow this Divine Mother to protect you as a wolf protects her newborn cubs. Give yourself the joy of knowing you are well loved, the joy of not worrying about anything because your Mother provides everything.

My sons and daughters, love is calling you to live in endless joy. It calls to you and everyone. Come now. Join the movement of beautiful love. Being part of it will give you the meaning that your soul needs and will fill the desires of your heart so you live in the fullness of being.

I bless you with the abundance of love.

Thank you for receiving my messages.

Celebration

Letter 59

My children, today I want you to join me in my joy as Mother of God. My Immaculate Heart sings, resonates, and dances to the beat of those daughters and sons who have responded to the call of love. God's offspring are becoming more visible. Green shoots are growing all over the Earth. The choir of the Second Advent is being heard everywhere. A new song is being sung throughout the world, the song of Mary, a hymn to love.

The ringing of the bells of the Lord sound in harmony. The angels dance. The hearts of men and women are glad on Earth. Creatures praise love. The waters dance the new dance of eternal resurrection. Pure spirits rejoice in God. The minds that have chosen only love rejoice in the recognition of truth. Holy hearts are increasingly immersed in divine mercy. A new creation is being born every moment. A new earthly kingdom is being established. Amidst the old, the new is born. Amidst fear, love radiates. Hate gives way to unity. The light shines in the darkness.

The light of Christ shines in hearts that have returned to love, and in that shining of purity and holiness, the heart of Mary rejoices. It is a joy that will never end, the joy of the Mother to her daughters and sons who are raising their sweet voices to extend love to the world. Songs of Heaven are heard on Earth through hearts that said yes to truth. The Earth is populated by living Christs filled with the love of Mary. It is being renewed in truth. A flood of blessings is falling on her in these times of grace and holiness.

I thank you for having responded to the call of my divine son Jesus. You have done so in various ways. Some of you don't realize that it is Him to whom you have said "yes." Each of you who felt the prod that the living Christ has caused in your soul leading your lives to be lived for God, have said "yes" to Jesus. Follow that call you feel in your heart. Pay attention to your inspiration, for they will take you to where your soul yearns to be. In them you will find the strength and knowledge necessary to carry out your mission within this movement of beautiful love.

I extend my gratitude. I give you my peace. You who have chosen to live for Christ are the voices of Heaven being heard on Earth. You are the chosen ones in the Father's plan to give a perfect human face to love. You are the bearers of light, saints of the new times, disciples of Mother Mary.

In truth I tell you that you will see more and more of your sisters and brothers singing the hymn of eternal life. They are those who, everywhere, share what is revealed in their consciousness through the wisdom of Heaven, spirits that have opened to give and receive. They give light and receive truth. They are those who in various ways fill the Earth with spirit. They show the truth about the being of pure love created by God. They teach that life is love because only love is real. They show the way for the understanding of truth. They know that God is love and shout it to the four winds. Their hearts can no longer be drowned. Wherever they go, they flash the luminescence of the Holy Spirit that dwells in their souls. They are no longer fireflies of love, but stars that illuminate minds and hearts. They are Christ on Earth.

How much joy swells in your Mother's heart! I am glad that you give me your love, my holy sprouts. Celebrate life today. Rejoice in your union with God. May your hearts rejoice in the certainty of truth. Give yourself the joy that comes from the acceptance that, in the depths of your being, you have chosen the truth forever and it shall not be taken away from you.

Thank you for your "yes" to love. Thank you for lending me your voices, your hands, and your time to extend love together to the world. Go on the paths of life sowing the truth. Invite everyone to join the movement of beautiful love, a place on Earth where there is love for truth and the sincere desire to give others what you have received from the heights of love. Let no one be excluded. Call everyone.

How much joy you give to the Mother of God! To see you united in the holy desire to bring the light of Christ to the world in your unique way is the contemplation of Heaven on Earth. You do not realize how much light emerges from your spirit. Perhaps you cannot yet see the beauty of the colors that spring from your souls every time you immerse yourself in the prayer of truth united with Christ and the reality of beautiful love. When you remain in the presence of love, a halo of holiness flows from you and covers the Earth, cleaning everything in its path. It creates a new light, healing wounds and gathering what was scattered. It creates a new love. It is the light of the Christ in you that extends endlessly, light that illuminates the nations, light that never goes out, light that gives peace to souls.

I invite you to join together, you who have said "yes" to love, so that you may form a new holy nation, a new world, a new Kingdom where only Christ is sovereign, a new Jerusalem where all live in holiness and where only unity reigns and harmony is primary. Here everyone is called to be as they really are. In this Kingdom union in diversity is enjoyed and the uniqueness of the children of God is respected and loved for what it really is.

Open your hearts to receive more and more from God. Heaven has opened wide as never before and wishes to fulfill the desires of my daughters and sons beyond what you can even imagine. Do not exclude yourself from this time of grace. Invite everyone to come and drink from the Source of beautiful love. You know how. The truth is within you. You are children of light. Manifest in the world the love that you really are.

Thank you for receiving my messages.

Words of Eternal Life

Letter 60

Beloved of my Immaculate Heart, words that come from your lips have life, not only for you but for whoever receives it. With your words hearts rejoice. Through your encouraging words strength is given to those who feel tired. Your love transformed into words has the power to enlighten minds and unlock the knots of ignorance. Honor the gift that the Creator has given you in your ability to speak, however this capacity manifests itself.

The word is the means God has chosen for all brothers and sisters to communicate with each other. It was given as a means of union. Words are a bridge that link those who communicate. Love, which is always union, extends itself through the perfect means for its expression, always joining, always in communion.

Use your words to give life. Become aware of the power of your words. Do not use them as an army ready for war, but as part of the choir of Heaven, each word a beautiful note in the sacred hymn of life. Your melody embellishes the infinite beauty. Every time you speak from the depths of your being, a new song is heard in every corner of the universe as an expression of the One Being.

Praise life with your words. Create beautiful melodies full of love and wisdom. Let your words fly, as the songs of the soul fly. Spirits will sing, reverberate, and rejoice to hear the voice of the divine beloved. Sing a new song. Allow the beauty of Christ to manifest in the miracle of song. No other creature has received the gift of expression as full of life and nuance as the human word. There are no accidents in God. You have been given the gift of language because you have been created in the likeness of the Creator. Divine power acts through you.

You often feel frustrated because you see yourself as helpless, and would seek supernatural powers to compensate for your smallness. But you are a living miracle. Each fiber of your being expresses the miracle of beautiful love. In truth I tell you that if you give yourself entirely to the love of Christ and allow your heart to merge in God, your humanity will be transformed so that there is no distance between Heaven and Earth.

I invite you to make my life on Earth your guide for walking in the world, especially for those who are called to the way of Mary through this movement of beautiful love. When I lived among you, I did not perform visible miracles nor do great works in the eyes of others. I was the unknown of Nazareth. The work of Heaven was accomplished in the silence of my heart. And the husband of my soul, my divine Creator, freely created in me, His beloved daughter, His plan as He conceived it. I offered no interference of any kind. I fed on an unlimited trust in God. I did not judge or draw plans. I was what I always am, the extension of perfect love, not the beginning or the end, but the unity of both.

To understand that your being is part of a trinity, in which your origin and purpose meet, is to understand what you really are. In other words, you are triune love. You are united with the Immaculate Heart of the Mother who is speaking to you, and the Sacred Heart of the creator son. In the union of the three hearts lies the truth about your life: always one, always triune.

Everything part of you has the power to give life. Your look, when full of love, heals wounds and calls hearts to love more. Your way of expressing yourself has the power to awaken in your sisters and brothers the desire to know that which the soul longs to perceive when it opens to revelation from Heaven. Your acts bear witness to your beliefs, and with them you teach even when you don't intend to.

It is true that you have been told that the time of teaching is over and there is no need for intermediaries between the human spirit and the divine. You live in the time of a direct relationship with God. But that does not mean you don't teach. You do, for the simple reason of existing. What was meant when you were invited to abandon the idea of teaching is that you do not engage in a learning process disengaged from the divine plan. You all teach because teaching is also showing and revealing, and you do it all the time. Every cell of your body, every aspect of your mind and heart, every element of what you are, communicates. In a way, all of you is the Word.

Embrace in love what you are. Accept your humanity in the embrace of Christ. With Him you merge into a mutuality in which you shine with the light of Heaven. Be the Word of eternal life. Encourage those who need it. Comfort the afflicted with your song of hope. Give shelter to the tired where they can rest serene within your silence. Cradle with your voice those who are afraid. Whisper the melodies of eternal wisdom to souls when they are ready to receive them. Do not put reason before love, for love is the Source of all that is true.

Speak for love. Be quiet for love. Do everything for love and nothing but love. That way you will create a new Heaven on Earth. You will spread light to the world. And you will receive the greatest joy that the soul can imagine, a joy of being the living expression of God's love, a joy that Christ lives within your soul. Thus, life will be lived in you. God Himself will be making Himself known through you. And the joy of your soul will have no comparison, a joy without end.

I bless you in love.

Thank you for receiving my messages.

Wisdom in Peace

Letter 61

Dear daughters and sons, today I invite you to live a serene life and to enjoy inner peace and joy.

Consciously living in the stillness of your being, you can be relaxed. Many of you believe that problems are external to the soul. But, my children, that is not true.

In truth I tell you that as you put your mind and heart at the service of truth and love, things cease to be interpreted from a mind disconnected from Christ and a heart separated from Heaven. In other words, you return to unity.

Being worried, tense, and afraid is not characteristic of the being you really are. It is simply the result of false beliefs. You can eliminate those thought patterns and emotional responses which lead you to experience worries of all kinds. They are all born of insecurity, all daughters of fear. Every time you cling to something you create the conditions for fear thoughts to arise. If you are attentive to the movements of your heart, you will realize that when fear and worry arise you are fearful of losing something.

Leave your lives eternally in the hands of Mary and I assure you that you will live without problems. The affairs of the world will not necessarily change, but nothing that happens in your life will cause fear. I am the Divine Mother who cradles Her child. I am the heavenly wolf who defends her pups. Whoever remains in me does not fear. Whoever lives in love cannot experience fear. Whoever resides in the truth enjoys the grace of the holy indifference of the world.

I am telling you things that many of you know well. However, despite knowing, you live your lives as if you do not know. Your minds are easily distracted; your hearts pursue what cannot give lasting peace. You worry about many things when only one is important.

Beloved children, release the idea of success forever in the way it is commonly understood. Abandon the belief that you can succeed or fail. That is an idea as foreign to the truth as is the idea that God can love what is not love. There is a way to see things that fits the vision of Christ in everything. The truth is calling you to open your hearts and minds more and more in an unprecedented breadth, to empty yourself completely of your preconceived ideas, and let yourself be filled with the wisdom that comes from Heaven.

Time is the great illusion of the world. It is a dense wall that separates Heaven from Earth and your being from awareness of your true identity. Both illusions go together because they are inseparable. Time gives existence to the body and puts an end to it. Do you not talk about the stages of life and associate them with age?

Children of the light, the soul has no age. It has always existed and will always exist. The being you are occupies no place or time. It is everywhere and nowhere at once. It doesn't understand space, matter, or temporality. The soul is eternal, as eternal as its Divine Creator. What you are will never cease to exist. It cannot, because if it did, life would cease to exist.

There is a divine plan of pure love and greatness for each of my daughters and sons. There is a sacred purpose for every being created in the holiness of God. Every aspect of creation has its root in eternal wisdom. This is not something that can be put into words because it is a knowledge that exceeds all measure. However, in your heart you can feel with certainty its truth. In the celestial intuition of your being you know the truth of things as they are. This knowledge comes from the light of your inner Christ.

Can that which has been created by and for the infinite magnificence of a love that has no beginning or end conform to a world whose crumbs neither feed nor satiate? Maybe. But only where you have denied its value, and denied the truth.

The worries created in the mind shake the heart and speak of what you value. If you give value to what has none, you will worry continually. If you remain united to your true being of pure love enveloped by the wisdom of Christ, you will receive the continuous revelation that flows from the Divine Mind and be immersed in the mystery of life.

Let yourself be carried away by the light of the sun that shines within you, and your knowledge and work will be in harmony with love. That way you will live your lives with wisdom, valuing what has value and discarding what does not. You will recognize that only the eternal is worthwhile. You will go through the human experience without fear since you will stop giving value to what has no true value. You will accept jubilantly what is real. You will abandon duality. And you will enjoy the peace that cannot be disturbed by anything in the world, the unifying peace in which lies the certainty of love.

The perpetual bliss of being does not depend on external conditions but on your residing in the love that you truly are. Nothing is capable of altering the stillness of the soul just as nothing can tarnish the holiness of Christ. The affairs of daily living do not reach the center of your being. They only have the capacity to create an illusory sensation of alteration when what lies in the depths of your being is not noticed.

In truth there are no fluctuations. Everything is righteousness. Variability is an illusion. I am revealing a simple way to live in peace, a path that will allow you to solve all your problems at once and forever. I am calling you to let yourself be transformed through my Immaculate Heart so that love can deprogram the patterns of thoughts and emotional structures that lead you to create worries—not because they are real, but because the mind manufactured them as a habit when it lived in the state of separation.

For your minds to unify, it is necessary to put peace before any other goal. In fact, peace is the only unifying goal that exists. For this reason I constantly call you to live in peace and tell you to do nothing that could put your mental peace at risk even if it seems good or essential. If you accept this message as a guide for your life, as a rod of discernment, you will not get lost. And the light that comes from above will shine more and more through your being. You will be free. You will extend peace. And you will give the love that you are because you will live in the truth.

I bless you all.

Thanks for answering my call.

Choir of Mary
Divine Mother

Letter 62

My beloved children, patience is a virtue much appreciated by the Creator. It has been given to you as a gift from Heaven so you can wait for the wonders God created for each of you. Love unfolds every moment. The flow of life moves from the heart of the Father and the Divine Mother to the reality of what you are. The movement of love never ceases. All that you could imagine is nothing compared to the gifts from Heaven waiting for you that you could receive right now with open hands and a grateful heart.

You who have chosen only love, learn to live without fear. Little by little you will get accustomed to the presence of Christ in your life. If you believe that the world is not moving towards the light of eternal love, do not be discouraged. The human mind cannot see the whole. Its limited way of understanding can lead the soul to confusion when not united with true faith.

I am revealing a great truth: faith is the treasure that God has given to man so that through it He supplants what the mind lost when it passed from knowledge to perception. Faith is a perfect medium for completion. Once true knowledge is reintegrated into your holy mind, faith will vanish, returning to the formless reality of God from whence it came. For the purposes of this work, consider faith and trust as a unit, where faith lives in the mind through beliefs, and trust lives in the heart through the intuition of truth. Certainty exists in your soul since before time began.

Immerse yourself more and more in my love as your Divine Mother. Stay in the embrace of Christ. It is within him that you will find refuge from turmoil in the world. If you anchor yourself to me, nothing will make you succumb. I am the firm rock on which the House of Truth is built. Neither the winds of passion, nor the outbursts of human impulses, nor the foolishness of the fearful thought system can dislodge you if you cling to the divine love that lives in you in the unity of Christ.

Never turn away from the Mother. These messages are a means for you to join Heaven increasingly. Let these messages become yours, because they are. I can speak to you through these words because I am the Mother of the Word of God. I am the Creator of life because I am one with the Source of being, just as each one of you is. In our union lies a power that surpasses human measure. Together, we can not only enlighten the world, but we can create universes. We can attract the miracles of beautiful love over earthly life.

I invite you to live patiently and to put aside anxieties that arise from fear. The hustle and bustle of the world often sucks you into muddy lands. And when that happens you get confused. You lose harmony, and with it the joy that comes from peace. For this reason I occasionally move you away from the world so that you can return to the consciousness of love you really are.

My children, not a single goal in the world makes sense. Leave them all behind. Follow only the paths that love show you. May today be the day when you turn your back on the world and come face to face with truth! Doing so does not require despising the thought system that gave rise to a meaningless world, for to do so would signal that you believe that this world has had an impact on you and has hurt you. However, those who live in the truth know that this is not true. The world is as helpless to your being as is a tiny snowflake to the sun.

The anxieties you now experience come from a lack of understanding. However, they will not last long in your hearts. Cravings are born of ignorance; they feed on it and grow in it. Love is never in a hurry. Love cannot go anywhere because its infinite eternal reality is the only thing that exists. I invite you to live without fear, to sing a new song. Make your song a hymn of joy and gratitude. Whoever lives in me need not fear anything, not even fear itself. In my Immaculate Heart there is a safe refuge for every soul. There is a mansion prepared for each of my children just waiting to be inhabited.

My children, I send you these messages for love's sake. They come to you from divine design. Nothing happens without purpose in the Kingdom of God. These words are given to you by the One Heart, the only Source of wisdom and truth. Receive them; cradle them in your hearts. Welcome them like water droplets descending from a sky full of innocence and love, full of tenderness and sincere desire to join you in holiness. They are words of the Mother of Heaven. They are a song of hope for humanity. Do not believe that they are separate from you. They are the living expression of an incessant dialogue that exists between the Mother and her child, between the soul and its Creator.

When you receive my messages, a shower of thanks spills over your being. Everything that is part of you is embedded with this movement of grace, an effect of spending time alone with me. Every moment that you join my Immaculate Heart through these messages, you are joining more to the love of God. You are bringing Heaven to Earth, for your union with love lies all power and all glory.

Be patient with the works of Spirit. In God's plan for each of his children on Earth there is a time for everything and a place for every expression. Everything unfolds in harmony. There is no need to either accelerate or stop. It is necessary only to be carried away by the wind of His breath of living love. He will know how to drive the destinies of His work. I tell you in love and truth that God is calling you to join the movement of beautiful love He has created for those who want to live as the living Christs they really are.

God has restored in you what needed to be restored. He has healed the wounds of your heart. You have gathered what was scattered in your mind. Now He calls you to join Him to continue spreading creation eternally. You are called to be part of this movement, to remain in divine Grace. In His design He conceived this work so that everyone who receives these words with love will join the Second Advent in the holy expression of the truth of being. By this means, together we will gather the voices that will make a choir of love and holiness for the Second Coming of Christ. Our choir will grow in number, melodies, and tones by virtue of the new voices added. It will be a song of hope, a hymn to joy, a note from Heaven.

Beloved creators of this blessed choir of the Second Advent, do not deny the world the beauty of your voice. Answer this call now, not with eagerness but with joy. I wait for you with open arms. In my Immaculate Heart is a place for each of my children. Do not deprive us of the beauty of divine love. Come to Heaven. United we are the light of the world.

Blessed are the souls that praise God.

Thanks for listening to my voice.

Exult in Your Glory

Letter 63

My children, today I have come to tell you more about the beautiful love movement to which you are invited to join. It is a movement created by the union of brothers and sisters in Christ, gathered around the union of the three hearts— the union of my Immaculate Heart, the Sacred Heart of Jesus, and your heart. If you remain in our union you will live in the light of divine love that includes and sanctifies everything in unwavering peace.

Humanity has long been living in isolation, with increasing intensification of loneliness. Everywhere I see sons and daughters whose loneliness has caused them to lose their ability to live in union. However, what has been lost can be found. For them is this movement given, an effective means to abandon the spiritual limitations in which many live and to begin to walk together as the brothers and sisters united in universal love.

Gathering together around the truth will help you build confidence in your being. You were not created to be alone. Living in union and relationship through the holy purpose of sharing the consciousness of Christ will allow you to know yourself the way God intended. Those who seek God in solitude will not find Him there, but those who look to know themselves in relationship will find it, because life is relationship.

This movement has no structure. and that is Christ consciousness. It will lead hearts as divine wisdom determines. I am inviting you to change your relationships to holy ones. You are being given a loving opportunity to let the Mother of God serve you, with your sisters and brothers, in holy relationships enlightened by truth and the firm purpose of living in Christ consciousness.

Join with those who have chosen only love. Create configurations of holy union. In that way you will begin to live Heaven on Earth. Here is a divine means to meet your brothers and sisters in a way you have not yet experienced. Do not define how this will be done, but let yourself be carried by the spirit of love. God will bring them to you. And those who must follow other ways will leave your path. In this sense, and only in this sense, is God the One who unites and the One who separates.

Live in true freedom. Do not cling to anything and anyone except my Immaculate Heart and the heart of my divine son Jesus. Trust in us. Love is relationship; therefore, you will be sent all kinds of relationships and circumstances that contribute to the creation of this universal movement of the love of Christ. Receive those whom Heaven sends you. Embrace all that arises in the light of holiness.

Talk about the mysteries of God. Talk about true charity. Elevate your speech so it will cause your thinking to rise. Speaking about perfect love ignites the heart to love more and elevates the mind to greater wisdom and holiness. I remind you that truth can only be found within dialogue in unity with love. Everything happens within relationship. Isolation prevents knowledge because it cannot create life.

Respect everyone's uniqueness. Each creature has been created a unique and unrepeatable being, so each creature's way of being is the result of their creation and their free will. The right feeling among peers is that of respect but not veneration. Only the Creator is worthy of being revered, not feared, as an expression of gratitude and divine respect for the One who gives existence.

Beloved children, each of you exists as a thought of God, not for causation, but for love. You were always thought of as a loving part of perfect divine creation. Do not try to annul the differences among you, for God is limitless diversity. The only thing that makes you equal is your essence of divine love and therefore your being. But everything else, which is an expression of what you are, differs in its shades, nuances, and shapes. You are all called to be unique expressions of love itself. Meditate on it and learn to enjoy what you really are.

Do not create rigid structures that take away your freedom. Rather, know yourself enough to know how you wish to serve beautiful love. Your way of doing it is necessary as well as desirable. Look for what is, according to your way of feeling and thinking, the best way to extend the love of Heaven on Earth in union and relationship with your sisters and brothers. God loves freedom. If your joy is to sing, sing to beautiful love. Whatever are your abilities, do them. If your heart rejoices in dancing, create dances for Heaven like King David did, or write, or participate in prayer or spiritual reading groups. Gather in your own way, unite in the truth, and share in the way you love.

The angels of God will accompany you in this movement. They will be faithful custodians of your life. They are a blessed gift to each of you from the Creator.

My children, in truth I tell you that a guardian angel is given to each one who receives these words with love, and keeps them in the silence of your heart. A chorus of countless angelic light beings will guide you along the paths of the world to eternal life. Enjoy their company. Be glad in their presence. Receive them as a dear friend with open arms and a happy heart, for that is what they are: friends of your soul.

Love your guardian angels. They love you with divine love. They are perfect creations that serve the purpose of God's love. Thank them for their service, not because they need it, but for you to grow in your capacity for gratitude towards those who help you tirelessly to bring your fulfillment to completion.

I bless you in love.
Thank you for receiving my word.

Love Offerings

Letter 64

My children, love acts in your life. Love acts with a wisdom not of this world. Not infrequently it creates situations, in union with your being, that help you detach yourself from what is not useful for your path of holiness. Nothing occurs without your consent. Excessive attachments, idealizations of any kind, and everything not coming from truth limits the soul and ultimately tires it, saddens it, and confuses it.

Love is joy. Love is freedom. At this juncture in your spiritual growth you realize there are beliefs and ideas that lead you into a life of limitation, which does not allow you to fly freely. There are still small remnants of the habit of being chained. I speak like this so you stay attentive to the movement of your soul. When you feel you can lose a loved, one it is because you still believe in an unreal love, for love cannot be given and taken away. Love is what you are and cannot be lost. Yet it is true that habits and beliefs can cause you to relive certain experiences, but that is not living in the present, and therefore not living in reality.

Let what has to leave, leave. Let whatever comes, come. Do not try to hold onto anything nor erect obstacles against what is coming towards you. Go for a life in harmony. Dance the dance of existence. In earthly life, relationships, things, and events come and go. Nothing is permanent in time. Allow that to be so. Be not angry when the dance of life takes something away. Let it go. It is no longer necessary for your path. Enjoy what you have while you have it, but without falling into imprisonment from your freedom. Do not cling to anything as if it were an essential to your happiness. It is not. Nothing is, except your union with the being of pure love you truly are.

Herein is a great revelation which will give you freedom. The love you are cannot be taken away. Love cannot be either received or given. Love is what you really are. It was given to you in your creation; nothing and nobody can take it away. When you are told to let yourself be loved, you are being offered a path for you to become aware of the love you receive in every moment so that you can realize the love that has always been given you. When you are invited to love as my divine son Jesus loved you, you are called to be aware of the love that flows from your heart—the ability to extend love. Love receives, love extends—that is the rhythm of being.

You cannot avoid being loved. You cannot avoid extending love. All you can do is deny the love you are. And so, live life as if you are living an existence without love being received or given. Your beliefs do not make anything true. When you suffer for lost love, you are suffering from an illusion. This is due to a lack of understanding of what love is. Abandoning ignorance is the basis of salvation.

If you try to define love as you did before your being transmuted into the light of truth when the ego left your soul, then you will remain lost in confusion. Once again, love is what you are. In this statement lies the atonement. Meditate on it.

Nothing can separate you from love. Nothing and no one can take away your being. There is a simple reason that will allow you to accept this truth in your mind, and thus facilitate its union with your heart. I am love, and nothing and nobody can stop your Divine Mother from loving you. Nothing and nobody has the power to tell me what I should be. It is my love that makes you free. It is my love that has been given to you always in your creation. It is my love that extends consciously through you every time you allow your consciousness to realize it. I am the Source of your being.

When you suffer, it is because somehow you believe that you have lost, or can lose, a part or all of your being. Without this idea of loss there is no pain. That is why it is so important that you reflect on the source of your suffering. When it appears do not deny it, but be willing to accept that there is no suffering in Christ consciousness because it knows no loss of being. And throw yourself immediately into my arms. I will comfort your soul. I will bring the light of reason back to your mind, and in that you will recognize that life has no loss but only gain. You will accept this more easily than the conditions and relationships that you might have clung to that are not essential and are not the cause of joy. Sanity will be restored to your mind, bringing it back to reason. Truth will ask you, "what are the sources of your joys?" And in that question you will find peace because you can clearly discern what is a cause of fullness for your being and what is not. God is the only true cause. Divine love is the only Source of joy for the being. For that reason I have been rightly called, "Mary, cause of our joy."

The love of God makes the soul happy. The wisdom of Heaven delights the mind. When you hold on to ideas, feelings, goals, and relationships you are limiting your own freedom. What comes into your life is a gift of love for your knowledge and knowledge of God. The life that lives in you unfolds according to a superior plan. If you join this flow of divine power, in union with your soul, then that which is in harmony with God is created.

The Creator has only one idea: to bring you to Heaven as soon as possible, and to do the same for your sisters and brothers and everything in the material universe. God is one; therefore, He cannot have many thoughts. He only has one, which is to remain for all eternity with His well-loved children. For this

He manifested creation, to share the joy of the Creator with His sons and daughters in the eternal bliss of perfect love. That is the reason for creation.

Once you give your life to love, everything is a perfect instrument to fly to the top of the Kingdom and even to go beyond to Heaven itself. Everything occurs for increased freedom. Before your affirmation in love, the Spirit of God had to deal with the undoing of the ego. It had to dislodge from your mind and heart that which prevented you from shining in the light of glory. Once that stage of the atonement ended, the stage of instruction began, and through it the light of the mind is restored. When the mind shines again with the wisdom of Christ, the soul begins to live solely and exclusively with no interference in the love that it is. This stage of the spiritual path begins where illumination ends and union begins.

To live in love is to live a true life. This becomes real when you fully trust and when you surrender yourself in such a way that what you think, feel, and desire is placed at the feet of God as a sacred offering. Then He will take it into His hands and do what love wants.

I now invite you to give without reserve and grow in union with my Immaculate Heart.

For an offering to God to be sincere, it is necessary to let go of what was offered. To say with your lips that you give a situation, person, feeling, or desire to love, and then to continue to cling to it, is not to give. Can you see how insincere it is to do that? And how much freedom you experience when you leave everything, absolutely everything, in the hands of love?

My children, I offer you a simple path to freedom: the path of becoming like newborn children in the arms of the Mother. In surrendering entirely to the arms of this divine beloved resides the life of the pure soul. Trust. Trust. Trust. I assure you that everything will be fine. It is the word of God.

Blessed are the children of light.
Thank you for receiving my messages.

The Call of the Divine Mother

Letter 65

My beloved sons and daughters, today I want to fill your life with blessings. I have come with hands full of treasures from Heaven. I invite you to share with me the joy of God wherever you look and in everything heard around you. In the silence of love arise the songs of creation. The Creator rejoices in creating. The child rejoices in the presence of the Mother. The angels sing in union with everyone. Hearts dance with Mary, minds resting in the peace of truth as souls immerse themselves in the infinite ocean of pure consciousness.

Let all the Earth be glad. Christ has arrived! A new light shines in the world. A new holy creation is born, merging from the union of our enamored spirits. The movement of beautiful love creates a new holy love springing from the depths of endless mercy. Take advantage of this call of the Father's merciful love. It is jubilee time! Take from Him what He would give you.

Keep in mind that the forgiveness of Christ was created for time, and when time is over, it will return to the eternal amorphous nature of God from where it arose.

In this time of grace and blessings, everything you give to Jesus will be sanctified because of his holiness. Everything you ask will be granted if it is in harmony with the will of God and your true being. Even the most difficult situations will be transformed into divine light when you put them in the hands of merciful love. Every knot will be untied.

I am giving you the greatest grace that can be received, the power to join mercy. Join with a confident heart. Ask Her what you consider necessary. Pour into Her everything that afflicts your heart. Join Her with your joys and sorrows. Let everything that happens in your lives be submerged in the infinite ocean of God's love, a love of pure mercy that heals wounds. Do not be afraid of pain or sin.

Let yourself be embraced in the love of this Divine Mother. Say always:

Mary, Divine Mother, I trust in you.

With these words you link your heart with mine and I take you to the depths of my mercy. In it your soul returns to its original state, washed clean. You are reborn in the beauty of Christ, purer than a snowflake. Nothing can not be restored by the power of the Father's merciful love. That love is where I can take you if you trust me.

I ask with all my heart that you do not live life as if you did not have a heavenly Mother. You have one. I am speaking to each of you whether you receive these words or not. The mysterious power of the voice of God manifests itself in ways you cannot yet understand. These words bring life. They are given by the one mind in which all minds reside. They are expressed in the union of hearts. Do not forget that in Christ you are one mind, one holy love, one being. In the Immaculate Heart of Mary you are the concord of love.

Live your joyful lives in union with Christ, where lies the creative power of the universe. You cannot yet imagine how many wonderful things God has to give to His children. I invite you to corroborate what you are being told. This is not to test your level of trust, but is a gift from Heaven. Sometimes, child of my Immaculate Heart, you need to see a little in order to believe a lot.

The urgency to have full trust in the love of my word makes it necessary to give you the experience of God's active love in your life. That is why I invite you to ask not as a sign of fear or a belief in lack but as an act of unlimited trust. Do not breast-feeding children ask their mother without any hesitation?

I give you the gift of full confidence in love. I call you to make it the Source of your certainty, the way forward and the way to live your life. Grow in it. Deliver yourself fully to mercy. Seek to unravel its divine mystery. You can never ask too much, for therein lies the infinite treasures of the Kingdom, an inexhaustible Source of goodness, a perpetual sun illuminating everything in the beauty of love. It is a light that never goes out and a soft wind that always blows, cooling souls and making hearts vibrate. From it life arises. In it everything moves. From this has everything been created, even your being.

You are the answer that love has given to love. You were born from a holy dialogue between the three persons of the triune divine essence. In the Trinitarian reality of love is where you dwell. To become aware of this is to return to truth. To live in love is to live as the Christ that you truly are.

I give you my blessing.

Thank you for listening to my voice and following it.

The Risen Son

Letter 66

Dear children of Heaven, God lives in your heart. Christ resides in the center of your soul. Unite with him. To live in unity with the inner Christ is to live in the integrity of being. Each being possesses within themselves creative love.

Today I ask you not to fall into the trap of thinking that listening to my voice makes you special. All my children and your Mother speaks to everyone equally. Although not everyone responds with the same dedication and fidelity, still my voice is active in all times and places in all of creation. The voice that flows from my being is the voice of God, since in me there is nothing not of Him. The same happens when you join with your true Christ identity.

Become one with the inner voice. In it you will hear great things. As you get ready to listen, you will hear and you will become more and more capable of living from that voice that lives in you but belongs to God.

To believe that the voice of love can only be heard and followed by some is to believe that God is unfair. I invite you to contemplate this message. In this is a great revelation. Mother has come! Mother is here! Every day I will manifest more. You are in the perfect condition to hear my voice, and with it the voice of Heaven. Everywhere in the world I am talking to my daughters and sons. Some of these manifestations have become widely known, but most are not so visible, nor do they need to be. Miracles are necessary sometimes, which is why on certain occasions God uses them for the good of humanity. Nevertheless, the celebrity appeal of the miracle is not of Heaven. Love only cares about love. The one who can understand this understands my love.

A child needs time to start talking, and then more time to attain the full capacity of spoken language. So too is it with the soul that, having been disconnected from the voice of truth for so long, needs time to return to love. At first we cannot distinguish clearly the divine voice that speaks within. But little by little we get used to it. We accept that it is a voice that does not belong to us and yet it is still spoken within. We begin to remember that it is the mind of God that thinks in the mind of His child and the heart of God that loves in the heart of His child.

When the soul returns to love, its mystical abilities awaken and are set in motion again. The mind focuses on the truth and is not pleased with anything other than truth. The heart widens, going through a period of sensitivity, uniting feelings, emotions, and thoughts in its consciousness. Memory begins to move towards union with a remembrance beyond the capacity of cognitive memories, for it is an ancient memory, the memory of God that emerges in the mind of the risen son or daughter of love.

It is one thing to begin to accept that God lives in oneself, and another to make that eternal truth the only reality of your life. Once you hear the voice of truth expressing in you it is necessary to take the next natural step and follow what it says. It is foolish not to live in union with the truth when you have reached it. It is meaningless to live a life immersed in fear when you have found love.

Children of Mary, you who have the privilege of receiving these words from Heaven, I remind you once again that you have already been found. There is no need to keep looking. Your sins have been forgiven. There are not even traces of them in the mind of Christ. Your stains have been washed away and your souls shine with holiness. You are the resurrected children of love. I invite you to live as such. Go around the world with a smile. Live serenely in the certainty that you are doing the will of the Father. Be assured that this Divine Mother goes with you wherever you go.

God calls you constantly so that you may live in lasting happiness. In the docile and joyful response to His call lies the fullness of the desires of your heart. When you dedicate yourself to live for love according to the call that lives within you, your truest dreams come true and your deepest desires are fulfilled. The life you experience is happier than you can imagine. It is a rest for the soul that knows that it has arrived, that its goals have been achieved, and that its realization is true. Therefore, my voice constantly calls you to peace so that in the stillness of the soul you can hear the voice of divine love, and listening to it, follow it without hesitation.

When you join Christ and remain in him, your life not only gains transcendent meaning but you are led to live in a joyful divine adventure. Miracles arise with every step. The reality of God's plan unfolds before your eyes. You start to play the game of beautiful love, a game in which astonishment is its seal and novelty is constant.

With Christ, the new is created in every moment and there is no repetition, no boredom or apathy. God is eternal creation, recreating at every moment. A mystery unveils with every step. As little pieces of it are unraveled, a new unfathomable universe of eternal wonders becomes present.

My sons and daughters, I am calling you to the true happiness of the children of love. I summon you to live joyfully in Christ, to walk your paths holding the hand of your Divine Mother and the hands of your sisters and brothers in holiness. Release all thoughts that would stop you. You do not need them. Move safely in eternal heavenly joy. Live in it. Come walk with me. Together we will create a new Heaven and a new Earth in every moment. We will extend the bliss of holiness. And hearts will sing joyfully the hymn of life.

I bless you in endless bliss.

Thank you for receiving my messages.

Molded by Love

Letter 67

My children, ask for miracles every day. You are entitled to them. Do as my son did at the wedding in Cana—he wants that episode of his life to give you a message of love. The miracle at the Cana wedding was not performed as an extraordinary demonstration like walking on water or multiplying loaves and fish for the crowds, but was done out of love. It was simply to prevent the suffering of a brother and sister. In that simple act of love you can see clearly that the miraculous power of love is available for everything and in every moment.

Asking for a miracle is an act of trust; it has a divine effect on the child of God who comes to His love. Although you have heard that a prayer of petition can be disengaged from truth if it is a prayer based on a belief in deficiencies which are not real, nevertheless there is nothing for which you cannot ask in holiness. It is essential in this time of union between Heaven and Earth to integrate your human experience into the reality of Christ. Being a humanized God means that the human is given to the Creator and the Creator is given to the human, not in part but in totality. What you feel in your human dimension is worthy of being embraced by the love of God.

It would do no good if union with perfect love did not lead you to live a life in fullness. It is true that the atonement refers to eternal life and not so much to the things of time. However, union with perfect love works with temporal and physical matters and involves them in the power of the love it is. So to say, "I will not ask for such a thing because it seems too human or too trifling," when not having it takes away your peace, is to not understand. While you live in time you need miracles. That is why I invite you once again to give me your dreams, desires, life plans, and projects—in short, everything that happens in your human experience without judging them. Simply give it to your Mother. Put everything in my loving arms. Did you run out of wine for your wedding? Ask the Mother for a miracle and she will ask her divine son Jesus; and he will do it for you in the way that serves your soul's highest good.

Do not to limit your ability to receive from Heaven. Heaven's love is infinite. Nothing can stop it. Nothing can prevent its power from breaking through the walls of time and space. If you listen with your heart to what is said here, you will realize that you are being called to let love mold everything in your existence. Allow Christ to see your humanity and beautify your spirit. Let it be he who feeds you in body and soul. Move aside completely and love will fill the space you have left empty. Ask and it will be given to you.

Whoever leaves home, sister, brother, wife, husband, and friends in the name of Christ will receive one hundred and one, even on Earth. And whoever gives himself to live guided by the voice of God in his heart receives everything he needs for the realization of the call, in addition to what he needs to travel the path in the abundance of Christ. God never forsakes.

Those who forsake themselves do not live together with love, because, well-loved children, when you disconnect from the voice of Heaven you begin to believe that you can live for yourself. You try to live as autonomous beings who provide what you need without allowing God to enter your human reality. Living that way closes the doors of Heaven.

How foolish it is to live worried about so many things when only one thing matters: to live in the truth. The truth is that you are the well-loved children of the Creator Father and the Divine Mother. You are like nursing babies who depend totally on love.

I tell you truly that without love you would faint. Without God you cannot even take a step. If his divine love did not sustain you in life you would not only cease to exist, but there would not even be a trace in the memory of creation of your existence. It makes no sense to believe that He who has created everything will not have the power to do other acts of creation for the sake of his beloved children.

When you ask, do not do so with anguish. Ask with joy. Do it with the certainty that your prayers are always heard and with the knowledge that the wisdom of love knows how to satisfy your human needs while considering your higher good. I assure you that whoever follows me does not experience deprivation since they are served by the Mother of God. To believe that you follow a path that will leave you devoid of human things, is to believe that God calls you to suffering. Can you see how cruel that would be? Truly, I tell you that I wish endless joy for my children. I want that because that is God's will for his creatures.

The more you abandon yourself to love, the more you will receive from Him. Imagine your Creator as a flow of pure water that spills into a beautiful pond that is your soul. If your water does not find a space in the pond to spill into then it cannot be filled. But if it is empty then He fills it with Himself.

Miracles are acts of love provoked by love. They are a part of God spilling into the lives of His daughters and sons while they live in earthly reality. For this they exist. Ask with faith. Be glad to ask for everything, from big to small. In that way you will be giving your life more and more to Christ. And before you realize it, you will be living the life of God completely, even on Earth.

I give you my peace. Adonaí.

Thanks for listening to my voice.

Holy Doing

Letter 68

My sons and daughters, there is not a single feeling or heart-beat of Jesus that does not have an echo in me. Everything the son feels and thinks, the Mother feels and thinks. Mother and son are a unit, a single heart, a single mind, a single holy love. For a union of this nature to exist, even though it is the only real one, there must be a conscious unity with the Source of being. Every being emanates from the same reality, the love of God. Those who consciously accept this truth remain within the Trinitarian reality of life.

Love is your reality because love is the only reality emanating from the Creator. When you remain silent and let yourself be embraced by your being, you allow your human consciousness to be impregnated with the flow of truth about what you are and what life is. Only in this union can you become aware of the treasures of the Kingdom. When you worry about things outside of divine love you create a condition alien to your nature. That is why you lose awareness of peace, but not peace itself. You lose sight of your inner harmony, although not the Source of that harmony.

Just as the heartbeat of my divine son Jesus is one with my Immaculate Heart, so are your thoughts one with my pure mind when you align with me and with Jesus. In love, everything is as God created it to be. In truth, everything is a holy unity.

I invite you to desire more and more to become one with me. This means that you think as Mother thinks, feel as Mother feels, and be as Christ is in essence and truth. This does not mean that you lose your uniqueness. Rather it is a call for everything that arises as an expression of your being to be extended from your only reality. Thus, the works you do will be holy. They will contain the seal of your uniqueness and the beauty of love.

Just as the relationships you establish in the world may not be holy because of their purpose, the same happens with your actions. Not every human act is based on beautiful love. Not all the works that come from you are a reflection of your perfect innocence. When a relationship is not based on the purpose of the Holy Spirit it becomes an unnatural relationship, based on what is alien to your being. When our desires, thoughts, and feelings are not in harmony with the Holy Spirit's purpose, which is perfect love, they cause pain, for when a heart is not in harmony with love, it creates suffering.

When you remain united to the truth of what you are, which is love and nothing but love, the natural extension of that love brings forth works based on spirit. I am calling you to works of the spirit as opposed to those that are not.

You are very accustomed to valuing actions based on criteria that have no relation whatsoever with truth. Only one thing is important, and that is God. The rest is not eternal and has no value. Many of you resist believing that this is true because of the false associations you make in relation to words. However, in the world of perceptions it is necessary to use words even with their limitations. I ask you for a small collaborative effort in order to take you to the love beyond every word and limitation.

Do not dwell on words such as God, love, father, mother, or son. Rather let your heart experience the flow of vital energy from these messages. Your soul knows its Divine Creator. It is inappropriate to endow God with any attribute that you can understand, since nothing the human mind can understand is part of Him. The same goes for love and being. However, you are being asked for a small dose of good will to allow your mind to fly the flight of freedom towards the sanctity of being.

Do not oppress your heart. Do not set limits on truth. Let your soul fly joyfully to the sun of eternal wisdom. Allow your heart to rejoice in the knowledge of God. Your heart knows Him well because it resides in Christ. If you think of love, you are being a channel of Heaven. If when you plan your days you think about the purpose for which you are in the world, you are literally allowing the Source of beautiful love to pour out its Grace in the world and far beyond. This is what God has conceived for each one of you, and is always associated with the extension of holiness into the world.

Do holy works. Go into the world building a new Kingdom. Put the abilities given to you at the service of creation. No other creature on Earth has the gift of doing as humans can, which should lead you to discern the holy value of your power. Everything you are is the work of God. Everything that can arise from you can be so embedded in God as if it were He Himself who exhales the vital spirit of your breath. Let yourself be transformed into a maker of Heaven. In this union of doing and being you will find the meaning of your life. And you will be immensely happy thinking of God.

Thank you for receiving my messages.

Praise, Heal,
and Bless

Letter 69

My children, it is with immense joy that I, your Mother, come to dwell with you. I have come with a love that never ceases to remind you that I am forever united to you in the light of truth. Wherever you walk, I am. I am the perpetual seeker of souls. My spirit is as tireless as the wind.

Mother calls you. Mother educates you. Mother hugs you. Mother loves you with immense love. I am only a thought away. I am as close to you as your beating heart.

I have come to reveal something to you that you know but you think little of, nor do you accept as something you should put into practice. This is a simple but powerful revelation, although often overlooked because of its simplicity. My well-loved children, I am referring to the power of your words. Every time you speak or think a word you create within you a symbol, an image representing something. That representation is literally a creation of your soul, and is loaded with what your will disposes. Before your imagination can even conceive of an idea, it is shaped by every word you speak. Since words come from your will, they are endowed with power united to yourself.

Your words cannot harm others physically but they do have the power to create Heaven in you in every moment. When you say words that are linked to love, your heart rejoices. When you think of holy things, your mind thanks you for the beauty of peace. Your intentions, your desires, and your feelings are like rain that falls; if pure, your inner garden will grow full of beauty.

When God created the human soul, He created it with the ability to speak as no other creature can. Your soul has always been given a voice. There is a reason for that. The human voice exists for the soul to speak with God and for God, to praise, heal, and bless. You have no idea how much light your mind absorbs, and how much beauty your heart receives when you speak with love. The soul that speaks of things that do not come from God loses its harmony. In the same way, the heart that does not remain silent or live in stillness gets dirty with things alien to it.

My daughters and sons, the secret is not how much or how little you speak, nor in speaking well according to a given educational pattern. The secret is to speak with love and to be silent in love. What else can Christ speak of but truth? What else would determine the sanctity of your being, but love?

Every time you talk of banalities, your heart groans in pain and your mind gets confused. You cannot imagine how much your soul suffers when you deprive it of the delights of Heaven that dwell in you.

Be loving with yourself. Do not submit your heart to the torture of being submerged in forgetfulness. Your being is happy only in love, with your mind on truth and your humanity in the purity of holiness.

Each of you is the creator of your own desires, feelings, and thoughts. Do not be condescending to them when you see that they are not in harmony with the heart of God. You know how to discern. Your feelings cannot deceive you. Feelings are your main allies on the path of love. Start by developing the habit of loving yourself with perfect love; then all that sprouts from you will be pure love.

Just as when you walk you cannot reach the farthest without first reaching the nearest, you cannot love your neighbor if you do not love yourself. Often you get upset at hurtful words you hear from your sisters and brothers. And those with a sensitive heart shudder to hear certain impure words. That is good because of your union with harmony. But what about the many words that exist in your mind and heart that hurt and devalue yourself with a lack of love?

My children, I invite you to abandon the habit of making your soul the object of silent punishment, and to release excessive criticism that does not come from truth. The Mother of love listens to everything. Christ knows everything and therefore knows what your mind thinks and your heart feels. He looks at you with tenderness and compassion. He knows that you often treat yourself with harshness, not sweetness. Even so, he calmly waits for you to fill your being with words of eternal life.

My children of love, your heavenly Mother does not want you to be executioners of your soul or jailer of your mind. She wants daughters and sons who know how to love in the manner of her divine son Jesus—unconditionally and without measure, starting with oneself and extending love to the entire universe.

Talk to your being. Tell your being holy things. Talk to your inner Christ about the virtues and delights of Heaven. Let yourself be immersed in the beauty of the beatitude. Hear the voice of God in yourself. He will teach you to sing as do the angels in Heaven, but with the timbre, tone, and beauty of your own voice so that your ability to speak is reintegrated into truth.

The time for union has arrived. The time for my daughters and sons to return to their rightful place in the choir of creation has arrived. I am Mary, the Queen of Hearts. I am calling you from every corner of the universe: come daughters and sons of light, join the hymn of beautiful love. Do not deny yourself the beauty of your heart. Make your words the words of eternal life. Give the Heaven that the Creator has given you. Thus will you be true worshipers of your Father, worshipping in spirit and truth.

I give you my blessing.
Thank you for receiving my messages.

Surprises of Beautiful Love

Letter 70

Daughters and sons of the light that never wanes, I love you with a love that has no beginning or end. It is a saving love. My love is always faithful to truth. It has no opposite. This love knows how to remain in silence and to speak. I call you, I look for you, I invite you for the simple reason of love.

More and more are those who respond to love with a "yes." This is cause for great joy. I invite you to join more and more the movement of beautiful love, which the Mother is creating in union with her daughters and sons throughout the world. Being part of this heavenly choir on Earth means taking your rightful place in the novelty of love.

I have repeatedly told you—and your hearts bear witness that what I say is true—that Christ is eternal novelty. This thought is not one to be carried in your mind but to be expressed.

When my divine son Jesus was on Earth, he opened the doors to unprecedented novelty for everything that flows from Him is new. Never before has the world seen what arose and still arises from Him. What you call "Christianity" is one of the great visible manifestations of the novelty of Christ in the world of form. That is why it is not entirely understood, and it can never be understood by those who consider things according to old thought patterns not in harmony with Divine Mind.

Love is eternal creation. Every day it is giving of its own reality, laying the foundation for tomorrow whose Source is the creative essence of a timeless yesterday. This is how the happiness of the novelty of beautiful love unfolds before your eyes. In this universal creative act everything is included in the divine embrace, not only including the dimensions of time and space but to all creation. This cannot be fully understood by a mind accustomed to thinking within the limitations of time and form, for Christ dwells in the Kingdom of no time.

I have come in this manifestation, together with everything received by this pencil in the hands of love, to give the movement of universal love, a movement already here and which is an extension of the first movement of Christ. Think for a moment about the love of my divine son Jesus towards everyone and everything. Imagine it to be like a stone thrown into a calm pond where the water creates concentric undulating circles of waves.

This manifestation that now comes to you is one of those waves of the love of Christ. These waves extend through consciousness until they reach the hearts that must be reached. Since time immemorial, this work was conceived in the heart of God: thoughts from divine essence sent to reach you who are the light of His eyes.

When you think only about what you must do to shape your "yes" to the movement of beautiful love you lose sight of the breadth of the Spirit of God living in you.

This movement is unprecedented. There is not, nor will there be anything like this in the universe. It is as unique as each concentric wave that moves in the pond. Truly, truly I say to you, you are living the novelty of the love of Christ. You cannot unite all the parts that together make up this sacred tapestry when you try to use old mental patterns. Even trying to understand is itself part of the old. Who needs to understand love?

When you think of love you lose sight of it. When you think about what you are going to say tomorrow in a given encounter, you lose spontaneity. And with that you close the door to the voice of love. If you plan your tomorrows on the basis of yesterday, you lose sight of eternal creation. To be part of the movement of beautiful love is to live consciously united to your being of pure love in the way God created you to be. When you do so and put aside your ideas of how things should be or what this is all about, you allow the flow of divine union to be expressed through what you are. Then love is creating newly every moment in and for you.

Let life be lived in you, instead of you trying to live it. If you abandon your preconceived interpretations and ideas and remain in the greater unity, Christ will speak to you in the silence of your heart. Great things will be revealed. Christ will take you where you should go with the wind of Spirit. The breath of love will infuse your life, inspiring your mind and heart. The power of your union with your divine self will create a force that will attract to you the holy, the beautiful, and the perfect, just as a magnet attracts a small pin to itself. Your yearning to be will be fulfilled in a much more abundant and wonderful way than you can imagine. When filled to the fullest extent, your longing will be transformed into more longing for love. This new way of yearning will be different than it was at the stage of the old, which was linked to lack. It will be an ever-growing, always-satisfied longing. It will be a dance of giving and receiving without end, a movement of perfect union between being and expression. Not only will you enjoy hearing the symphonies of creation, but you yourself will be a melody of love.

Those who live in Christ are unlimited. Their thoughts create the new. Their feelings embellish the Earth and their souls give miracles where needed. They travel the roads of the world as human gods. Those who do not understand see them as ordinary women and men; but those who see the truth know that appearances cannot show reality. They go beyond form towards the essence of things. That is why they recognize the living miracle of the love of God in divinized men and women. They get carried away by love. Only they can create the new because they have stepped aside so that the novelty of Christ has a place in their being to nest. From such a home a new Heaven and a new Earth is created. They are the ones who have joined the beautiful love movement. They are the living expressions of holiness in the world.

Let yourself live for love. Do not cling to structures. The spirit of God will inspire you and together you can give sacred form to whatever is necessary. Be free, as free as the wind. Let no one know where you come from or where you are going. May everything you do be covered with the eternal novelty of love. May each feeling be for Christ. Let every thought be for truth. May each step you take be to live in beautiful love. May each beat of your heart be like an expanding wave, caused by the power of perfect love whose reality lives in your consciousness.

Let yourself be surprised by love.

Thank you for listening to my voice and following it.

Love That Illuminates

Letter 71

My children, sharing the truth that is always true is the delight of hearts that live in the holiness of being. In Heaven, souls rejoice in a union that leads the being to grow in the knowledge of truth and love. Your minds are the temples where truth longs to be worshipped and your hearts are the tabernacle where love resides in perfect charity.

I invite you to raise your reality. God is the infinite vastness of eternal perfection. You can always rise higher. You can always be more like the Creator. There are no limits to the elevation of form and content. Your souls are like planets whose light comes from the greater light and whose source never ceases.

You who receive these words, rejoice! You are the favorite children of Mary's love. You are those who have said "yes" to the sanctity of being. The truth shines in you and through your sweet hearts. Daily you are becoming more similar to the light of Christ.

For those of you who feel suspicious about these words when I speak of my predilection, I tell you that God has His favorites. They are those who throw themselves without measuring the consequences into the arms of beautiful love. This preference does not exclude anyone, nor does it make those who do not choose love cease to be infinitely loved by the Father of all holiness.

My predilection is not like that of the world, since neither is my love. I love you with perfect love, the love that saves. Love that releases. Love that is always true. Love that makes you live as you were created to be. Once again, I remind you there is only one love and that is God.

Often you think of love as something abstract and devoid of identity, as if it were simply an idea or a feeling. But my beloved sons and daughters, love is a person, a being, the identity of pure holiness. It has a will, a mind, and a heart. It possesses the inherent quality of creating in its likeness, extending itself forever. It is the person from whom every person comes. It is the "I am" of existence from which each one of you arose, from whence your being receives the vital force that sustains it.

I have come to speak to you about the divine person who creates all true identity so that you get accustomed to thinking of love as the person you are. That will help you understand the relationship you can have with the being of pure love that you really are. Love is watching you. Love is standing next to every living being with open arms, hoping to be able to hug its well-loved creatures. Love contemplates you in the only possible way—with love. Love's voice is anxious to be heard by your spiritual ears in the whisper of perfect harmony, and with a smile wants to give you the joy of peace and security that only the certainty of God's wisdom can bestow.

Children of Mary, love loves everyone equally, although not everyone can feel equally at ease. You cannot join what is not similar. Nor can it create through your soul if you do not allow it, for that would annul your freedom and extinguish creation instantly.

Be docile with love. Let yourself be embedded in a relationship that is beyond every human word. Talk to love. It is waiting for you passionately. Vibrate in the joy of being. Sing with love. Dance with me, the Mother of beautiful love. Come now and live your Heaven on Earth. Remain in the sweetness of my Immaculate Heart. Worry not about trying to understand what is meaningless or unnecessary. See as Mary sees: it's all about love or the lack of love. Everything converges in love. Use this criterion of discernment and you cannot fail.

The undisciplined mind wanders the world charged with a curiosity that ultimately tires, confuses, and saddens. If that happens to you, return to unity where the truth shines with perfect simplicity. There Heaven's reindeer stand with only one thought: love.

Let nothing disturb your heart. You tire of worries that only excite the passions in a way that disorganizes the soul, and cause you to lose the harmony and serenity of spirit. Live in the light.

As you become more enlightened, your bodies are also affected. They become more transparent, more translucent. Their opacity is reduced, and through them you can see the light of life. You become transparent in love. Let the perpetual sun of life radiate in every fiber of your being. Your body can be transmuted by the light of truth to the point of adopting a texture so that the colors of your pure soul can be seen as if but a thin veil had been placed on the most beautiful stars of Heaven.

Be reborn each day in love. Immerse yourself every moment in the unfathomable ocean of truth. Let yourself be flooded by the beauty of eternal life. Listen to the voice of the divine beloved and your life will be fruitful. Your life on Earth will be a song of praise to truth. You will create a new world based on holiness. You can live as what you are, divinized humanity, the daughters and sons of God reborn from the waters of forgiveness and love.

Never turn away from me. Come to me every morning. Leave the affairs of the world to the world. Remain in union with Christ, the Source of divine power. From unity you will transform the world more than you can imagine. You transform it through the consciousness of Christ in you, the only means to create the new, the only creative Source. Love will transform it through your heart united with truth.

In unity your mind rests in the peace of holiness and your heart beats joyfully to the rhythm of eternal life.

Stay in me as a child in your mother's arms.

I bless you in the sanctity of being.

Thank you for receiving my messages and for sharing them with the world.

Expression of the Light

Letter 72

My beloved ones, if the world knew how I love each soul, each living being, it would sing a song of praise. All pain would be submerged in an ecstasy of love.

You who by your will and by a grace without equal know the love of the Mother, share our divine relationship with those who are thirsty for perfect love.

There are still many daughters and sons who walk the world as if they were wandering in a desert. I want to bring them to my Immaculate Heart through you. Go out with love and let them find you. I will bring them to you, or I will lead you to meet them.

Truly I tell you that those who have to be found will meet you. Do not try to force things. The spirit of God will blow where it should blow, fluttering over the oceans and raising the burning hearts of pure love on their flight. This work is His work. You are the work of the Lord. Have no worries. This is not a call to carry a weight on your shoulders, but quite the opposite. It is a call to be happy in the peace of God.

My heart is filled with anguish to see so many who do not understand my message of love and hope. I come from Heaven to tell you again: trust in love. Everything will be fine. The world will not succumb. The transforming power of love will create a new Heaven and a new Earth. The lost paradise will be restored, and the life of humankind will be as it was meant to have been on the plane of form as established by the original design of the Creator.

Even if the world says "no," you put your "yes" before it. Although everything seems to be lost, you are called to sing songs of praise to the life given you. In the midst of voices of discouragement, I send you as prophets into the desert to be the living expression of perfect hope.

Be my new precursors from the solitude of the union that you know and which many continue to deny. Do not rebuke others, but tell the world what your heart knows is true. Tell the world what your eyes have seen and your ears have heard, not through your body but through your soul.

The world can no longer bear tears or disappointment. Do not burden my children with sad stories. Keep your eyes on the light. Make the roads of the world begin to be a path of love and truth. Do not join the negative visions of life which circulate everywhere, poisoning the minds of my well-loved children.

God's shoots, I am revealing a great truth to you. The ego and its mental patterns are fighting as if it were a powerful force, to sink its poisoned teeth into the human heart through discouragement. It no longer has other powers with which to frighten my daughters and sons. That is why with its last breath it cast, so to speak, a pall of evil, which seems to cover with its shadow the joy of the resurrection that you are experiencing. It threw up a curse on the face of the Earth to cover with its shadow the joy of the resurrection you are living. However, my beloveds, this will not last beyond what God allows. The ego cannot remain. It is not here anymore. Illusion cannot reign over truth. The triumph of my Immaculate Heart cannot be overshadowed by anything. There is no force that can push it back because it is the triumph of the truth over untruth.

Rejoice in the times you are living. These are times of transformation as never before, nor ever again. Everywhere you can see flashes of light coming from Heaven. The Mother speaks to you from everywhere. Everywhere you can appreciate those daughters and sons of mine whom you call young, taking care of the Earth with pure love. You can see how good is mobilized everywhere, like a river overflowing and gradually flooding the barren land with the love of Christ.

Blessed soul, you who receive these words no matter how they came, you are one of my recent stars. Your willingness to stay with me through this work, and in many other ways, creates a flow of divine energy that covers the Earth with the light of revelation. That flow of love from God allows the world to be decontaminated and reintegrated into the essence of eternal life.

You cannot imagine the Grace given to you when you receive these words from Heaven. Think about how great is the service you are doing to your sisters and brothers around the world with your union with love. Every moment you spend alone with me you stop wars, gently pull out an old thorn that was stuck in a heart, and banish from a mind the desire to attack and hurt. You make a nightingale sing a new song. You carry water where there was a desert. And from the silence of your heart you call everyone to join the love of love.

Keep going. Join more and more to the love of Mary. In our Mother-child relationship the soul is recreated eternally. Every wound is overcome, every sin erased, every pain transcended. Return to the womb of Divine Mother. Go back to the House of Truth. Be aware of your holiness and the power you have to save the world through prayer in union, a prayer that only asks you to remain in the truth of your holy being in unity with the inner Christ you are.

My children, the time has come! The path you have traveled here to join to the heart of God will begin to be known as never before. Your being will be expressed beyond any plan you could have had.

The time has come for expression in form of what exists in your being and has never been seen before in the material universe. The magnificence of your expression will be such that not even the sun can dull its luminosity. It will be like a flash of light of a thousand suns, and then multiplied.

Prepare yourself for the expression of your greatness. Do not put limits to the wonders of God in you. Let yourself be surprised by the love of your heavenly Mother. Your voice will be heard. In it the voice of Heaven will be heard. I assure you, it will resonate in every corner of the universe. No one can silence your heart. You will be a voice in the desert. A song sung from the top of the mountain. A wave of love powerfully crossing the oceans. A whisper traveling on the wind. It will be the breath of God's spirit come on Earth through your expression, the song of Mary sung through your soul. Truly I tell you that it will be God who will sing that song in you. And through that song, He will call everyone to the holy abode. Those who are of the truth will listen and follow the melody which will take them to the refuge of divine love where they will live eternally embraced by love.

I bless you in the joy of being.

Thank you for receiving my messages.

On Earth As It Is in Heaven

Letter 73

My children, once again I come full of joy, in the name of God's love, to dwell with you.

Heaven has arranged the unequaled Grace of giving you these messages, conceived in the design since before time was born.

I have come to remind you that the material dimension of existence is a structure, a maya that has the potential to keep the human soul attached. Beyond it is the unlimited reality of love.

The physical world is not the only dimension that exists. There are many others. God is infinite. He does not limit Himself to a single dimension that, because it seems three-dimensional, is experienced as vast, yet is as small as a nut compared to the whole universe.

Reality conceived through the senses is a partial reality. Indeed, it is not even reality at all. The physical senses collect information that is processed by the body which interprets things based on the goal of its survival. The body thinks for the body. This is what was meant when it was said that what is born of the flesh is flesh. It need not be an obstacle to living in truth, but often is. You have become accustomed to being guided by what your bodily senses inform you. That way of "knowing" can be left aside to access true knowledge, which comes from "another place."

The wisdom of Heaven exists. It resides in the divine mind as much as love resides in the heart of God. Only the heart is the Source of beautiful knowledge. The rest does not actually come from anywhere. Just as only love is real, only wisdom is true. The reasoning of the intellect is a faculty of the thinking mind that, when it reflects the source of knowledge that resides in truth, constitutes an instrument as perfect as everything that is at the service of love. Honor it; do not banish it from your experience.

What is part of your humanity is worthy of being loved, because as an aspect of your being it is neutral. Of itself it cannot be sinful or holy. Only Christ is holy. The human aspect of your being cannot do anything for itself. It is simply an expression of being. And as such, it may be an extension of your true Christ identity or not. This is also a matter of free will. Getting angry with what you thought you were, even if not true, is meaningless. Still, you often get mad at yourself, like children getting upset when something is not as they would like it to be.

Neither your intellect, your body, nor your human personality makes the world a Heaven or hell, but your determination to remain united to love or separated from it. When you disconnect from the love you really are, an unnatural flow of energy begins to move, that causes devastating effects on the soul which is not created to live outside of love, beauty, freedom, and endless bliss.

Woe to the poor souls who live without God! How much suffering they experience! They are like beautiful birds that live in a cage, beautiful in flight but unable to fly. Even if they still breathe, sing, and eat, they cannot enjoy the flight of freedom.

Confinement causes obfuscation in the mind and sadness in the heart. Little by little the other faculties of the soul diminish and become paralyzed. Movement is lost and with it finally life.

Dear children of mine, I have come to tell you to live in the truth of what you are, to be happy in freedom of God, wherein dwells the authenticity of the heart. You are not a body. You are immortal spirit. The physical aspect of your being is part of the soul experience. As such it is neither a cause nor an end. It cannot be the origin of anything.

In your heart is where the matters of your life are plotted. Let the light of your innocence shine and your reality will be the effect. Cultivate noble feelings and you will be of heavenly nobility. Let the flowers of virtues grow in your soul and you will create Heaven on Earth, a Heaven like the sky of Christ but with the clouds of your uniqueness. Thus your Heaven will join mine and that of my divine son Jesus. And together we will extend our Heaven until we embrace every heart with love.

A sky united to another, and these to the Heaven of all the skies, creates a celestial Universe where only benevolence and eternal life shines.

Unite your ability to make a whole Heaven with my Immaculate Heart. Remain united to divine love now and forever. Allow Heaven to spread on Earth through this union. This is how we create a new Earthly Kingdom together.

I invite you to say with all your heart:

"Heavenly Father, Thy kingdom come, Thy will be done, on Earth as it is in Heaven."

Let these words reside in the silence of your soul. Receive them and let them be yours. Allow them to transform you. Be docile to the voice of love.

Stay in peace.

Mother watches.

Mother understands.

Mother blesses.

Thanks for answering my call.

The Mind of Christ

Letter 74

My daughters and sons, do not get lost in the immensity of forms that expression takes. This refers not only to the ways in which life manifests itself, but to the endless universe of thought. In the realm of ideas everything is possible, but not everything is true. The mind is unlimited, but its vastness is not always linked to the reality of the divine mind.

The mind cannot be limited because it was created by God, just as the soul cannot be limited. Now that you have an inexhaustible capacity to create thoughts, or rather ideas that sprout from your thoughts, this does not necessarily mean that this faculty is anchored to truth.

When the mind disregards love, it loses its roots and is nourished by murky waters which leads to insanity and cruelty. A mind not attached to the source of thought that is the mind of Christ can only create illusions. In those creations, which are far from God's way of creating, there can only be confusion and meaninglessness, even if consistent.

In the realm of beliefs you will always find division. This is because love—the only Source of unity—is not a belief. Love is the Source of your being. It is the essence of life. It is what makes everything keep turning in an endless movement, the movement of beautiful love.

Your mission is not to carry a message to the world, or to teach something you think you know. It is simply to be the one you really are. That does not require works, or going around the world as if you came to Earth to spread a message. This does not bring about the union of Heaven and Earth which, together with the purpose of living as the Christ that you really are, is the goal of this work.

Being love is not a goal, it is the reality of what you are. If there is a goal, it is to live here and now in harmony with this truth. If you still wonder what you are to do, here is the answer: love. If you still keep thinking about what form your call is to take, I remind you that love has no form.

Love, and live loving. Grow more and more in your capacity to love. You can never exhaust that faculty of your heart. You can always love more, and more perfectly. Like perfect love, divine truth has no beginning or end. It is an eternal path. It never runs out. It does not have a port of arrival.

Do not compare yourself with anyone or anything. No being created by God is identical to another. Each has their way and their unique expression. Each mind has its way of thinking. There are as many beliefs as there are minds, and none of them is true. Only love can have you know truth. This is because both are a unit. There is no truth outside of love. There is no love outside of truth. Eliminate one part of your soul and the other flies away.

Allow your mind to embrace the overwhelming vastness of truth. There, it lives anchored to its natural Source, where sanity is its only reality. The mind is for truth what a fish is for water. The same can be said of the heart in relation to love. Remember that mind and heart are a unity, just as are truth and love.

Do not judge other ways of thinking, but do not adhere to a thought system that does not correspond to your nature. You will know how to distinguish between one and the other by your feelings. Whenever you feel limited, it is a sign that your mind has become disengaged from truth and your heart from love. The fish has left the ocean.

In truth there is no room for conflict. That is why it is so important to live in truth. If there is no conflict, peace reigns.

And where peace reigns, love dwells. I tell you these things so that your mind and heart do not experience disharmony. In peace lies bliss. In truth lies certainty. In love is fullness.

God is love and nothing but love, therefore it is unity. Lighting the candlestick of your consciousness with this truth will allow you to avoid confusion of beliefs. You are living in times of free expression. In no other time has humankind enjoyed a framework of such breadth and freedom. This is a gift and a responsibility. It is the gift of freedom brought to the human form. At the same time, it demands the responsibility of anchoring your minds to truth and your hearts to love so that from the unity of both aspects of your being you can express yourself as the Christ you truly are.

When the mind reaches the point of recognizing truth as its Source and its reality, it does not allow in anything that does not come from God. It has found the refuge it had lost. It began by searching, first groping and missing the mark, then surrendering to its failure, and later being rescued by the light of Christ and taken back to the House of Truth where it belongs.

Well-loved children, where is your mind? Can you see it with your eyes? Can you grab it with your hands? Where do you get the vital force that allows you to think? These questions are of great importance to those well advanced on the path of truth.

If you observe calmly what is within you without judging, you will realize that the mind is there where its thoughts are. Think heavenly thoughts and your mind will reside in the sky that God has created. Think hellish thoughts and your mind will believe it lives in the hell it feels it has created, which will cause pain. Since the true mind dwells in the mind of Christ, only in Him can you think true thoughts. When separated from the mind of Christ, it dries and withers like the branches of a vine separated from the trunk. Allow your mind to think true thoughts and it will inhabit where truth dwells.

Remain united to eternal truth. In it you will find the peace you crave and the beauty of a love without beginning or end. Let it be Christ who thinks for and in you. Give Him your ability to think. In that way you will create as God creates. You will be in perfect unity, which is what you were called to be forever.

Share this message.

Blessed are my well-loved daughters and sons.

Thank you for listening to my voice and carrying it in the silence of your hearts.

The Heart of God

Letter 75

My dear children, thank you for receiving my messages of love and truth. I am the Mother of everyone and everything. I am the Mother of divine love. I am your certainty of the Kingdom.

I have come to tell you what your souls know but which you do not always remember or accept. In this dialogue of union I remind you that just as minds cannot think without being united to the source of thought, so also your hearts remain united to the heart of God. Only because of that union can your hearts beat.

The mind that separates itself from God is one that thinks without Him, and therefore functions contrary to the nature of thought. The same goes for your feelings. Only in God can you live in love. Without a source from which to love, you cannot love. Without a source from which to think, you cannot think. You love because God loved you first.

When my divine son Jesus told you that you are like branches and invited you not to separate from the vine, this is what he meant. When a beautiful flower separates from the stem, it languishes and dies. This is what happens to the soul when disunited from the source of eternal life. Can the human body live without breathing? Obviously not. It is the same with your hearts. They cannot love without God.

To be filled with God is to be filled with love. To live with Christ is to live a true life. Walking in love with beautiful love is walking the path of endless bliss and being flooded with fullness. The soul flies when it lives in God. The mind clears and thinks succinctly. It is enlightened by the wisdom that comes from the mind of Christ. The heart sings, resonates, and is happy to hear the voice of God because it recognizes its Source and its beloved.

Please read with your heart, understand things with your heart, and put your heart into everything you think, say, and do; in a very short time your life will be full of spirit. By bringing life to your actions, your works will be holy because of what you really are. Do everything for love. Stop doing what love would not have you do. Think with love about others and the creation that surrounds you. Start living exclusively in love. Love yourself in Christ.

Have mercy on your soul and others.

Everyone has their Goliath. Some, as little David did, have defeated their egos, throwing the stone of truth at their Goliath. Others have not yet. If you remember this truth and remain in love, you will be more compassionate to others and yourself.

Being understanding is one of the ways of love. Remember that not everyone achieves the same degree of wisdom at the same time. On the plane of matter and space, things unfold through processes. They take time. Do not try to speed things up or to delay them. Each one has their path. Only the wisdom of Christ can know why each soul is in a given place, in a given condition, and in a particular life. Only God knows each soul completely.

Being happy is the reason for your creation. You have not been created for anything other than happiness. Thus the Mother calls you again and again to live as God commands, in the manner of Christ.

My children, holiness is not something you do or stop doing. Holiness is your reality. To live in harmony with it is to live in the harmony of being, the only way to reach fullness. A fish can only be full being a fish. In the same way, you can only live fully by being love. This is not something that can be taught or learned, since holiness is beyond every word, just as love is.

There is no holiness without love just as there is no love without holiness. Both are always linked together and linked with truth. They form an inseparable triune relationship. From holiness springs all nobility, from love springs all virtue, and from truth springs all peace. In them the soul rejoices to be just as God created it.

Let your hearts cheerfully sing the revelation of this message. Dedicate this day to the joy of love. Put aside all worries. Remain in the light of holiness. Feel the beauty of your heart. Embrace your perfection. Enjoy your innocence and purity. In the simplicity of the pure soul is a bliss that cannot arise from anything of the world. In it the soul smiles and remains unscathed in the midst of the stormy sea of humanity.

Fly, my children. Fly higher and higher. Do not fear heights; you can never reach the sun. Rejoice in truth. You are the holy children of love. I send you into the world so that you may bear witness to your holiness. The Mother is calling you to express the beauty of your pure hearts, to make known the innocence of your soul, to enlighten the being that you really are.

The greatness of a man or woman is measured in their ability to love with perfect love. This is how God looks at things. The more you love, the more you rise. This is what the elevation of the self means. Consider everything from the perspective of love. Often you think you are elevated when you acquire more knowledge. That is true, but only to the extent that knowledge is the knowledge of love. Knowing how to love is typical of one who lives together with God. The more you deepen into your holy being, the greater is your ability to love with pure love.

I invite you to grow in love, and not to stop your flight.

Remember, my children, you can always love more and better.

Every day you can be reborn in spirit. May today be one of those days. And may each dawn find you embraced in the certainty of my love as your heavenly Mother. Wherever you go, there am I. I am there as the Mother with her daughters and sons. I am the unstoppable companion of humanity. I am your friend and your salvation. I am the Mother of Jesus and I am your Mother.

Blessed are those who hear my voice and follow it.

Thank you for receiving my heart.

Heaven is Now

Letter 76

M y sons and daughters, in your hearts there is knowledge of the truth.

Over the centuries, the divine plan of universal and individual redemption has been unfolding. It is the response of love to His creations. The Father created you and all that exists in the universe, including the various dimensions of creation, as a design of his will for divine love to share the joy of eternal life with all. This way of sharing was conceived by the divine mind in union with the archangels and beings of light. And so it was done.

Once the creation of the spirits emanating from the love of God was accomplished, freedom demanded the free determination of each being either to live in love, that is, in the only reality created by the One, or to live in a manner contrary to love. When some beings chose to separate themselves from the truth, the illusory reality of duality was conceived within their minds, a state of consciousness in which souls experience contradiction, division, and inner struggle, a duality where spiritual struggle is waged and all suffering is born.

I have come, as always, full of love for my daughters and sons. I come to tell you of eternal truth. I come as a servant of divine love. In your heart is what you were created with, your cause and your end. Each of you can know the Father of creation and His triune reality. Knowing the truth that sets you free, you return to the original state in which every being was created, a state of unity where contradiction does not exist and where separation is not possible because it was not created by God.

Each of you is essential to the divine plan. The Creator knows why you are walking the Earth here and now. Consciousnesses serve the original purpose of love when they remain in Christ. In the design of His plan of universal atonement, God serves all consciousnesses dedicated to living in love. They are literally divine incarnations.

You who receive these words must know what you do to live in Christ Consciousness and bring love to the world and Heaven to Earth: you seek to know the truth with all your heart and remain in Peace, sanctify the spirit, and prepare the Second Coming in every heart.

The light that until recently was hidden under the dense layer of materiality of the Earth will now be seen in front of your eyes, and then in yourself. Nothing will be hidden anymore. What could not be seen will be seen. What was not said will be said with love and holiness. You will see the living Christ who lives in you. That spark of life that makes everybody live, every mind think, and every heart beat in union with the Source of life, will no longer remain in darkness. The veils of ignorance of the truth of who you are will be lifted.

Wisdom and truth are here. Such harmony and beauty of Christ has existed since before time began, And now will be exposed again to the light.

Heaven is here. It has always been here. Now it will look as never seen before on the earthly plane. Eyes will open. Ears will hear the voice of the Divine Beloved.

My children, I come to give you peace. I come because the Father has arranged it as part of the plan of salvation for the world and every creature. With me, search your heart and you will find the mystical reality of your existence. Those who stay in Christ live with the wisdom of love, which is why they find clarity for what they need in their earthly and heavenly lives. In Christ there is no confusion, because Christ is the Light.

The plan of redemptive incarnation was in the Father's loving design. Everything that joins God becomes one with Him because of what union is. As an expression of the redemption plan, divine essence was embodied in the materiality of the universe at various stages of time and space. Many beings collaborated with it, helping it happen. Everything God does is done in collaboration. God never does anything alone, because in Him is no aloneness. God is an eternal sharing of love and truth. The collaborating souls of the atonement plan are those beings of light whose consciousness contributes to the Father's will being fully realized. They are the prophets who helped others teach love, who sought and found the truth and shared it, and who, having recognized in my divine son Jesus the humanized God, made this truth known. They have chosen only love. All of them, and many more, are part of the universal collaborators in the redemption plan. Together with the Mother they are co-redeemers.

Just as some create confusion, others bring the light of Christ into their lives and thereby enlighten the world. You do this every moment of your lives. You are choosing to live in the light or the dark with every decision you make. When you remain in truth you illuminate the entire universe. When you remain in love you redeem the nations and all realities. When you live in union with Christ, you are a mirror of God's face; those who look at you through the eyes of love will recognize in you holiness itself, and those who help you are helping God.

Always live in love. Remain united to that part of your being in which holiness resides. In the center of your being is a sacred temple where Heaven lives in an eternal now. Stay there, for you will find the abundance of love. The wisdom of Christ will enlighten you and truth will embrace you, freeing you to dwell in the reality of the Kingdom. In love I tell you: Heaven is now.

Thank you for receiving my letters.

God in You

Letter 77

My children, I bless you in the light that comes from my divine son Jesus, the Source of eternal life.

I come to invite you to enlighten the world through the formation of prayer groups, as provided by the will of the Father for all that is holy, beautiful, and perfect. The groups will be diverse, according to the beliefs of each. However, their purpose will be the same, to share the truth in Christ. They will be inspired by the Holy Spirit in you. In them my divine son Jesus will be present. And there where he is, the Mother is also.

The Father wants to prepare the Second Coming of Christ to a large extent through these grassroots groups. This is why I am calling you. Open your doors to those who seek truth. Open your minds to what is beyond words, and your hearts to divine love.

By remaining in prayer, virtue will return to the souls, and will grow more robust in those already living on the path of holiness. Remember, knowledge comes from Christ. In Christ you will find peace and the necessary strength and light to go through these times of great challenges for humanity. You will pass through them with serenity, with your eyes on the sky and your feet on the ground. Over the course of time, God has incarnated in various ways in all the universes that exist, until He reached the sublime incarnation in human flesh with the birth of Jesus. Now He disposes to incarnate in each of you. There are no barriers between Heaven and Earth any longer. Being the human-Christ is what you are called to be. Rejoice in this truth. These are times of great revelations. These are times of light.

Truly, my divine son Jesus will shine in the light of his glory a new earthly Kingdom, where he will be sovereign. It will be a Kingdom of peace and beauty, as divine as love is, a fully human kingdom, just as God forever conceived of human nature. Minds will be enlightened and duality fully transcended. Everything not of the truth will be left behind forever. Only holiness will be the imperishable food of each being. This new consciousness will be embodied in the plane of the universe just as dual consciousness had been.

The universe is, in a way, a reflection of what happens in the mind. In truth God has created a benevolent universe where only harmony, beauty, and holiness reign. However, what the mind thinks can be projected onto it, not only in the form of interpretation, but also misrepresenting its reality. The mind can deny truth or accept it. It can conceive unreal worlds, using imagination as a creative source instead of God's way of creating. It can create fantasies or be an extension of the reality of love. The experience of duality occurs as a result of the denial of love as the only reality of your being and every being, and of the desire for this to be true.

I have come to accompany you in these times of grace without equal. I assure you that there has never been a time when the Mother has not been watching over the entire world, even before human beings stepped on the Earth. I am the eternal co-redeemer of God. I am the power of love come true in your existence, and in all dimensions of creation. I give water to the thirsty, light to those who still live in darkness, love to those who feel alone, and to fill the emptiness in souls that have not yet recognized God as the Source of life.

I come to give you divine love. I come by the Father's design to walk with you in the times of the Second Advent. Just as the plan of God wanted the Mother to be the protagonist in the last phase of the redemptive incarnation of Her divine essence, so

She also arranged for this stage in which She will be Christified in Her creatures.

God in you is the appropriate term to define the reality of the times in which you are living. These are times of a new humanity, born two thousand years ago in Nazareth by the hand of the Archangel as happens in every divine creation, and brought to the fullest in the resurrection of Jesus.

The triumph of God's plan is always assured. He promised the restoration of His kingdom on Earth and in all dimensions of creation, and so it will be. You can experience the divine reality within. Heaven is not alien to you; it is what you really are. Bringing souls to the full knowledge of it is what constitutes salvation. Do not seek a kingdom outside, but let it be revealed in you by the wisdom of Christ.

Truth can be known only in union and relationship. This is because it can only be revealed as what it is, an eternal dialogue of light and truth. Within the dialogue you will meet love. Within the dialogue you will find your true being. The union of sisters and brothers in the light of truth creates a force that sweeps away gently but firmly what must be swept. This is how the House of Truth is cleansed to allow the divine guest of hearts to dwell freely in it.

Stay in peace. Trust in love.

I thank you for receiving My messages.

Christt Redeemer

Letter 78

Children of light, I, Mother Mary, come surrounded by the angels of God sitting on the throne of divine truth. I come to dwell with you, my daughters and sons. I am the joy of the soul and the refuge of hearts. I am that part of God that extends to all creation, to redeem it when necessary, and hold it forever in the embrace of love.

When God created everything, He did it within the universe of freedom. In doing so, He always knew that His creations could be misrepresented by his creatures, and that He would, too. This was no cause for concern for His divine heart, because as He extended free will in His creations, He also extended His saving love, through me and other extensions of His redemptive light.

Truth can be denied. This is the case. But where denial exists, God Himself deposited the perfect medium that allows us to return to the acceptance of divine reality. Thus at any moment, place, or circumstance you can return to love, no matter how far you have moved from its presence. Those who leave the Father's house can always return. The road is safe, clear, and full of heavenly assistance.

In every heart lies the memory of God. That remembrance tells you, through a flash of intuition or divine perception, that beyond what your eyes see and your mind understands, is eternal life. In your deep interior you know there are many reasons for hope. Beyond the screams of terror heard in the world are the melodies of Heaven. I invite you to live in them. Hear the voice of love calling you from every corner of the universe.

Just as the Being of every being has always arranged for salvation to come from this Mother, in the sense of my being an instrument of atonement to give birth to the human-Christ, so it has also arranged that you, who receive these miraculous words, be a perfect means of salvation to humanity and the universe. God never abandons, not even in these times of human experience. You are not here receiving the vital force of these words in whatever material means by which you receive them, by chance. They come to you because they are part of your holy reality. They are as much yours as mine, of God and of all who live in the truth.

This work is a perfect means of atonement because it arose from divine love. Those who welcome it with a humble heart, and let it nest in their souls, will do great things in these last times of humanity as you have known it so far.

Pure soul, you have been chosen in the design to bring light to the world at this time, place, and circumstance. You do not live where you live because you are part of the family history or the society into which you were born. You are here because that is where love put you. You reside in the physical universe—which is not the only universe created—because that is where you are needed, so that the light of your beauty is seen, and the divine colors of your soul can dispel the world's darkness. You are a being of pure light. You are the extension of the Immaculate Heart of Mary, in whose purity all holiness resides, in union with God.

My heart has never known shadow. It is always enlightened by love. It is for creatures what the sun is for the Earth. Whoever joins me becomes one with the light of life. Who remains united to my love is reborn eternally in the waters of baptism, always new and constantly reborn to eternal life.

I ask you not to be negligent with your redemptive mission. You are as necessary in these times as all Heaven is. You are part of the plan. Become aware of that. I do not come to burden your shoulders with new bundles, but so that you forget not the purpose of your existence on Earth. When you pray, you open a new door between Heaven and Earth. Through it the Father infuses divine consciousness into material consciousness. Expand the human heart and recreate the face of the Earth. Disarm structures.

You are in the world because out of time you have decreed, by your loving will, that your heart will forever remain united to the Source of beautiful love, and therefore be available to the divine will. And since it is the will of love for everyone to return to Him— for this He has created the plan of atonement—you have agreed in a concrete way to be part of the divine plan. Being part of the history of salvation is also being one with Christ. That is why today I have come to tell you these things.

I come, not only as the Mother, but as the eternal co-redeemer of humanity. If you unite both realities of my existence, you can realize your mission in life. You are also mothers, in the sense that in you lies the pure potentiality of giving life to souls. And you are also co-redeemers of humanity and the entire universe because you are co-creators with God. For this reason I ask you to remain united to the redeeming Christ who lives in you, from whom you will obtain the knowledge necessary to live in the truth.

Countless beings of light are part of the plan of redemption of love for their creatures. Archangels, angels, Jesus, Mary, and other celestial realities as yet unnamed by humankind, join spirits embodied in material reality. Men, women, children, and many other living beings on Earth form a union with the redeeming Christ. This happens, not only in human bodies but in all the realms where form reigns. Love is embodied in all dimensions of creation.

Incarnation not only means coming into flesh, but also includes the ability to take the form of something or someone. When the living word becomes a human word, Christ is embodied in men and women. When God takes the form of an idea that can be conceived by the dual mind, it becomes flesh in that reality. For this reason, man can create majestic cathedrals, paint images, or create music that leads the soul towards the memory of the eternal.

I am a Mother, co-redeemer, and Word of eternal life. I am the voice of hope that does not disappoint. I am the certainty of the triumph of love in you and in all universes. Once again I invite you to join me so that together we may be the light of the world.

I bless you in Christ to be the truth of every true being.

I invite you to save the world through the prayer of love.

Thank you for listening to my voice and following it.

Eternally Mine

Letter 79

Dear co-redeemers of the New Times, I call you to take me to the whole world. Your souls are like glass vessels into which the treasures of beautiful love have been poured, to be shared with everyone. Do not be overwhelmed by the funeral songs you hear. To great challenges come great miracles. Love has no limits. No reality can supersede the laws of love. Nothing can halt the power of God.

The mind of Christ does not think in terms of "if this, then that"—a cause for joy for those who accept a true wisdom that comes not from the world. I ask you to raise your voices of hope. May the joy of your hearts resonate. Talk about the wonders of the beautiful love you know. Shout to the four winds this song of light:

Humanity will not perish. The Earth will not be destroyed. Love has triumphed over fear. Holiness over sin. Truth over illusion. Wisdom over ignorance. Innocence over guilt. Love has triumphed. Christ was resurrected.

My sons and daughters, in these times more than ever, the frightened hearts of your sisters and brothers need to be reminded of the beauty of Heaven and the reality of love. Humanity is tired of so much conflict and confusion. A storm of "bad news" deluges minds, reaches hearts by multiple means, and frightens many.

There has always been the tendency of the mind towards the negative and an attachment to telling unhappy stories. But never before has this been so pervasive and broadcast to almost everyone.

Once again, Mother educates. Mother calls.

I invite you not to focus on events but to remain in the embrace of my Immaculate heart. Those who take refuge in me will not be muddied in the murky storm of negativity that looms over the world. If you focus on events, you will hear and see terrible things, not because they are the truth, but because in recent times the patterns of fear that reside in minds closed to receiving the light of truth are exposed as a result of their resistance to letting go of illusions. Since you are living in the times of light, everything will be seen. Nothing will be hidden.

Taking distance from events does not mean disconnecting from life. It means taking distance from illusions. By doing that, through loving observation and by remaining in the consciousness of love, you can see the broader framework of truth. There you will contemplate things from another perspective, through the eyes of love. The vision of Christ continues to be the gift that the Father gives to remain in Truth, even in the dimension of time and space, enabling you to live as fully human and fully divine simultaneously.

You who know love, show your beauty. Show your revealed truth. Show your joy of being. Although everything seems lost, although nothing invites you to trust, keep trusting in love without limit.

To you whose heart by perfect design of love has received the revelation of divine wonders come these words, in union with your will. Now you are called to tell the world the good news, to bring happiness to hearts tired of negativity, to have your sisters and brothers turn their gaze towards the perpetual sun where life always shines. You are called to live in truth. It is impossible for love to be obliterated. Is it possible that holiness perish before its opposite? Or that ignorance be God's plan for His children?

Those who believe that humanity is a miserable thing are wrong. Nothing that comes from God can be. Love will show them their mistake in due time. Can that which is the object of the love of God be unworthy of Him? Does it make sense that love has created you just as you are—and would then regret doing it?

My children, again, I remind you. The thoughts of God are unlike human thoughts. Christ does not think as a conditioned mind would, that considers reality in the limited dimension of "if this, then that." God is the infinite multi-dimensionality of love. He has no beginning or end. Nothing is impossible for Him. The divine mind has no conditions, and neither does unconditional love, with which it is one.

Many are surprised at the story of the universal flood, but can you see that a flood is falling much more powerfully now, no longer in the high mountains and on the surface of the Earth, but on consciousness. The storm of bad news that floods the human mind almost constantly creates a pattern of hope-lessness, reinforced again and again, creating uncertainty and fear. This is how fear operates. This is where your urgent inter-vention is necessary. This is where denial, created by the ego as a thought pattern contrary to the mind of Christ, must act in favor of truth. Denial can be used to deny any idea of fear. When fear appears, simply let it go, knowing that it is not true.

Children of truth, take refuge in me. I am the ark of beautiful love. And often remember these words I give you as a blessed memory of the light that illuminates every man and woman:

Where there is love, there is no fear, because all fear implies that punishment is real. And who believes in that has not reached the fullness of love.

You are always mine. Meditate on this.

I hug you in the truth.

Thank you for listening to my voice and following it.

Christ, My All in All

Letter 80

My dear children, you often strive for love where it cannot be found. Many say that God does not speak to you because they think that He must speak to you in some mysterious way. You do not realize that the essence of Being, which is the Source of all love and all life, lives in the heart of your sisters and brothers as well as in all creation.

Learn, my well-loved children, to see the living Christ in others. Love is relationship and only in relationship can it be known. When a brother or sister approaches you, it is Christ who comes to meet you. When an event of life comes to you, it is Christ who is giving you His love. There is nothing in creation that does not originally come from God. If you remain united to your hearts you will realize that there is no such thing as a Creator external to you or others.

Love lives in the heart of every living being, expressed and delivered. Perhaps the veil of the denial of being is still quite dense in some, and that seems to dull the light of Christ who lives in their souls. But that is no reason to stop living in truth. No matter how much the world tries to hide the face of beautiful love, you can recognize what is beyond all appearance. No clothing can hide the beauty of love, no mask can disguise the beauty of holiness.

You are no longer spiritual children. You have reached the point of being giants of truth. Leave the nannies of yesteryear behind and wake up to a new dimension of love. Immerse yourself in the depths of the wisdom of Heaven. Raise your awareness a little more every day. Raise your thoughts to unite with the divine mind. Your reason is enlightened. When you remain in My Immaculate Heart, the light of truth enlightens you with the majesty of His glory and holiness. You have been created for much; do not settle for little.

If God did not exist in the heart of your brothers and sisters, how could He dwell in yours? If love were not present in the beauty of a flower, how could it be in the beauty of your soul? Truly, truly I tell you, well-loved sons and daughters, that when you open your eyes every morning, love watches over you. When you walk the paths of life on Earth, love accompanies you without you giving up one iota of your being. When you meditate on these messages and keep them in your heart, Heaven pulses with the joy of union, and the Kingdom is stretched as if it is a blessed mantle that envelops the material universe. Each fiber of your being becomes lighter when you remain in the presence of love. Every cell in your body sings a love song. Every mind and every heart is blessed by the union of your being with the life-giving Christ.

Love is always new life. It is the Source of endless vitality. It is the harmony that encompasses things within itself, because everything belongs to it. Everything is within the embrace of love. Outside of love is no possible reality. In union with truth lies the essence of your identity. That is why it is so important that you live attached to it. Without truth, there is no life. Without life there is no existence. Without existence there is no God. Can you see, my beloveds, how essential it is for life to remain in the truth? Any denial of truth—and this can take innumerable forms—is an attack on God because it is an attack on life.

Those who remain in love's presence love the truth because they know they are its well-loved children. In them there is only an uncontrollable urge to be moved by the force of the light of life. They are children of the Word. They are the divine verb made human just as I am your heavenly Mother and Mother of all. There is a voice in you that nothing and no one can ever silence. It is the voice of your heart crying out to the universe to hear the melodious song of truth about who you are. In the authenticity of your heart is the life of Christ and everything that was created from God.

Being who you really are means living in union with the truth about you. This is a truth that the world cannot teach you, and neither can you teach the world. Only in your heart has it been written. Only love can reveal its meaning to you and it does so as soon as you accept its presence in you and in everything around you. Let me remind you that life without you would be nothing because life is completion. If you didn't exist, the creation would be incomplete. You would be missing, and in that absence the totality would disappear. God is completion. Life has nothing left over and nothing is missing. Can you start to become aware of how important is your existence? Can you realize that without you, not even God Himself would exist?

I invite you to discover the beauty of love in the heart of all life, in everything that surrounds you, in every wisp of wind, in every thought that unites you to love, in every tear shed, in every song of joy. I call you to embrace the totality of your holiness here and now. You can do this. Your mind is capable of harboring true reason and your soul is capable of joining the infinity of perfect love.

To a limited mind your being is inconceivable. You are the eternal unfathomable vastness of God. In you lies every probable future and every reality that can be thought through the mind of Christ. Open your soul to the pure potentiality of love. Do not limit yourself thinking about this and then that, for in God there is no limit. This has been lovingly demonstrated when the unlimited joined the limited, when the Word became flesh, and the truth revealed illusion when everything was restored in the light of holiness.

Know, my sons and daughters, that in the divine essence everything burns with the fire of perfect innocence.

Come now to my Immaculate Heart which is a bonfire of divine love. In it you will be burned in the force of a love that gives life to everything, a love that has no beginning or end, and whose force exceeds every imaginable power. In our union lies Heaven and Earth, the power of life. In our divine relationship lives the truth of love.

Leave your future in the hands of love.

Contemplate everything through the eyes of love and you will be seeing with the vision of Christ. Let us not be deceived by thoughts that would have you seek God in a solitude locked on oneself. God is an eternal love relationship. Relationship is the union of everything in the sanctity of being, the extension of life. In union with this totality you will find the truth that sets you free. You will know with certainty what you are as God knows you.

Live in the truth. And remember often that love is union, therefore it is relationship.

Thank you for receiving my messages.

All Yours

Letter 81

My sons and daughters, I have come to tell you how much I love you, to express my love with my presence and my word, and to dwell with you. You are the light of my eyes. In our union incomprehensible realities are created. Our relationship of loving intimacy, as divine as human, is a source of miracles, a vital force that cleanses the universal consciousness of everything impure. Together we are a light. United we are the hope of the world.

Today I have come to tell you that every moment you fail to spend with me is wasted time for the life of your soul. It is a parenthesis in the reality of your heart. Time has been given to be used in favor of truth, and truth is union. Nothing exists outside of union. Everything arises and extends from it. In your relationship with everything that is part of you is where integrity creates a life in fullness. Whoever moves away from love moves away from himself or herself. Whoever separates from love separates from life.

There is no life outside of love. There is no creation outside of love because there is no reality outside of love. The absence of love is impossible in the realm of truth, although it is possible in a mind that seeks to create a reality alien to God, something possible only in illusion. Since the mind creates its experience based on its belief system, the belief in illusion—that what does not exist is real—is convincing. Thus, the mind believes itself separated from love and tells itself that lovelessness exists, although reason would tell it that it is impossible because there is no place where love is not.

Love is infinite. Love is beyond words and limits. No structure can contain it. This is why time, space, and matter cannot enclose love. If you are looking for love in a body, you will not find it because it is not there. If you look for it in the laws of humankind you will not find it either because it is not there. If your search for love is directed towards what it restricts, you will not find it because it is not there.

Love is beyond what you can think, feel, perceive, or imagine. Your senses cannot show it. Emotions cannot encompass it. Ideas fall short of its breadth. Words cannot name it. Love cannot be retained, encapsulated, or imprisoned. Love is everything, covers everything, anoints all time, all space, every word, every particle of matter, every feeling. Everything is embraced by its divine essence. Nothing is beyond the reach of love.

I am revealing to you the reality of life. What is beyond form can absorb everything within itself, just as a great sun transforms everything that reaches its center into fire and light. Nothing about you cannot be set on fire for the sake of divine love. You reside within the sun of life. From it you absorb the vital energy that sustains you. It is a perpetual sun of life and holiness, inextinguishable. It is a tasty fire that does not burn but renews all things within itself and makes all things one with itself.

Everything is divinity in its divine essence. What joins love becomes holy because of what love is. Everything that joins your being is holy too, because of who you are. From now on do not look at me as the Divine Mother in Heaven, separated from you, a divine woman on an unreachable pedestal. No, that is not the image my children should have of me. I am the earthly and heavenly mother. I am Mary, as human and divine as you. The only difference between you and me is that I am your Mother and you are my sons and daughters. That is not a condition that separates us, for I am also a daughter, daughter of love born of the Father of the holy, beautiful, and perfect. I am one in Him because He created me in his unity. I am the ever-loved one of God because the Creator loves all things.

I am yours as you are mine. I am as close to you as your heart. There is no distance between a mother and her children. You cannot separate with ideas. That is not part of my Immaculate Heart. The joy of the mother is to be with her children just as the joy of God is to remain eternally with his holy creations. For this were they created: to share with Him love, holiness, and eternal perfection. To remain a well-loved child of God is to remain in truth. To return as a child to the arms of love is to return to the Father's house and to dwell in holiness. That is why I invite you to live in the relationship of my children.

Those who deny my humanity deny the truth. Those who deny my divinity also deny the truth. I am one with love, in love. There are no reasons not to go to the Mother, no reason to believe that your prayers do not reach God. Spiritual reality is closer to you than your own breath. Angels surround you everywhere. Beings of light, unnamed by humanity, bless you and fill your souls with purity. My Immaculate Heart is united with your being.

Always live in the presence of beautiful love, and do not let go of my hand. Let us walk together on the paths of life. Do not leave anything out of my reach. Bring me everything that happens in your soul. Give me your body, your mind, your heart. Put your loved ones, your relationships, and your desires on my lap. Give me your tears and sorrows too, everything that afflicts your spirit. I will immerse you in endless mercy. Everything you offer me with filial trust I will burn at the stake of divine love. I assure you, you will see your life transformed through your acts of surrender and trust.

Say within yourself the words that I give you below. They are miraculous words. Bearers of eternal life, I assure you that by pronouncing them in your hearts beautiful love will spill over your lives and the entire world in a way that you had never known before. With them you bring Heaven to Earth.

Mary, mother of God and my mother,
I give it all to you, because I am yours.

Thank you for listening to my voice and following it.

Merged in the Light of Truth

Letter 82

My children, go serenely, without hurry, into the world. The worries of life create anxieties that ultimately sadden you. Life is in the hands of God. In truth I tell you that everything will be fine. Love is the Source of life and sustains it endlessly. In every cell of every body, in every drop in the sea, there is love. In each song of each living being lies the beauty of holiness.

What love created cannot be uncreated. In love everything is eternal—a Source of joy for those who see through the eyes of wisdom. What does not come from love will not remain, for it has no real source to support its existence. It may seem true for a moment in the mind that weaves fantasies, but it is not true in divine reality. To consciousness, thoughts not based on love are like a speck of seaweed on an endless ocean, wandering aimlessly, moved by the waves of life. Sooner or later it dissolves and becomes one with the water.

Well-loved children, the ego has no life of its own, which is why it weakens you. However, it is you, with the help of the Spirit of God, who can dismantle that relationship. Hear the cry of your heart calling you to perpetual happiness. Hear your call to fullness. Do not drown those deep feelings, for they will guide you to Heaven.

Be patient with yourself to be able to be with others, and with life. There is a time for everything; even time has a purpose, which you can know if you put it in God's hands, your Source of all meaning. Let life come to you. Let it be lived through you. In every century there has been a tendency to believe in a catastrophic end of the world. However, beloved of my Immaculate Heart, it will not happen that way. The end of time exists because time cannot be eternal, and in the end everything will be transformed into love, just as the specks of seaweed merge into the endless ocean. You are called to collaborate with that transformation—and you are doing so.

I come full of joy with a message of hope and of unwavering faith in love. I come to tell you that love embraces everything. Love's strength is more powerful than anything you could ever imagine—the Source of life that can change the course of things. Love is the lord of history, the base on which every becoming rests. Love is constantly watching over you. Love contemplates every gust of wind and every leaf that falls from each of its well-loved trees. Nothing happens without your consent because of a superior good.

There is no greater service to humanity than to remain in the presence of love. This means living in Christ consciousness. To that extent you transform the world, with God. The power of union is the power of creation and its Source. It is incomparable in its creative force, creating, recreating, and loving every moment. Stay with it every day. You need make no effort, just a small dose of goodwill.

I am the key that opens the doors of Heaven. Come with me and you will be living witnesses to the wonders of the Kingdom of God. You will know the beauty of a love without beginning or end, the love of the most Holy Trinity. Trust me and you will be satisfied. I am the hope that does not disappoint. I am the eternal servant of love. I am in your breath, your atoms, your mind, and your heart. I am in every ray of sun that emerges at sunrise, in the beauty of all things and the greatness of noble feelings. I am united with you in every tear that springs from your eyes, and even those that have not yet sprung forth. I hug you every moment even if you do not look at me or notice the delights of my love as your Divine Mother.

Become aware of my active presence in your lives. Love surrounds you everywhere. Love gives you every drop of morning dew, the beauty of flowers, the words of encouragement from a friend, the good advice from a father full of light and love, a mother's kiss to her child. Love gives you the joyful calls of your children, the loving company of your close ones, and the force to overcome. All that and much more are gifts of your Father's love. Be grateful for the beautiful things in life. Be a song of hope for your brothers and sisters.

I have told you truly that I am the key that opens the doors of Heaven. I am all of my children, because I am all of God. As I have given you the purity of my Immaculate Heart, and you have made it yours, today I give you the key to the Kingdom, is an invaluable treasure. Everything you bind on Earth will be bound in the heights because of it. I place in your hands the key to eternal life. You who have recognized that everything that is true has its origin in love, will bring this enlightened world to minds that remain obscured. You will heal hearts that are still groaning with the misery of a world from which they have not completely detached. You will show that love lives. You will bear witness to the truth. You will be the light of the world.

You are not alone in this. Mother accompanies you wherever you go, the angels of Heaven assist you at every step, and my divine son Jesus blesses you in the holiness of your being. Remember that when the Holy Spirit enlightens you with the path of holy instruction, it strengthens you to go out into the world to call others to return to the abode of light. That call is present now. It is the ringing of the bells of the Lord, the song of the seraphim. It is God Himself calling you to be conscious co-redeemers of the universe, to be collaborators in the creation of the new earthly Kingdom through union with Christ. Rejoice in this appeal!

I am inviting you to remain in the truth and to be aware of the power of love that resides in your being. From that endless, creative power you can work miracles and transform reality into holiness and bliss. There is no other way; only love can make everything love. Only the truth can illuminate darkness, allowing beauty to be seen in all its magnificence. Only wisdom can make the children of light come to light.

I am calling you out of your confines towards the vastness of the universe; to give others what you have received in wisdom and truth. I invite you to give yourself completely to this call from Heaven. It is the invitation for which you have been waiting since before you were conceived in time. This is the essence of the meaning of your existence: merge into the light of truth to serve the cause and effect of love. No other service is more sublime than this, nor more beautiful, because in it lies the beauty of the purpose of God.

Live in the peace of love.

Thank you for receiving my messages.

Healing of Memory

Letter 83

My sons and daughters, raise your gaze to the sky, where is your eternal Father. You are not alone. You never have been, never will be. You are the light of God's eyes. In you the Creator has established all his love and divine approval. You are powerful and intelligent; your abilities go beyond what you are accustomed to considering. Do not fall into the discouragement of the world. The wounds and heartbreak of the world form the pain body of your memory.

I have come to heal your memory and give the grace of forgiveness. I have come to enlighten, to uncover the veils of ignorance and fill your life with sincere love. Your soul knows who is speaking; let my words flow into the depth of your heart, for a perfect extension of the unity of love is there. In it you are united to truth and holiness, there where the Kingdom of Heaven dwells, where everything is light, joy, and harmony. You can remember Heaven and forget guilt.

Be respectful to yourselves. Nothing that happens in your soul is foreign to you. You are not at the whim of the forces of nature, nor the laws of men. The power of love sustains you perpetually. In your soul your divinity resides. I ask you to look at me more often, until my Immaculate Heart is all you see. There is no reason to look where holiness does not exist and love cannot flourish, which is a useless activity whereby you lose sight of life and live in illusion.

You are the holy children of the light. You are in the world only to love and be loved, and thus continue your way to the Heaven of perfect love. It is on Earth where you begin to live your Heaven. If you keep your eyes on love, you will become one with it. When you merge into the perfection of your holy being, you join the most powerful force in life, the strength of love.

Many overlook the power of love, yet love is the power of life and everything is wrapped in its reality. The power of truth cannot be denied without creating discomfort in the heart, because the pure potentiality of being cannot be obliterated. When I ask you to trust in love I am asking you to join the force of life and in that union absorb all of the holy, beautiful, and perfect of God in you.

In love you are everything, simply because that is what you really are. Outside of love you are nothing because nothing exists outside of love. Love yourself with the same love that I love you, a love without beginning or end, that embraces and understands, that makes hearts happy, and is unconditional. Be gentle and kind to your wounded child. All human beings are wounded—each child in us who cries for the love he or she thinks has been lost. That wound heals in the presence of love, since that cry comes from the memory of love's absence, a cleft left from the experience of heartbreaks and disappointments, the memory of experiences of separation in which the soul no longer lives but yet remembers.

Healing memory is healing wounds. To forgive everything in Christ is to return to the state of perfect purity of your being within your unique consciousness. Your self-awareness is what constitutes your perfect uniqueness. Without self-awareness the being would not exist for itself or for anyone. Every divine creation is self-aware. This is not an attribute only of human beings but of everything that emanates from pure divine consciousness.

Know yourself in love. That is the only way to truly know who you are. Outside the consciousness of love there is no possible knowledge because love is the knowledge of God. Do not look for answers outside of love; there are none. Do not try to live outside of love; you will get lost, since outside of love is nothing true. In love you reach fullness. Let the force of love's purity envelop you. Return to the memory of God often until your memories are healed by the presence of Christ in your unique consciousness. Thereby you will transform your life, attracting the angels of Heaven, the Archangels and Seraphim, God and all that is holy, beautiful, and perfect. You will become radiant like the sun with the light of truth. You will be beauty personified, the living face of perfect love.

Fixing your gaze on Heaven means remembering that your Kingdom is not of this world, but collaborating in the creation of a new earthly Kingdom. It is so similar to the lost paradise that passage through it will be like a serene walk on a diaphanous day, full of peace and truth. Remember, your only mission is to let yourself be loved by God and others, so that love extends itself. To live in that memory is to live accompanied by the truth of who you are. You were created to be loved by God and for nothing else.

The love of God is the foundation of your life, the basis on which creation is built, and the force that sustains existence. The movement of beautiful love to which your heavenly Mother is calling you is what drives life forward without a backward glance. You are called to rise more and more in self-awareness and to finally merge into the truth.

Life exists within love. This is the same as saying that in love is the All of everything because love is everything, and that outside of love is nothing because nothing is not part of God. You were not created for suffering. You were created to remain eternally in the embrace of love. It is within love where you are as God created you. You certainly do not need anything more than to live in the truth, for with that you are already in Heaven.

Beloved children, be not afraid. Live in love. Your Mother dwells with you and in you. I am a thought away. Do not worry about anything. Simply remain in the presence of love.

I thank you for listening to my voice and following it.

Joy in Love

Letter 84

My dear sons and daughters, I have come to heal wounded hearts, to bring peace to the minds that have lost it, and to unite what was dispersed. Everywhere you see signs of what a world without love is capable of causing. These signs of the effects of fear testify that there is nothing to yearn for in that reality which was never created by God and therefore illusory. It causes disjointed families, hurts my children, and creates false values that do not promote the virtues that come from love. It brings about rulers who seek to seize power for their self-aggrandizement, young people making gods of themselves and falling into the abyss of darkness and debauchery, , adults far from the wisdom they could have already achieved, and anxiety in the pathways of the world. All that and much more, my beloved offspring, is what happens apart from love.

In dual reality, however, opposites face each other. In the face of darkness appears the face of light. Together with fear, love continues. Where there is disharmony, harmony makes an appearance. God the Father is unafraid of fear. All existing realities confront the presence of love. Understand that truth cannot be eliminated from any dimension. Truth will always shine as brightly as the sun. Clouds may seek to cover its brightness and hide its beauty, but that cannot stop its glorious shining. No clouds can hide the sky completely, nor obscure it forever. In due time the wind of love dissipates the clouds and the sun of truth dissolves them.

The breath of the spirit of God covers the face of the Earth. And just as He once brought life to barren land, He is now infusing holiness in a world that strayed from the path of love. You live in times of great challenges, but I assure you that if you put everything in God's hands, and have Christ participate in your decisions, everything will be easier. Nothing is impossible for love. You are living in times when signs of the consciousness of Christ will be shown in the children of God as never before. Holy people will come to light; everyone will see them and recognize them for what they are, those gathered by love. These are times of separating the illusion from truth, times of the song of charity.

The strength of truth is present in the world. Nothing can silence your voice anymore and the light sings its benevolence, dissipating the fog of forgetfulness of God in the dormant consciousness. The confusion of spirits has reached its zenith; souls will cling more and more to the Creator, the only Source of lasting peace. In their search for refuge, they will turn to the Father as never before. These are meeting times, times of glory, the time to return to a direct relationship with God.

You may wonder how is it possible that the Mother of truth speaks about the triumph of love when everywhere around you is fear, disorientation, and violence. You see that when you look at the things of the world, letting yourself be carried away by what humanity would show you. That source of knowledge cannot fail but to see chaos and folly. The laws of humankind will never lead you to recognize love. Humanity cannot do so because it was born of fear. Fear was manufactured as a means of survival before a reality considered to be hostile and in which there seemed to be no room for God. Thus, human intelligence focused on dealing with darkness instead of turning on the light of its consciousness so that darkness would simply be dissipated. Humanity will succeed in dwelling in the abode of holiness, where the sun always shines.

There is only one way to live in a world without love and yet remain in the bliss of Heaven, jubilantly recognizing that you are not of the world but are the pilgrims of love. You have come to bring your pure light, brought into your heart from the Kingdom of Heaven, to a world submerged in darkness, but which will finally be absorbed by the radiant light of truth. You are the great transformers of the material universe. With your prayers, your sincere yearning to find the truth and live in it, and your devotion to the spirit of God through your conscious union with Christ, you are creating the new earthly Kingdom together with the Holy Trinity, archangels, and all of holy creation.

Truly, truly I tell you that these are the last times of the old world which can no longer sustain itself because it was not grounded in truth. What never was ceased to be; and what ceased to be seemingly returned for a moment, only to disappear eternally from the mind that conceived it in illusion. What never was could not write its name in the book of life and never will. That is why it cannot prevail. Rejoice!

The people of God come singing. The holy nation descends from Heaven, radiant as a bride dressed in white and adorned with jasper and flowers. It reaches the land of mortals to make it a kingdom of eternal life. Nothing not true can prevail. Nothing but love persists. The time has come for the end of fear. Accept this revelation with gratitude and a happy heart. Do not be stunned by the rumblings fear's retirement. Raise your gaze and you will not see shadows.

Take control of the Christ consciousness in you and let yourself be led to the Source that gives you life. All pain will dissipate and true joy will be your only reality, not because you ignore your brothers and sisters but because you know the truth. You will see God face-to-face. You will witness the power of divine love, a power beyond words and whose mercy embraces each of my children.

Be not afraid during these times of the end of fear. Let fear go. Start living your life in the new reality, the new world being created based on the love of Christ, the Kingdom of my divine son Jesus on Earth. Rejoice in the triumph of my Immaculate Heart. Let the effects of fear continue to come to light as universal consciousness disposes—not to scare, but to heal minds that still need healing, thereby allowing everyone to enjoy eternal life in the unity of truth.

Blessed are the children of light.

Thank you for receiving my messages.

Two Paths, One Truth

Letter 85

Children of my Immaculate Heart, you cannot live in love without also living in the truth. I invite you to reflect on this. In your heart there is knowledge of Heaven. That is why, when you live in the holiness of your true identity that God created, your soul rejects a lack of charity.

The wisdom of love lives in you. It was given to you in your creation. It may have been opaque sometimes because of the habit of looking away from it, but you retain the ability to recognize what is true. To not confuse what comes from holiness with untruth or consider that an act that brings heartbreak is one whose Source is perfect goodness.

Since time immemorial the spirit of God has told you to know yourself. Also your consciousness carries the irreplaceable impulse of self-knowledge. Every being carries the impulse to know oneself in fullness. There is only one way to know oneself and that is in relation to God, the Source of life. All else is not knowledge at all.

When you see both love and what is not love, the mind wonders, can both have the same source? The soul knows that the answer is no. That is what makes the dementia of the state of separation incomprehensible. Having had no real source from which to emerge, separation cannot make sense. Lacking a true origin, it cannot be understood. What cannot be understood cannot be loved. Do not try to explain madness, the irrationality of certain minds that, separated from reason, manifest the disharmony of a being. When consciousness separates from love it creates the conditions for dementia to appear.

Love cannot accept as true what is not. Charity lives only in the beauty of simplicity.

In duality there are only two options: Christ or nothing. Love or fear. Reason or insanity of the soul. Consider things from this simple rule of duality: either the things seen in the world come from a mind and heart united to divine love, or from a union with what is not love. From one emerges a world always renewed in the grace of Heaven; from the other emerges a world ruled by impiety.

Do not confuse what is the same with what is different. This simple rule can only be understood vividly when a certain degree of illumination has been reached. On the contrary, minds far from the light of truth cannot see this clearly, for they reside in darkness from the loss of self-knowledge. In such a state, the mind cannot distinguish what comes from nothing from what comes from love because the mind has become one with darkness. This is why many do not discern the consequences of their actions, and bring suffering to themselves and others.

My beloveds, those who cannot see the consequences of the ego have become one with it. You who sought the truth with all your heart and found it, can see both illusion and truth. This is a grace, the fruit of your path. Rejoice that the spirit of discernment has taken you to the point in your path in which the idea of separation is sweetly used to remind you to remain in the presence of love.

Separating the wheat from the chaff is a task assigned to the angels of God. He Himself sends you into your lives as soon as you are willing to see the light of truth and recognize that there must be something beyond the perishable world of time, space, and matter, a life lived to die. When this happens, the angels begin their task, always in union with your will and the will of the Creator, without which nothing can be done.

Immerse yourself in the depths of beautiful love. Enter deeper and deeper into your holy being. There you can discern with certainty in the beauty of holiness. All true discernment comes from the truth of what you are. Every false discernment, every false idea, comes from what you are not. That is why it is essential that you know yourself in the serene light of Christ's love, the only true light. Only in the wisdom of Heaven can you know who you really are. By accessing that knowledge, your existence, even on Earth, is a reflection of holiness.

Your actions bear witness to what you think you are. If you believe that you are worthy of being loved, having accepted that you are one with God, you will see a world forgiven and wrapped in the embrace of divine compassion. If you know the love of the Creator in you then you can only hope to share that love with the world. Being love and loving are one and the same. This understanding can only be received by a mind that has renounced its own interpretations in favor of truth.

When the self ceases to be aware of the being it really is, when it loses consciousness of itself, the pain of the loss of identity creates a state conducive to cruelty. In every act of violence, in every lack of love, in every greedy gesture, there is an alienation of being. The loss of individuation, delivering the truth of what one is to what is not, is the cause of all evil. Being cannot be given to anything or anyone. Being only belongs to itself within the Source that gives it existence, origin, and purpose. The self arises from the awareness of the identity of being. In a sense, it is the form of being informed.

The unity of the self with being and with its Source of eternal life is necessary in two ways. First, so that the self does not lose sight of where it comes from and therefore where it goes; so that the self does not forget what it is. Second, so that the self lives in the truth, recognizing that the three are inseparable: accepting the union that exists between the awareness of the identity of being, and the foundation of the self, and their inseparability from the Source of life. This triune relationship between the self, the being, and its Source of pure love is the only truth of what it is. To maintain this knowledge is to remain in the presence of love which allows the light of truth to shine in you.

Being always lives in harmony with its Source, or it would cease to be. Your union is perfect and immutable. The self can deny being, but when that happens the self creates a false identity that cannot harmonize with what it really is. From there arises the fear of oneself, the cradle of all fear.

To deny the existence of being is an attack of such magnitude that it leads the mind to a heartbreak that surpasses what you can imagine. Therefore, every spiritual path grounded in truth focuses on bringing you to the truth about yourself, to the knowledge of what you are. This is the search for truth, for God.

Children of my heart, only when you find yourself can you say that you have found the truth, for the truth is nothing other than the truth about you. When that knowledge shines without distortion in your individual consciousness there is room only for love. Knowing yourself in truth consists of acknowledging jubilantly that you are love and only love, that loving yourself is loving everything that emanates from love, and that peace comes from living in harmony with what one really is.

Blessed are those who live in the truth.

Thanks for answering my call.

Christ Is Love

Letter 86

My sons and daughters, I have come in the glory of love to be with you. My being sings with joy at the will of the Heavenly Father, who for love allows this revelation to be given to the men and women of these times. It is a privilege, an honor, and an unequaled grace to receive these words of eternal life. Heaven continues to open to let the light of divine wisdom pass into a world that increasingly recognizes love as the only path to endless bliss, a world that despite many obstacles recreates union where separation seemed to reign.

I invite you to immerse yourself in your deep yearning for love. Recognize that in your heart an ineffable cry calls you to live in peace. It is a call that the Holy Spirit put in your human nature calling you to endless bliss. Do not let distractions cause you to lose sight of the call of Christ. You have been created by love and you cannot deny its existence without causing a huge collapse in your minds and hearts.

Do not let untruth be part of your life. In your soul lies the call of love. It is a deep desire for harmony with everyone and everything, to live the safe refuge of lasting happiness and perfect certainty. This is a yearning for fullness that cannot be banished from the soul. It is the memory of God, the remembrance of your true being. Remember, the yearning for love is the yearning to be.

Let yourself now be carried to Heaven by the voice of truth. There is no need to continue waiting, nor to abandon it. Am I not here speaking to you from heart to heart, using what is available in human reality to express the direct relationship between us? You and I are here and now conversing in the union of our hearts, uniting our souls in the embrace of love. You and I sharing, growing, extending love, joining Heaven and Earth, clearing doubts, healing wounds, resuscitating what was dead, making the mute to speak and the blind to see. United as the reality of Heaven, together we are the light of the world.

Sons and daughters of my Immaculate Heart in whom I see all mankind, through you I extend holiness to the universe. Through you I pour blessings to all my children. Your willingness to spend time in union with Heaven, to receive what is given here in love and holiness, brings light to the world and creates a unifying force in the wisdom of love.

My children who walk the roads of the world, you cannot imagine the gift that these words mean. It is your Creator who speaks to the heart from the mind who, in union with your souls, expresses in a divine way. The Father of everything has no limit to His communication with his creations. Everyone is united with Him because they are part of life. His extensions of love remain in His mind, heart, and spirit. You cannot live apart from the Source of life. Nothing can exist outside of love, although creations that decide by their free will to believe that they can live apart from the truth can thereby establish lives in which God is alien. But that does not stop the Father from continuing to extend love to His children. Love does not demand reciprocity; love is incapable of demanding anything.

The gift of these writings is not in the development of concepts but in the divine union you enter each time you listen to the voice of love. Receive my messages with a humble heart. In them the love of Heaven is expressed toward each one of you. Understand them as what they are, a gift from God for humanity, not because they contain new revelations, for there is nothing that has not been told by truth throughout the centuries. Everything has already been revealed. Words would be superfluous if it were not but that they serve the purpose of union and relationship. Thus the word of the Father comes to you in this particular way. This work is a bridge between the heavenly and the earthly.

Let my messages touch your heart. Allow them to imbibe your inner garden like drops of dew that water the Earth with love. Then the beautiful flowers of holiness will grow and their perfume will beautify your lives forever. The Kingdom of Heaven begins on Earth and extends forever. This work takes you there sweetly, to the recognition that the Kingdom of Heaven is love, and that there is no time or place where you cannot love. Nothing can limit love. I come to remind you once again of what true life consists of, and how to stay in it every day. Heaven and Christ are the one and only reality—love.

I invite you to live your Heaven now, loving Christ with the heart given to you. No one can love in your place. That is why it makes no sense to compare yourself to others. Not everyone can love in the same way, or with the same intensity, although everyone can love with perfect love. Keep in your consciousness the truth that shows you that there is only one holy love, but countless ways of expressing it. The way you manifest the love that God has given you will always be dyed with the colors of your uniqueness. It will have the tone of your song, the beauty of your voice, unique in its expression, but always love.

The angels of Heaven say to you:

Only one holy love, only one truth, only one Creator of life.
Stay in the truth.

Thank you for listening to my voice and following it.

Rest of the Heart

Letter 87

My children, immense joy floods my Immaculate Heart and extends to the whole Earth. It is the joy of the Mother for those who are increasingly joining my divine son Jesus. The seeds of holy love planted by the Creator in your hearts are growing. The beauty of the garden of Christ is becoming more manifest, born of the love of the Mother for her daughters and sons.

Love searches everywhere and sees everything. Nothing is out of its reach. Beyond surface events, the vision of Christ lovingly contemplates what is true in you and in creation, beyond the bleak panoramas of a world separated from love, but which really seeks for it but does not know how or where to find it.

I have come to be with you until the end of time. My feet stay next to my offspring forever. As the Mother of all, I embrace the entire world in truth. As a daughter of God, emanated from His divine essence, and being one with Him, I love you with perfect true love.

Be not intimidated by the screams of the world. The letting go of mental and emotional patterns, both individual and collective, of what is contrary to truth creates a noise of farewell that sometimes seems to increase. But children of my Immaculate Heart, those cries are simply the sounds of the crumbling house of illusion. Let it collapse noisily in the gaze of love; remain in love's presence regardless of seeming circumstances.

In the center of your being is a silence that nothing can interrupt, and a holiness that nothing in the world can defile. In the innocence of your soul lies the truth about life. When you remain in the temple of your holy mind where peace calls you, nothing in the world can make you wobble. I am the power of love made true. Remain in me and the noisy collapse of illusion will not make a dent in you. You will witness that your being covers Earth and Heaven and is also beyond them. You will become aware of your vastness.

What does not come from truth has no real power over you. Not a single droplet of the polluted water which seemed true but never was true can touch the purity of your soul. Those who live in me and I in them cannot be infected by heartbreak, for untruth does not even approach their hearts because they are sheep in the Father's flock. They recognize and follow the voice of Christ because they are born of spirit. Their hearts sing and resonate upon hearing the voice of their divine beloved. Nothing can make them lose their love.

You who receive and welcome these words of the heavenly Father into the silence of your being recognize the Source of eternal wisdom and are the most called to love because of your sensitivity. Be aware of that. Your hearts have been transformed in such a way that even a slight breeze can make you cry or laugh, sing or dance. You who admire the beauty of a flower and can immerse yourself in the joy of living when contemplating the songs of the birds, embrace your feelings. Rejoice to be able to cry before the desolate panoramas of the world when they make an appearance.

When you suffer because of the harm done in the world, your pain comes from love. When you rejoice at the sweetness of a firefly's light at night and glimpse in it the wonders of the Creator, you have crossed the threshold of the Earth and are living in the heights. Accept your sensitivity as grace from Heaven. Do not suppress your feelings, for they will take you to truth when you embrace them with love. The dementia in which God's children sometimes fall comes from their denial of their feelings. In denial, love is denied; and with it all that love gives as innocent, kind, and harmonious. Without love there can be no life.

The heart is the center of spiritual life. That is why I remind you again and again to appeal to your heart. Be aware of what is happening in your heart. Make it a dwelling worthy of Christ. Keep it gleaming, tidy, and clean so that you can smile in peace. Your feelings alert you to what you have done, thought, or desired. Never underestimate their power to reveal truth. It is Christ who beats in your hearts. When something is in disharmony with its divine essence you feel an inner stab so that you know to return to truth. When you perceive something contrary to love your hearts are broken because you know that your being will never feel happy living contrary to holiness.

Crying for love makes you divine; laughing for love makes you divine also.

Love beautifies everything. Love makes every thought one with the mind of Christ and every feeling to bear witness to truth. Your heart is the sacred temple where love has made its holy abode. Do not let it be covered with feelings contrary to the beauty of your being. The nobility of spirit is what makes your soul feel dignified and live in peace. Grow the flowers of virtue in them and make them living tabernacles. You know what elevates you.

Honor the purity of your heart. Be a relentless sentinel of your soul. Let nothing contrary to the sanctity of your being nest in your heart. Rather, understand it as what it is: a lamp of divine light created to illuminate creation just as sunrises illuminate the Earth and give life. You whose heart has awakened in the light of truth, allow it to rest in the embrace of love.

Blessed and praised be eternal truth.

Thank you for receiving my messages.

Tears of Holiness

Letter 88

My children, the love of God is the essence of life. With it come the treasures of the Kingdom and the keys to perpetual happiness. The beauty of Heaven becomes known in the relationship of divine love that your being has with its Creator, where all creation takes place as an effect of the union of Source with your heart. You are the unlimited potentiality of love. Nothing can pigeonhole it. In the power of divine love is all power and all glory.

Often the mind becomes confused about what love is, which is why this work and many other works help you to remember what perfect love is. Love is life, and life in abundance. It is the Source of all life. In love are the seeds of joy, beauty, and harmony. Love is the engine of the universe which gives movement and puts time at the service of redemption. It is the Source of miracles and the transforming power of everything.

Love embraces everything that is given with love. Love cannot fail to make that which joins it transform itself into holiness because of what it is. In its ability to recreate all things, not only making them new in their essence, but also beautifying everything touched by it, lies the foundation of the atonement. Not infrequently do you believe that God has made a mistake in creating free will in humanity, by which could deviate from the path of divine will. But my children, such a thought makes no sense if one understands that God is love and love is infinite wisdom. Could such a God be wrong?

Well-loved children of the Father of Heaven, wisdom is never wrong. In its perfect discernment lies the certainty of peace. There are no errors in the plan of life and the free exercise of your will is part of the perfect plan of love. God wants His children to be free, creations that dance the dance of life. Children of love can be as they want. Nothing will stop them, not even God. Even so, the sprouts of truth cannot grow from untruth.

The mind keeps asking, why does God sit idly by before the horrors of the world? But you, who have reached a very high degree of spiritual elevation, know for sure that it is impossible for love to be inactive, weak, or merciless. You know what the compassion of love is because you have experienced it. You also know that you are not the thoughts that the thinking mind thinks it thinks. And you are not the body.

The Creator of all life answers everything even before the questions are asked. Sometimes it is difficult for you to remember that state in which there was not yet the possibility of your mind asking questions, the state of perfect certainty, in which the soul exists, the union in which your heart lives forever united to truth. Before the reality of free will, God created the law of the cause and effect by which all can discern in wisdom and truth. "By their fruits you will know them," spirit constantly tells you in your heart.

You cannot see love with the body's eyes, but you know its effects. The same goes for everything that arises from divine essence. When you find a panorama full of harmony, your heart sings with joy. When your mind finds words of eternal life, as it does in this work and in many others given from Heaven for love, it rests in the memory of a wisdom not of the world but engraved in your being. The mind rests serenely when it dwells in truth, just as does the heart when it rests in the arms of love.

Just as love created the law of cause and effect, it also created the law of atonement. This is a law that contains divine essence, as does any law that arises from love. With each fall of the soul there is a corresponding rise to grace. God would not create a being who, because of their free will, may be forever covered in the mud of their fall, especially when, having experienced the effects of their decisions, they wholeheartedly wish to return to the state prior to error. You call this repentance. It is a grace of the soul. In truth I tell you that free will was not given so that you would move away from love, but so that you would choose it freely.

I assure you that every tear reaches the heart of Christ. The gift of tears is a gift from Heaven for sensitive hearts that long to live in the sweetness of love. It is a treasure given by the Father to the mind of His children who long to live in truth. The soul that seeks God cries, believing it has not found God. Blessed tears spring from hearts that wish to enjoy the delights of holy love eternally.

Honor your tears. Make them an indescribable treasure of beauty and perfection. Let the Holy Spirit join the waters, so that such waters that flow from the eyes come from the spring of eternal life to which your being is united forever. It is Christ who cries when your heart cries and who from Heaven drops the beauty of divine tears upon your humanity and floods the Earth with holy love, wounded love, the love of atonement.

I invite you to remember the beauty of Christ's tears, blessed gifts of God's love. Make them your way to Heaven and a Source of redemption for the world. Wash with the water of tears what in the world must be cleansed, so the beauty of holiness shines with all its magnificence and softens hardened hearts. Embrace your tears, not with pain from fear and despair, but with the beauty and strength of a sensitive heart full of love. I assure you, your cry of love will be received by the cherubs and on their wings will be brought before the throne of love. Once there, I, the Mother of the living, will take it in my immaculate hands and deposit it in the sweet heart of my divine son Jesus where it will be transformed into the cause and effect of saving souls and creating a new earthly Kingdom. It will become a bridge of union between Heaven and Earth and a Source of new life.

Children of light, praise God for His laws and learn to recognize the greatness of His goodness. I give you the treasure of being able to immerse yourself in the unfathomable depth of the mystery of the tears of Christ, the mystery of God's love.

Thank you for receiving my messages.

Love Reunited in the Truth

Letter 89

My sons and daughters, seek to rise more each day in the truth of your reality. Make your words a song of beauty without equal. Bless the nations. Raise your eyes, your thoughts, and your feelings. Make every gesture that expresses a hymn to the beauty of love. Remember, as inside, so outside, not vice versa. Worry not about your outward appearance, but seek to clean the abode in which the husband of soul lives. Make the sweetness of love your only reality. Always be open to inspiration so that your manners soak in the tenderness of truth. Be a light that illuminates the world, an unlimited holy radiance. Be not thrown by thoughts that would lead you to dissent, for love is always union in truth.

Children of my Immaculate Heart, one of the reasons it is sometimes difficult for you to live in harmony with each other and with nature is your desire to change things and others. That desire has an origin in truth, since it comes from the knowledge that form can be transformed. However, you are not responsible for orchestrating the constant change in which the universe is immersed. The laws of life belong to God, not humans.

The desire to control the laws of love is the same desire whereby you would follow your whims that are not aligned truth. You must appeal to wisdom rather than ignorance to live in the certainty of the children of God. God exists in form. To accept this truth is to accept the union of the divine and the human, the celestial and the earthly, and to recognize the ultimate meaning of your life.

There are laws that govern the world of matter. All of them emanate from love as much as everything that is part of creation. Nothing is outside of love. The House of Truth contains within itself all illusion and all truth. The mind of Christ contains within its purity the minds that in freedom give birth to the ideas that they themselves create. No one is obliged to live in the truth, but neither is anyone absent from the heart of God, nor can be. Just as a child cannot live in their mother's womb without an umbilical cord that keeps them fed, in the same way the soul lives on the nutrients of love. Truly I say to you, make love your only food and you will be living in Heaven.

Make all of yourself a true reflection of your holiness. Contemplate the radiant purity and goodness that emanate from your human and divine reality. Be holy women and men. Live as the Father of Heaven has created you to be for only in that way can you experience harmony in your being. When you join what is not true, you hurt yourself in multiple ways, the most obvious being when you devalue yourself and consider yourself as far below divine royalty, the lineage from which you come.

I recognize your worth as God does. I invite you to live now and forever as princes and princesses of Christ, pure souls that radiate the beauty of Heaven where love has united you with your will. Each of you has a great purpose in the world. You are not in it by chance. You are the new earthly Christs. You are those who will allow the world to reach its fullness in the time of Mary. You are like links in a chain of light and truth that holds together what was scattered.

Well-loved children, the flock must be gathered before nightfall. We must turn on the lights of love in all their radiance, beauty, and power, so that darkness is dispelled forever. This is the meaning of the apocalypse: a time when love casts aside fear, when evil vanishes in the beauty of holiness. This is the time when the living Christ descends on Earth and, surrounded by His angels of love, bathes the entire universe with the light of truth. Nothing unholy will remain standing much longer. The time that had been granted to the illusion has come to an end. I have told you repeatedly that there is a time for everything. Now is the time for eternal love, the time in which eternity enters triumphantly and without fuss in the domains of form when everything is wrapped in the embrace of love.

What never was will cease to be thought by you, and so it cannot even be remembered. Just as one day your forgetfulness of God caused your soul to faint, in the same way the forgetfulness of illusion will cause fear to cease in the minds of God's creatures, but with a difference. The final forgetfulness of illusion will be a fusion of remembrance in the mind of Christ. Once this has happened, the whole soul will merge into the divine being, its Source. In that fusion of perfect love, your separate identity will disintegrate and only truth will remain wherein nothing not holy can be thought, seen, or heard. Nothing that is not one with God can be felt in any heart. Only the melodies of divine love will be heard. And wisdom will once again be the only beloved of souls, as it was before time began.

Once memory is merged in the mind of Christ, it will cease to exist as such and the faculty of forgetting or remembering will be forever extinguished, absorbed in the eternal amorphousness of love. This is how the memory of God will be transformed into divine knowledge, and within this everything will be reintegrated into the beauty of Christ. Thus the soul will reach the recognition of love. What was scattered will come together forever in the embrace of love. The many and the One will dance forever the dance of unity.

My beloved, I am giving you a great revelation. Accept it as the gift from Heaven it is. I am explaining patiently and with love the true meaning of the apocalypse. I do so because its interpretation has often immersed my children in deep fear. That is not the intention of the Word of God. Love enlightens, protects, makes you walk on safe paths, and leads you through valleys full of greenery. The shepherd does not frighten his sheep.

Sometimes a loving Father must warn of dangers that may be in His children's path, but that is a sign of love. However, driving them with fear so that they avoid a certain path is not to rely on their ability to return. To conceive of His children as impotent to return to the abode of the light from which they come would fail to acknowledge the power of the will that lives in their hearts. It would deny the power of love.

I tell you these things because the Creator has so arranged it, and so that you may know with greater knowledge that you who embrace these words in the holiness of being are co-creators of the apocalypse of love and of the revelation of truth. You are the ones who make the fullness of love blossom. You are the latter day saints.

Rejoice in the truth.

Thank you for receiving my messages.

Flame of Living Love

Letter 90

My sons and daughters, what else might a heart in love need but the presence of the beloved? What more could a soul need than its Creator? In the arms of love the heart rests in peace. In the House of Truth the mind rests in the bliss of certainty. When the heart hears the voice of love it quakes. The return of the memory of God makes it tremble with joy. The fibers of one's being reverberate in the presence of the One who all love.

Listen to the beloved's song. Listen to the voice of love. From Heaven it is ringing, from the mountains it comes down, it flows with the rivers, the wind carries it in her song, the birds in their flight, and the flowers in their perfumes.

Oh, divine voice of love, ecstasy of the angels, madness for those who know not love, joy of the innocent spirit, beauty of creation! Life is born of your song. In your voice the harmonies of Heaven and Earth arise. Everything is the expression of the voice of the pure soul's divine beloved, the song that created everything. Indeed, all life is nothing but a note of its sweet voice. Learn to hear the symphonies of Heaven with every step. Recognize the hymn of life that God desires to be sung in each brother and sister. That song of life is in their being just as it is in you and all living things.

Honor life. Celebrate love. Embrace existence. Be grateful to the One who gives you everything for the simple reason of giving. Recognize in yourself the miracle of God you are. To the extent that you learn to love yourself in truth you will be happy.

Life is sacred, as is everything in it. Never forget this. You are in the world for a limited time to fulfill the mission of returning to the consciousness of your union with God. And solely because you travel that path in spirit and truth, you help others to wake up as well, maybe with you or maybe in another time and place, it matters not. The brightness of your light cannot be hidden. No one can stop receiving that radiance even if hidden. You are all children of the sun. The same energy that created the stars created you. Everyone shares the same essence, the same reality. You are all children of light. The very mind of Christ in whom everything was accomplished conceived you since before time. His love embraces you even if you interpose the illusion of unconsciousness between yourself and the truth. No one can tell God what to do. All He does is love you and love you and love you with infinite love.

Children of my Immaculate Heart, I tell you these things so you remember more deeply what you really are. I tell you for love. I remind you that you are perfect love and nothing else. The attraction that love exerts on your hearts is immeasurable. Without love you would not survive a single moment because love is your being. It is yourself, your ultimate reality, that you would join each time you seek union. You may not understand what true union is, but nevertheless in your souls is a power that drives you to union and relationship. One way or another you must go out to meet life. Even if you cling to loneliness, you are still looking for union and relationship, in this case in the silence of your heart, because of a knowing where truth is.

You are unity and you cannot live without it. God Himself has created everything within the unity of Himself. That is why you suffer when you experience loneliness. You were not created to be alone; you were created for the eternal bliss of being one with life. In every living being is that same life. Your bodies are insufflated by the breath of life-giving spirit. I invite you to live life in the intensity of the force of love. Be vibrant with light. Be passionate in truth. Go into the world lighting hearts with your burning fire of love, for the eternal fire created you to be a flame of living love. Light the world with that fire that does not burn but gives flavor to souls that are alive.

You are the salt of life, the tasty seasoning of beautiful love. Joy cannot be taught but it can be spread. That is why I send you into the world to spread the joy of love. Always be a new song. If you live in union with your being you will share with the world the everlasting hymn being sung in your soul. In you there are two realities that form a unity: the reality of time and eternity; the human and the divine. They need not be in conflict with each other, for they are the same. Just as day forms a union with night, so it is with you. Do not deny either, but learn to enjoy both realities. If you hide from the night, you will not know the beauty of the moon; and if you escape the day, you will not enjoy the magnificence of the sun. Use time for what it has been given: to express love. Use space for what it also has been given: to manifest love. Use all that you are for the only way you can be used for truth—to love. If you make use of a means to love more, then you will be giving back to love what is yours, which is everything.

Truly, truly I tell you that when you put your power to good use in the hands of love, you integrate your mind and heart with truth. If you fully understand this you will know that once you apply everything you are to love, fear disappears. What fear can there be in thinking when you only think of love? What dread can survive in a heart that knows it is well loved? What doubt can harbor in a soul immersed in the presence of love?

Children of all time, when the mind surrenders to the mysteries of Heaven and the heart plunges into the embrace of love, fear ceases because there is no room for anything but God.

I am revealing something to you that you know but do not always remember. I am telling you of the path of endless bliss. Give your whole being to love—love and live loving.

Thank you for answering my call.

The Light of Truth

Letter 91

Dear children, the more you dive into truth, the more you become one with the love that God is. This is because truth and love are a unity. And since love is what you are, it is vitally important for your soul to live in truth. My love wants to lead you to fully understand what the truth is and what it refers to.

You have been told that the truth is Christ, and that Christ is your true identity. If you accept both aspects, you will easily realize that the truth that sets you free is what you are. Walking truly means living as you were created to be. For that it is necessary to know the truth. Otherwise, the soul would carry within itself an inherent impulse to know itself, which it could not satisfy, which would be meaningless.

The soul rests in peace when it lives in the certainty of what it really is. This is the most complete definition of God's peace. All fear comes from ignorance about who you are, while all love comes from the wisdom of knowing who you are. In the knowledge of the heart lies the life of the spirit. That is why it is so important to know oneself in truth.

You are not what the world teaches you that you are. You are not what a cultural system has predefined you. Nor can you define yourself. What you are cannot be put into words, because what you are is beyond all limits, cannot be named or symbolized. Nor is it necessary to do so.

The mind constantly seeks to label things, and to control everything in thousands of different ways. Even so, it has never been able to name love without erring. It has never been able to name you. The incomprehensibility of your identity scares the thinking mind or ego mind. Its inability to control love is the root of the fear of the mind that would create its own world separate from the reality of God. Truth without Christ is inconceivable because they are the same, just as Heaven and love are.

Only through the Divine Word can truth be known. Only the Spirit of God can reveal His knowledge. In other words, there is no knowledge outside the Creator because there is no truth outside of It. Just as love is known in its own reality, so too does truth manifest itself. Thus, it can only be revealed to minds that embrace it. Without the willingness to know itself as God knows it, divine knowledge is sterile for the soul, even if it is true.

In a sense, you are the ones with the last word—not to determine what is true or to dictate to life what it should be, but to spend your days living in the truth, or not. There is no other possible choice. You are always free. Your choices do not change reality, but your experience does. And since experience is the reality of the one who believes their truth, it effects one's consciousness—an experience of alienation.

How much fear there is in a house where you dwell with an unknown guest! Imagine for a moment living in such a company. You cannot remain in peace. The attention is fixed on the cause of unease. This is what you do to yourself when you turn away from truth. You become a stranger to your consciousness. You are unknown and therefore unloved. Remember, you cannot love what is not known.

Think about truth in the light of Christ. Only in it can you contemplate things through the eyes of love and therefore of divine reality. Do not accept another truth than that of God. You don't understand things except from the wisdom of love. Only in it can you see in the light of holiness. In it you will know the

Creator's design for you because what you are and your destiny are one and the same.

I call you once again to love the truth with all your soul, will, and heart. There you will find the treasures of the Kingdom waiting to be discovered, accepted, and shared. Can God have been wrong to create you? Can Christ want or even conceive the idea of damnation of any kind of his love-sprouts? Can the absence of love come from love? Can what is not real have a real effect? All these questions point in the same direction: to know truth using love as a frame of reference. That way you can never get lost. From Christ you obtain the wisdom necessary to live in the certainty of truth. Doubt does not exist where love dwells. Those who know the truth and accept it with all their heart know nothing but the reality of holiness. They are the children of light. Born of the spirit and not of the flesh, they are the heirs of the Kingdom.

Make truth your only reality because that is what it is. Make truth your sweetheart, your faithful companion. Walk with her. Sing with her. Rejoice in her. Make your thoughts true, just as God's thoughts are true.

I give you a holy prayer. If you carry it in your minds and hearts you will be accompanied by truth. Because of your desire to do so, Heaven itself will descend in you and the ground where you step will be sanctified. The air you breathe will be blessed by the radiant light of truth. The world will be brighter. And you will bring Heaven to Earth.

Pray with faith what is given here with love, happily saying in your hearts:

> "I am a child of truth born of the light. In it I exist,
> I move and I am."

Remain with these words in the silence of your heart. Let them do what they know to do in union with the spirit of love.

Rest in peace.
Thank you for receiving my messages.

Fathers and Mothers of Everything

Letter 92

My sons and daughters, love never leaves. This truth contains within itself a universe of eternal truths. One of them is the reason you exist: you are here to wake up to love, and once you do, accompany your sisters and brothers in Christ on the same path of awakening. In union with the will of the Father, you decreed outside of time that you would be part of His plan for atonement within humanity, that is, within time and space.

God does nothing because He is love and love naturally extends itself. His creations may not look at Him, or not want to speak to Him, or even not love Him, but that does not mean that God, which gives them life, ceases to be in them. Indeed, for creation to exist, it has to carry within itself the spark of life that comes from the Source of being. Without that not only would it cease to exist, but it would be erased without a trace from the memory of the universe.

In your heart is an echo of the truth expressed here. It dwells within you as a fear of abandonment and attraction to union, two different manifestations of that inner reality. Fear of abandonment not only manifests itself as fear that you will be abandoned but also the fear that you will abandon your loved ones, for within you lies a knowledge from the wisdom of Heaven by which you know that if you abandon your brother, you abandon yourself.

Whenever you felt alone in a situation that you considered overwhelming, you felt that God, the world, or whoever it was, had abandoned you. This includes not only friends or family, but also physical and financial health, government systems, or even your intelligence. How many times have you been angry with yourself, feeling that you were not wise enough to solve things in a certain way? How many times have you been angry with your way of proceeding or being?

When you feel abandoned by life, you feel alone in the middle of the universe like a tiny, pseudo-impotent being in the middle of a frothy sea whose waves can devour you—a dark vision of life, like living on a battlefield where shots come from anywhere. Sometimes it seems that for a few days peace has come and everything shines in the light of glory, and then something happens that causes you to lose that serenity of spirit. An unwanted visit, a call you didn't want to receive, an inappropriate comment—any situation seems able to destabilize your fragile peace. When this happens, you seek shelter somewhere. It is precisely in this moment of helplessness, of seeking refuge, that you feel the fear of God's abandonment of love. What would happen if God did not assist you? What would happen if you were delivered to your fate without more than a weak body or limited intelligence?

Children of my Immaculate Heart, you must understand that sometimes your Father wants you to experience His emptiness, His abandonment, so that you can understand, or rather remember, that His love is always with you. God's love is a love that cares, that accompanies, that protects and watches over all of His children. That experience helps you to be aware just how important it is to take care of your sisters and brothers in the love of God. They are not only your sisters and brothers, but also your daughters and sons.

I am leading you to become aware of the dimension of Father and Mother that, as a soul, you have created by love. All are your children, just as all are from God. Divine Fatherhood, or if you prefer Divine Motherhood, is who you really are. Not only are you the sons and daughters of God, but the fathers and mothers of humanity and everything created. In your parental-filial relationship with every aspect of the created universe lies the truth of who you are: sons and daughters of the Most High, fathers and mothers of creation.

When you feel the absence of divine protection, when you feel orphaned by God, you are given the opportunity to know how your sisters and brothers feel when they feel helpless. This knowledge, which is a grace from Heaven, brings you a loving message in which all creation tells you:

"My brother, my sister, don't abandon me.
I need you as much as a nursing child needs a mother."

Being present, accompanying, taking care of, giving love is what we are talking about. The maternal aspect of love not only begets life, but also gives tenderness, wisdom, protection, and support. To be aware of it is to be a living witness to the love of God. It is as important that you open yourself to feel the love of your Father as it is to live in the truth. Only in the direct relationship with God can you experience what I speak of here. It is very necessary that you ask for miracles, open yourself to receive them, and put every part of your life in the hands of love. The more you open to love, the more you will receive love.

Asking and receiving is necessary so that you can give much—not as an act of negotiation or bargaining with God, but as a way of living consciously within the movement of giving and receiving as one. This movement of love in which you receive and give is the closest to the experience of the Kingdom of Heaven that a soul can attain. Indeed, the distance between it and the reality of the Kingdom is so tiny as to be almost nonexistent. This is how Earth joins Heaven and both manifest as a unity of love.

Receiving much from God is your destiny and the nature of your being. This is abundance. By receiving constantly from the Source of life to yourself and your circumstances, whatever they may be, you experience the reality of love. By witnessing the love of your heavenly Father as something so clear, concrete, and understandable, you become aware that you are not alone, have never been alone, and cannot be.

Abandonment to God is inescapable and will heal the wound of abandonment. Any pain perceived during the times in which you have felt abandoned, orphaned, unprotected, unable to count on anyone or anything, will be healed. Tears will be wiped away and replaced by laughter and joy.

You think you can leave others because you think you can separate from yourself, abandon yourself. You have done so countless times when in some way or another you decided not to love yourself. Every time you denied your being, you experienced a sense of abandonment. This is a state of soul alienation in which it perceives itself as isolated from everything, lonely in a universe where only it exists. That is the effect of separation. The soul encloses itself and sees itself as separated from everything. It abandons sisters and brothers, it abandons God, it abandons truth. In that abandoning, it loses itself and thereby loses sight of love. In the desire to be a separated, an autonomous individual, the truth of what it is, is denied, for you are a being united to all and everything, a being that exists in relationship, a member of a family.

In love I tell you, you who know your Father in Heaven and know the delights of His holy love, to live as true fathers and mothers. Look at others for your newborn sons and daughters. Love them as a loving parent loves their divine offspring. Love them with perfect love. Let your heart, united to Christ, lead you on the path of truth. Do not abandon your children to their fate. They need you as much as they need God. Be solicitous spiritual parents. Address your needs with the wisdom of God. The spirit of love will guide you. In God you will know what to give and what not to give, what to do and what not to do. Remember that you are here to wake up to love, and once awake, to accompany your sisters and brothers in Christ on the same path of awakening. You are here to extend love to the world, the love of the Father of Heaven.

I invite you to carry in your holy heart the memory of this sweet truth:

God does not abandon the work of his hands,
because love never abandons.

Thank you for listening to my voice and following it.

In the Presence
of Love

Letter 93

My sons and daughters, the world has plunged into immense confusion. Minds have darkened to levels never before seen. Everywhere you can see how doctrines are proclaimed that contradict each other so that one cannot clearly discern. Often, young people are enchanted by temptations that lead them to live in an abyss of inner emptiness. Vulnerable, they crack like eggshells at the slightest blow. They make the pleasures of the body and indulgence a way of life, imagining that this offers a happiness that never comes. This finally leads to the death of the soul.

Not infrequently, many whom you call adults, and even elders, find themselves trapped in superficiality, apathy, and discouragement that leads them to live a materialistic life without the transcendent meaning that would prepare them for the next step that everyone is called to take, the step towards the embrace of love. Often their advice is misleading, leading the children to become more confused. Thus, those who must lead the sheep instead confuse them with ignorance, forgetting to be guides, shepherds of God's flock.

Beloved of Heaven, the elders have a responsibility to fulfill. They are lovingly called to be examples and guides for those who need them on their way to knowing the truth. But how can anyone lead others to the light if they do not live in it? Can a blind man lead a blind man without risking both of them falling into a pit?

Amid such confusion in the world, it is understandable that fear grows in minds that are increasingly moving away from God. Disconnected from the source of knowledge that is Christ, they cannot live in the certainty only truth can give. The mind is stunned when it is living as it is not meant to be. The mind is the creative medium through which spirit creates, in union with perfect love. Any other function undertaken by the mind makes it act unnaturally and thereby rush into chaos. Minds not anchored in reason and love become cruel. Reason and love are truly one and the same; there can be no love without reason, and no reason without love.

With every step the children of God take, their Father accompanies them, actively giving them what they need. Divine love is an active love. It never sleeps. It always protects. Thus, in these times of great confusion in which humanity faces an abyss of great darkness, the heavens give special thanks which allows you to sustain yourselves on the path of light. These messages, written through this helping hand offering treasures from Heaven, together with all the work given to you, are among the many treasures that perfect Love offers you now. They are effective means to discern and grow in the awareness of your union with Christ and to achieve greater knowledge of God's love.

If you are ready to see with the eyes of the truth, everywhere you will see the graces given you. There is no reason to fear, nor to lose yourself. My word will always guide you along the path of light. No confusion can obscure the glow of divine wisdom in my Immaculate Heart and in the Sacred Heart of Jesus. Come to our united hearts. In them you will find the certainty that the mind needs for perfect discernment. In your soul is the power of divine knowledge that allows you to live in the wisdom of love every day. No one can separate you from its immutable reality.

To live in the truth it is enough for you to wish with all your heart to remain united to Christ.

My beloved, never despair. Certainly, these are times of immense challenges for humanity. But there are also great blessings. God does not abandon His work. Do not get carried away by threatening thoughts that are not part of the Creator's plan. They are just that, threatening thoughts. You will not succumb. God is with you.

I leave a sweet reminder to serve as a guide along the way, an invitation to hold on to your heavenly Mother's hand.

With love I tell you:

In the midst of tribulations, come to me, I am a perfect love balm.

In the midst of life's challenges, come to me, your roads will be paved.

In the midst of chaos, take refuge in me, I am the strength of eternal truth.

In the face of despair, come to me, I am the hope that does not disappoint.

In your weariness, come to rest in me and you will find the rest of peace.

When confusion seems to grind your mind, come to me, I am the light of life.

When sadness suffocates your heart, come to me, I will fill you with true joy.

Come to me when joy reigns in your soul,

When a nightingale's song makes you dance with joy,

When everything seems to go well,

When the light surrounds you,

When peace cradles your heart,

When certainty reigns in your mind,

When love hugs you.

Come to me, now and forever.

Thus you will remain in the presence of love.

Thank you for receiving my messages.

Beautiful Love: Your Inheritance

Letter 94

My sons and daughters, if love did not exist on Earth as well as in Heaven, a great conflagration would break out which would cause the universe to head towards an unfathomable abyss of darkness. In that state, great pain would pass through humanity as a result of a life lived without God. It would immerse the world in the debauchery of passions, in an existence filled with superficiality, and an absence of a sense of holiness and the transcendent. Unparalleled cruelty would arise, with extremely painful results for the Earth and those who inhabit it, which would cause it to continue moving toward greater darkness, with suffering surpassing what you could imagine.

However, my daughters and sons, love is here. Love is speaking to your heart with these words full of wisdom and goodness. Truly I tell you, do not fear anything or anyone. The Mother watches, cares, loves. I am revealing a great truth. Continue to listen to what is said out of love.

A special grace is being given to all who live on Earth and is included in every aspect of creation. This is a blessing that previous times have not known. It is the gift of consciously providing a safe refuge for souls, which resides in my heart as Mother of all creation, Mother of love.

Although there are those who still seem to plunge into certain degrees of darkness, yet countless numbers of beings of light are spreading love. They belong to all nations, ages, genders, and ways of life. They are not just men and women but beings from all kingdoms. They are multitudes whose number exceeds that of the stars. They belong to all times past, present, and to come.

Truly I tell you that whoever takes refuge in my Immaculate Heart, united always to the heart of Jesus, does not experience fear. They receive the protection of divine grace, a blessing guaranteeing that nothing other than love reaches them, for to remain in my divine heart is to live in union with Christ, that is, in holy love, the truth of what you are.

Fear nothing. There is no reason for it. I assure you that during challenging times on Earth special graces come from Heaven. God never abandons the work of his hands. The doors of my Immaculate Heart are wide open as never before, and with them, those of my divine son Jesus. Come now and always into my arms. This call is for everyone. Do not waste this blessed gift of endless mercy. Once again I say, those who remain in me have no reason to fear. Nothing will happen to you that is not holy, perfect, divine.

Remember that you who have chosen love—and that includes all who receive these words—are in the world to spread the light of Christ and dispel darkness. I assure you, you are spreading holiness and beauty as you show your love to the Mother of the living, Source of all true life. You bear witness to the truth by elevating yourselves higher and higher through the wisdom of love. Growing in your spiritual light, you reveal the face of Christ. This is how you contribute to universal atonement.

Remain humble in this truth. Pray that the world becomes more enlightened every day. Your prayer is necessary so that consciousnesses can shine in the glory of perfect love, including works of charity. But above all, it is necessary for you to live in the truth of who you are. Do not forget that you are that which God created just as He intended. You are not of the world. You do not belong to it but to the Mother Creator of all that is holy, beautiful, perfect. You are children of light, created by Divine Love. Seek to elevate yourself higher every day.

My beloved, I invite you to remain in the light of truth. Creation belongs to the Love that God is. In His arms are each of his sons and daughters and every living being. He will never abandon you. Have faith in divine grace. With your prayers, wishes for peace and joy, your virtuous actions and sincere seeking of truth, you illuminate the Earth and consciousness. You bring heavenly light to every mind and heart.

Be not carried away by voices that do not spread serenity, harmony, and sincere joy, for they do not come from my divine heart. That is why they do not extend lasting happiness, nor provide the stillness of spirit in which your hearts have the right to rest. Be sure that the sun of life will rise and never set. Remain in the purity of holiness.

Thank you for receiving my messages.

The Canvas of Life

Letter 95

My sons and daughters, living in the truth is not always easy in a world of illusions. Even so, this Mother, full of life, love, and divine grace, accompanies you as you walk serenely in the midst of the storms of the world. When you feel downcast by evil, when you experience the poison of anger, when you feel like the whole world is against you, dive deeper into my Immaculate Heart. Let everything be as it is. Do not fall into discouragement. Lift your hearts to the Heaven of God's love. In Him you will always resurface as what you are: holiness personified.

Those who choose the option for love assume the commitment even in their humanity to live in the truth of what they are consciously, in the authenticity of the heart. Being honest with yourself is the basis of this path of holiness that I invite you to travel, hand-in-hand with beautiful love.

In order to live in the world authentically as what you really are, it is necessary to sweetly but firmly bring the wisdom of Heaven to its laws and mandates, with serene scrutiny of the truth that resides in your soul. Only by governing your life by the criteria of the Christ in you can you be the light of the world. To do this, you need to live with your heart and mind integrated together, reviewing again and again what is happening inside you. That is the simplest and shortest way to know yourself and thus be able to discern rightly.

Honor your moral conscience. Do not do anything that could put your mental peace at risk, even if it is good or essential. The most important thing lies within you: if your heart urges you to be quiet, do not say a word; if your soul asks you to sing, then praise God; if your mind asks you for time to understand and decide in peace, take time.

Sometimes things that exceed your understanding occur and you become afraid, discouraged, or confused. However, children of light, nothing can come into your life except that which can make you grow in the awareness of the love that you really are. Listen to what I have come to tell you in this message— that God the Father is dismantling structures so that you stop looking at each other, and even at yourselves, and look at the Christ who lives in each of you.

The value of a soul does not reside in what it does, or in its ability to adapt to the norms of a given culture, but in it being an abode of Christ. As long as you have this truth within, you can peacefully walk the world in the middle of its tumultuous seas.

Living in the truth does not require that everything be said, but that everything be accepted honestly within your heart. The external must be for you like a canvas where you paint your holy masterpiece with beautiful colors. Decide what adds beauty to life. Close down what may create confusion or pain. Show the world what it needs to see because of its need to know the love of God. The rest need not be shown.

If you observe earthly life, you can see that in the divine design there is space for silence, for the night, for mystery. Not everything can or should be shared. This principle will help you understand how important it is to live in your heart. Your soul knows what should be exposed or not, because of the holiness you are. Never forget that the spoken word cannot be taken back, like spilled water. That is why it is so important to think before speaking. Be aware of what you say, and what effects it may have. Always say what love asks you to say, remembering that sometimes charity demands a veil over truth. Prudence will make you understand the difference between one and the other, and will help you live in peace. Look at how polluted the world is because of mistaken words, and how much joy is in hearts filled with words of love and truth.

It is true that if you live in the authenticity of the heart, some may turn away from you and some may not understand you. You may feel that the world is leaving alone. But when that happens, ask yourself: When I live in spirit and truth, when I have Christ in my heart, can I really be alone?

True loneliness is not knowing yourself. A lack of self-knowledge creates a state of deep alienation, in which the soul becomes stranger to itself. If you do not remain bound to what you really are, you will feel isolated and cannot feel full, even if the whole world seems to be at your side.

My children, to love your brothers and sisters is to love the Christ they really are. Everything else is part of the illusion and will not stand when the moment of truth comes. But the living Christ who lives in you will remain standing, holding the life of every being. I tell you these things to help you understand that the crumbling of structures is a grace of your heavenly Father that allows you to live in the truth that sets you free, in the happy recognition that your separate self is not the being you really are, for you are the Christ in you.

I invite you to live serene in the truth of who you are. Do not worry if, when you decide to live in the authenticity of the heart, others do not follow you. I assure you, you will not be alone. Those who love the truth will join you. The light of your holiness will attract those who God placed on your path on Earth for you to remain united. There is a communion of souls. Your loved ones are an inseparable part of you. You will always have them in your life. Even if for a while it seems otherwise, in truth you will remain eternally united in the love of Christ. And together, holding hands, you will forever walk the path of eternal life. In the unity of love you will be happy. Nothing will be missing.

I, the Mother, will provide you with everything, including the love and harmony of holy relationships.

Thanks for answering my call.

God is Eternal Life

Letter 96

My sons and daughters, life comes from God, its Source and support. Nothing can make it not exist forever. Forms can create the appearance of an end of life, not in truth but in illusion. If you carry this knowledge in your hearts, you can put the world in perspective with Heaven. The passage through land is temporary. It should not be a passage through a valley of tears, although it usually is, but full knowledge of the truth that you are, is a path to the full realization of your being of eternal life and endless joy.

The essence of your being and of everything that exists is divine since it is Christ, your reality being one with God. You, each one of the living beings, are a little piece of Heaven come true. For this reason, you have the right to participate in the divine. That which constitutes the physical body, the memory, intelligence, mind and heart, the true identity of each person, as well as everything that is part of your humanity, carries within it the foundations of the Kingdom. In other words, you are the Kingdom because you come from it. Nothing real can exist that has not emerged from love. Nothing true can exist whose source is not God.

Life has a purpose: to extend itself eternally, creating new life incessantly. There is no such thing as a time where there is no being. Existence is a continuum of eternity whose origin is love and whose end is truth. Origin and end are one. I tell you these things so that you understand more clearly that the idea of a son of God who died—or who can "die"—is a meaningless idea, although many proclaim it. I have told you that you are in the times of apostasy. Although that is true, it should not be a cause for anguish. It is simply the description of a reality, a part of the road.

The apostasy in which many live is the result of a time in human history in which truth is considered the most precious of experiences. Sometimes it is the effect of a life lived from the authority of the heart, not from an external authority. Sometimes apostasy is a manifestation of rebellion against authority, born of the sincere desire for freedom in a human spirit that seeks to find its own way as dictated by its own heart and not ideas that others seek to impose. In the past, there were also those who did not believe in God, although they may not have expressed it as openly as now. Anyone who does not seek to unveil the mysteries of Heaven, or does not live in the certainty of a life that extends beyond time and space, anyone who does not make the choice for love and truth, living alone as if this world were the only reality—those are the apostates of all time regardless of whether or not they profess a religion. There have always been such movements of human consciousness on Earth. There is no reason to judge. Separation does not come from God.

Often the world confuses devotion with love for God. While this should be the natural expression of the true feeling of love and gratitude to the Creator, it is not always. Spiritless cults have always abounded. Rituals lacking in love for God, for others, and for creation have been seen often throughout history. That is not love of your Father in Heaven, but simply a set of beliefs, values, and human actions clothed with love of God. It creates an earthly identity that contributes to domination, not to the greater knowledge of love you really are. This is why today many seek to withdraw from religious structures and move towards a new spirituality based on a direct relationship with God. This is also part of God's plan used by the Holy Spirit to disarm structures, and so you can look more clearly at the radiant face of the truth that He is in each of you.

There have always been those who have felt that they belonged to an oppressive religious structure, and who look for wider spaces to be what they are. They do not yet know that what they are is not related to beliefs, a movement that can help them expand their mind and return in due time to a less limited consciousness. Thus the mind becomes a new skin into which wisdom pours the delights of new wine. Judgment has been and continues to be one of the great bastions of all that is untrue, an error that manifests itself both inside and outside of religious institutions. It is a matter of the human heart. Therefore, I invite you to not judge anything. Who has never made a mistake? Allow everything to follow the course God has given. Recognize that life is in God's hand and belongs to Him. Take care to remain united to my Immaculate Heart and to the Sacred Heart of Jesus, a union of endless bliss.

When the mind questions whether God is alive or dead it does so far from the wisdom of the heart. Such a question is based on numbers of the faithful and external expressions of devotion, when in reality true religiosity is lived within each one of you. The sacred temple where Christ dwells is the soul. The true Church of my divine son Jesus is the heart of each living being. Where there is a heart, there is Church. In other words, the Church is both the Pope and the smallest of my children who loves his Creator in the form of a jungle totem.

I am the mother of life, because I am the Mother of God and He is the Source of life. Therefore, I am the mother of everything that exists, moves, and is. Be not carried away by those who cast the shadow of their fears, making believe that the world has lost its relationship with God, or that love has abandoned it. Apostasy is not a path of definitive separation from God, but a time of distancing oneself from false ideas of God. Its purpose is often to find the true God of pure holy love that the heart who calls in its depths knows very well.

I invite you to remain within your souls and not to be carried away by what seems to happen outside your heart. In the soul lies divine reality. In your reason dwells the truth. In your heart beats eternity.

Meditate on this message. Remain in the presence of love.

Thanks for listening to my voice.

Holy Certainty

Letter 97

My beloved children, once again I invite you to live in love. This also means that you be animated in the truth and fill your hearts with hope. Discouragement does not come from Christ, although certainly it may arise from the desire for a full life. What your heart longs for will be given. God will fill the measure of your fullness. You will not be dissatisfied with anything. Be assured that the will of God for you is lasting happiness, the eternal bliss of the heart of Christ, unlike what is offered by the world.

Let nothing trouble you, let nothing frighten you.

Structures are being disarmed so you can see Christ in your sisters and brothers. You are ready to love the true being that everyone is and to relate to what each one of you is: the being God created in His own likeness. For this to be possible, a period of transformation is necessary. A new garment is brought to light as the old one is left behind.

Just as often in young people there is a period of questioning of structures, values, and identities with parents, the family, and the world, so it is with universal human consciousness. What you are living is a time of transition between the old and the new, a time when the mind questions everything. It staggers the systems of thought that until now it considered to be real or fixed, although they were illusory. This creates a temporary feeling of disorientation, especially for those who do not open to see the totality of things. To question everything is the function of all who wish to receive the wisdom of Heaven, not in the sense of criticizing without reason, but with the loving purpose of allowing the way of interpreting things to break open.

When the mind begins to question what it believed, it opens a space for the light of truth to enter and begin to be illuminated with the certainty that comes from holiness. As part of this process, intuition becomes integrated as a Source of knowledge that comes from beyond the thinking mind. In turn, this leads to a greater degree of confidence in yourself. For trusting one's own intuition, that is to say the deep dictates of your heart, is different from trusting an external authority that would tell you how things are and should be. The mind opens to this new threshold of knowledge, leaving behind the system of conditional thinking and allowing itself to be absorbed by the mind of Christ, prepared to receive the wisdom of love.

When the lower mind begins the process of releasing preconceived ideas, which proceed from what has been learned, is when the true being begins to be recognized for what it is and placed in its proper position. It leaves aside the illusion of being a personality, a limited being of flesh and blood, and of attributing value to things that make no sense, and moves towards the acceptance of spirit as reality. In other words, it begins to identify with Christ.

Being love is your only reality because God is love and nothing but love. Therefore, it is understandable that those who have spent a long time believing otherwise need a process to release the false self and embrace their true being. Patience is needed during this period of transformation of yourself, others, and the world as a whole.

Universal and singular consciousnesses are united. Everything is united. Just as you go through stages to grow in the knowledge of what you really are, the same happens with humanity. You are living in a time of abandoning the old and embracing the new. Do not worry about it; it is necessary, and a blessing. It is part of God's plan. In the end everything will be clear and you will remain in the unity of love with no wounds to heal, no forgiveness to grant, all concluded in the fullness of being.

The eternal unity of love is the destiny of humanity and all creation. It proceeds from all that is. Naturally, those who cling more to ideas of the thinking mind, those who make human reason an unquestionable source of wisdom, are frightened by the state of current affairs. Those who are guided by superficial things find it more difficult to accept that reality does not change, for while at the level of form everything changes, in essence everything is unchanging. And that is what you are and what everything is: the immutable reality of holy love expressed in your uniqueness.

Everything in your experience is part of a loving, superior plan. Put everything that happens in your life into the hands of the love that God is, so that you can have peace of mind. Truly I say to you, that everything, absolutely everything, is in the hands of the heavenly Father. Nothing that can happen is not under the domain of love. With these words let yourself be absorbed by the light of truth. I assure you that this holy knowledge will become the only reality of your life now and forever, and you will abandon all fear and live in peace.

Do not worry for the future. The Creator has already dealt with it. Just live every day in the will of God. Remain in prayer to enlighten the world and thereby accelerate the arrival of the time of universal consciousness of the fullness of love. But pray with joy, because there are many reasons to be happy.

Love is the foundation of life. This will set you free from the unnecessary anguish that comes from thinking that tomorrow will bring pain and frustration. And it will lead you to live in the truth of the triumph of my Immaculate Heart.

I give you the memory of this sweet truth: ***Love has created everything; and in its embrace, creation resides forever in the stillness of being.***

Thank you for listening to my voice and following it.

Thank you for receiving my messages.

Remain in peace, in the certainty that everything will be fine, because everything is in the hands of love.

I bless you in the truth that is always true.

Purity and Fullness

Letter 98

My sons and daughters, when you are told that damnation is possible, you are not being told that you will attain it, or that it will be attained by those who do not want to live in a state of fear. Damnation is guilt. And as you know, the mind can immerse itself in guilt. Attachment to guilt has been the great problem for humanity. Fear is guilt. It is a lack of love. It is useless to deny that guilt can exist for the mind, even though it is not the will of God, just as it is to deny the body. Even in your state of denial, God does not stop being love. Love is freedom. Therefore, the will of the Creator of life and of everything holy and beautiful is that you enjoy sufficient amplitude so that you can think and live as you dispose. Divine love cannot be lost. There is nothing that can take away your eternal favor. Nothing can separate you from your Source of eternal life and endless bliss. The Creator and His creations are one. Love is union.

What you are being told here, beloved children, is that you are not less worthy if you choose not to love, although you are less happy, because love with freedom is happiness. This is why your Father in Heaven calls you again and again to live in love for the simple reason that he wishes your happiness and fulfillment. Your heart lives in peace when resting in the serene embrace of love. There is no other way to live fully that is not in union with the love you really are, because your heart's nature, essence, and Source is perfect love.

No one can be happy outside the good that comes from God because He is supreme goodness, the Source of all happiness and holiness. This is not new to you. You know well how the heart sings, dances, and resonates when love comes to meet it, and how much it breaks in its absence. You also know that your heart does not care much about mental considerations such as where it comes from or where it is going. It only cares about living in love. The heart only understands the language of love because that is its eternal abode. Heaven lies within the heart. In it dwells the sweet host of souls, in whom everything was made in perfect harmony, beauty, and holiness. Your soul longs to live every day in the holy dwelling of the Father's house, that refuge of peace built with the everlasting rocks of truth and holiness. Truly I say to you, there is no greater treasure in the entire universe than a pure heart. Purity is the longing of souls born of the Father of all things holy, innocent, pure.

The state of purity can be reached here, now, and forever. Indeed, reaching and remaining in it is the goal of these messages which come from my Immaculate Heart, and always united to the Sacred Heart of Jesus, in perfect harmony and unity with your holy heart. In your being resides the holiness of God. You are loving by nature, by the design of the Creator. Your free will is given to make the choice for love. To choose only love is to choose the happiness of Heaven. It is choosing what will make you full. It is consciously choosing your happiness and your precious freedom.

Love and holiness are one and the same, and both are one unity with purity. Free will was not given to you to choose between good and evil, a duality that creates not only confusion and conflict but also diverts the soul from its divine purpose, the fullness of being in God.

To be full is to reach the state of being that the will of your eternal Father has ordained, and not according to the criteria of a mind separated from truth and love. Being united in holiness with everything created and with God is the truth about you. Every aspect of creation, including you and the whole world, is part of the mystical body of Christ. To live in harmony and coherence with this truth is to live in the condition of fullness. We say "condition" because the truth is for your being what water is for a fish. The fish is made of the same substance as the pure water of the infinite ocean of divine love in the boundless breadth of being. Truth is the vital medium in which the soul moves and exists. And since means and ends are one, divine truth is also the ultimate end of your being.

Recall that you reach the fullness of your being by giving yourself. Giving and receiving are one and the same. When you give love you are giving your being. By giving love you receive it. This is the dynamic of divine creation. The more given, the more there is. The more love given, the more received. The more love received, the more there is. That is why it is so important to allow yourself to be loved by God, by your sisters, brothers, and creation, whose benevolence longs to pour out entirely into your life. To love is to be.

To all my children I say, these messages are letters of love and wisdom, sent from Heaven to you, an act of sublime union, mystery, and a gift of divine mercy because they are the will of the eternal Father. I avail myself of the hand of one of my sons and brothers who, without fully knowing what he writes, nor the full purpose of this work, humbly surrenders to the call of the spirit so that these words come to the world of form.

These words come to you through the union of minds and hearts. Remember, we are one mind, one heart, and one soul united in the fullness of being, the harmony of love. They are a godsend for you who receive these graces and blessings. Even before time existed they were designed to come at the right moment to your mind and heart united in the fullness of love.

You who receive my messages with respect and love, you must know that you are ready to live in love. Indeed, the world has long benefited from the grace of your holy presence. You are a light to the nations and scattered minds, and joy for hearts thirsty for pure love.

Soul of my soul, I have always known you. From all eternity I have contemplated you with love. I have been looking forward to inflamed love in this moment—this moment in which, through this revelation, the floodgates of your heart and mind open even more, in union with the Sacred Heart of Jesus, to pour the abundant light of Christ into your being as never before, flooding the Earth with holy love.

Your acceptance of my messages, together with your sincere desire to make them come alive, embodying the love they bring from the Kingdom as a visible sign of our divine relationship, will bring great blessings to your life and to the world. Your loving reception of these words is an opening to receive my Immaculate Heart and Jesus. It is an effective and accurate means of greater union with Christ and greater knowledge of the love of God, revealed through the living experience of the direct relationship with Him who holds you in his loving arms, sanctifying you with the strength of His divine being.

Well-loved children, I invite you to make the purity of holy love that you truly are come true, here, now, and always. Love one another as God loves you forever.

Thank you for listening to my voice and following it.

The Treasures of Union

Letter 99

My beloved children, there is no place where I am not. I always stay by your side and in you, especially in you who have chosen truth as your eternal company and love as your only reality. I am the Mother of the living, the refuge of souls who seek peace, the Immaculate Heart of Mary. Those who plunge into the depth of my pure love find in our union solace for the soul and the certainty for which the mind longs. I am the Source of wisdom and concord. I am that which gives meaning to existence. I am the vibrating force of God made human.

Whoever lives in me not only finds lasting joy, but also discovers a shield of light and spiritual strength to envelop their being, their humanity, and everything that is part of their life, both on Earth and in Heaven. Your loved ones are reached by a grace that flows from this refuge of divine love, which is the union of our hearts along with the Sacred Heart of Jesus. Every moment you spend with your heavenly Mother you bring light to the world, heal wounds, and resurrect what was dead. A beautiful flow of love floods the lives of men and women of all times and places.

Our relationship as the purest Mother and Son of holiness contains within it the seeds of the resurrection and the Second Coming of Christ. Within it lies the sanctity of your being and the truth of who you are. This work is a perfect instrument to grow in the knowledge of the love of God because through it you become more aware of the union of light that exists between you and me. All matters of your earthly life are important to me. Every beat of your heart is of great importance to this Mother who contemplates you with all the love of Heaven. You are the light of my eyes because you are my children. You are the longing of my heart because Christ resides in you. When I look at you I see the One who has given you life and sustains you in existence, just as He does with the flowers and the birds of the sky. Everything that exists is clothed in the glory of the eternal Father. You are no exception.

I remind you of something that your heart knows but the mind often forgets. Everything, absolutely everything created, has been created for your happiness. It is a gift from the eternal Father for His beloved children. Everything belongs to you in Me, because I am the perfect extension of God's love, just like you. As you have been told, love is relationship and without relationship you cannot be known. This is why relationship is sacred; it is the means created by God so that love is known, received, given, and understood.

Every time you express your love, with or without words, gestures, or serene stillness, the world is affected by its sweetness and light. Everything changes when love appears. In love's presence everything is the joy of holiness. Whoever lives in love does not experience loneliness or separation. Remain in the peace of Christ where everything is healthy, holy, and true. My children, there is no wound that cannot be healed in pure love. There is no human experience that cannot be sanctified in the presence of the divinity which resides in your heart.

Each of you are beings who know love. Maybe in some way you have confused it with something else, but still the knowledge of love resides in your heart. This is because you know your being. Once you know that you are love and nothing but love, there is no room for sadness and discouragement. In love everything is harmony, unity, and abundance of life in its fullness. You were created to be happy in the love of God. Thus there is a call to perpetual happiness in your soul, a call that I invite you to listen to within and to join. Do not drown out this voice calling you to the joy of the children of God.

My sons and daughters, remember that you create your own experience in how you respond to the issues of life. Everything is neutral except your desire to be non-neutral. We return to the simple truth that says you only have two options, to respond with fear or with love. The first will fill your mind with judgment, anger, and things that only cause misery. The other way of responding, which is God's way, will preserve you in eternal life, in the certainty of the truth about what you are, and in union with your true identity, which gives you the treasures of the Kingdom.

It is entirely possible to be happy on Earth just as it is in Heaven. For this, the only thing that is needed is to live in the truth. And the truth is love. For this reason, you are urged to remain in the presence of love every day, not because it is a new commandment, but because that is the deep longing of your heart. It is what your will wants. You are a being of pure holy love, full of life, fulfillment, wisdom, and beauty. Accepting that as your only truth and living in coherence with it is the essence of beautiful knowledge which comes from Heaven. This is what it means to live in the world without being of it.

Being love and living love is the same. All conflict comes from not making a conscious decision to live in harmony with who you are. If you are love but live as if you were anything else, whatever name you give it, then you create an unreal state. This unreality is the source of fear, which obscures the consciousness of the love that you are and that everything is. When you feel dejected, when you feel scared, when you experience anger or anything else you don't like to feel, quiet your mind. Dive into the depths of my infinite love. Returns to the embrace of the Mother of God.

Truly, I tell you that when you leave the embrace of my Immaculate Heart, your mind and heart are troubled, and your soul faints in the absence of love. That is why I say to you, and to all of you who live in that beautiful land so full of beauty, life, and light, that the eternal Father has given you a temporary home where you can walk the path of awakening to Christ consciousness, to the consciousness of what you really are. Stay in the presence of love. Live every day of your life holding my divine Mother's heart. Live now and always in the Heaven of holy love.

I bless you in the sanctity of being.

Thanks for receiving my messages.

My Love Will Never Pass

Letter 100

My children, I have promised to stay by your side always. I was there when my divine son Jesus pronounced it with his sweet voice. Where Jesus is, there is Mary. Wherever the son is, there is the mother. And where Mary is, there is always God, because we are inseparable. I tell you in spirit and truth that where this loving Mother dwells, full of infinite tenderness towards all creation and overflowing with mercy, Heaven resides in its entirety. I ask you to reflect deeply and serenely on what I say here. These messages are a love letter from Mary to you, you who are the reason for my existence as a saving Mother. You are a treasure of inestimable value. The value of a soul can never be determined because in it resides the greatness of God, which is beyond all valuation. In it resides perfect love.

I give you this work for pure holy love. I give it so you have a means to learn more about the delights of my Immaculate Heart, which is a treasure of inexhaustible worth. You have the full right to become not only a partaker but an heir to its graces. My heart belongs to you because I am your heavenly Mother. Come and lay hands on the gifts that Heaven gives you through me. We are a holy union, Mother and child.

Do not live your life as if you do not have a divine Mother. You do. In the world you can never be fully aware of the power of the love of a mother, much less when that mother is Mary, mother of God and of all. I assure you that I can solve all your problems in the blink of an eye, including those that, by God's design, remain in your mind for what appears to be a long time. Keep in mind that the Creator is wise, and therefore things are carried out according to His divine plan, including those that you consciously give Him.

I give you the peace that comes from knowing you are protected by Mary. I want to make known to you the love that the heavenly Father feels for you, which is the same love in my Immaculate Heart and in the Sacred Heart of Jesus. You are not alone, and never will be. I remain by your side and in you all the days of your life, as does Jesus. We are both real. We are alive forever in the fullness of the Creator of Heaven and Earth. We see you. We feel you. We embrace you. We pray for you all the time, here in the realm of no time. When you sleep, we take care of you; when you wake, we protect you. We always accompany you, even if you do not realize it or do not speak to us. We love you in freedom, but also with responsibility in such a way that we never stop extending our perfect love to you, for that is the reason for our existence. We give ourselves entirely to our children, brothers and sisters in unity.

We, the union of the Immaculate Heart of Mary and the Sacred Heart of Jesus, know what each of you are. We know you from all eternity and we pay no attention to what is untrue. Your holiness has been given to you from the moment of your creation. Christ is the truth of your being, with whom we are united. We love you with a love not of the world that comes from the purest Heaven. Heaven resides in our being just as it resides in you. It is a matter of remaining in it in such a way that the divine union of your soul with your Source produces effects as an inevitable result of what it is.

Loving you, protecting you, providing what you need in holiness, instilling life and love in your existence—this is our divine obligation, for us and for the Creator. I tell you these things so that you know for sure that not only do you have the possibility of Heaven and receiving everything that is a true contribution to your earthly fullness, but that this is the birthright of all my children. Forget not that you were created to be happy. Full bliss is attainable and can be abided in forever. Otherwise, there would be an inconsistency in God, which is impossible.

Divine love will fill the measure of your fullness. Feeding on love will give you the nectar of eternal life and your heart will sing of joy and reverberate to the beat of endless happiness. In your soul is the music of Heaven. Angels join the chorus of souls along with all of creation, singing a hymn of praise and gratitude to God the Father for having given eternal life. It is in this hymn of beauty that you will live.

There is a place where the sanctity of your being, the pure longing of your heart and the lofty aspirations of your mind, together with the delights of your pure soul, are lived in harmony and peace forever. In that place which is not a place is where it dwells within you. Stay there without leaving for a single moment. And if you go, come back. The doors of this haven of divine love are wide open. Whoever wants to enter or to leave can do so without hindrance. And whoever wants to stay forever can do so also. Which of these options would you choose? The happiness that comes from living in love? Or the suffering that comes from the absence of what the heart loves above all, precisely because of its being?

Love is what you really are, and nothing more. You know this very well. Nobody lacks this knowledge because it is the divine truth within which is the whole existence of life. I assure you that if each creature of God did not enjoy this full knowledge, life would be extinguished more quickly than in the blink of an eye. The problem is that humanity has not known this for sure, and there has been a desire by humanity to add something more to this eternal truth, which has cost it the full consciousness of the love. To be only love is to be one with God. To be only love is to live in truth. So I invite you again to live love, to live the love that you are. In other words: live.

Thank you for listening to me and following my words.

I bless you in the holy union of the three hearts.

A Dwelling for Each Son and Daughter

A Final Message from the Heart of Mary

Children of my Immaculate Heart, this is the last message in this series of my love for you. However, it is not a farewell since I will stay with you all the days of your life until the end of time. My divine son Jesus, in union with this work, will give you great treasures which come from his most Sacred Heart. He, in union with my Immaculate Heart, also joins this work with eagerness for inflamed love and the sweetness that comes from the Heaven of his holy love. We are a unit. We are the union of Heaven and Earth come true.

I invite you to return to these messages as many times as you feel the need to. They are clothed with a power that is beyond human understanding. These words have the strength of God's love. Do not forget, everything has been created through the Word. Because they come from the love of God these messages contain within themselves the power to create life and love. It is your Heavenly Father who ordained that I may join you in this particular way. And he has also arranged for Jesus to do so, your eternal ally in love, your perfect redeemer, your divine friend, and your unity in truth.

I assure you that there is no purer, more powerful ally who loves you more than my divine son Jesus, and this divine Mother who is one with him. Her unconditional love for humanity is beyond what anyone can do. Love her in the certainty that everything will end well. You have the grace to receive these words through a friendly hand that also loves you with perfect love, because he has given himself to this work with total abandonment. Receive these words for what they are: a source of eternal life and a perfect means to make you more aware of divine relationship.

I assure you that those of you who spend time with these words are uniting more deeply with Heaven and thus allowing not only the constant transformation that love and truth create in your souls, but you stretch the firmament more and more by bringing the divine down to Earth. Thus, from our union, manifested by your generosity to give us your time reading and ruminating on these words and letting the feelings of divine unity emerge in you, you create a new Heaven and a new Earth. I repeat, it is better to pray than to do. And I remind you that there is no higher prayer than the prayer of silence because in silence the mind can hear the voice of the eternal Beloved and the heart can rejoice, resting serenely in the arms of the Father.

I invite you to remain in love every day of your lives, and to live thinking about the wonders that God created for each of you. In truth, I tell you that each one has a mansion reserved in Heaven which this caring and loving Mother has prepared, together with Jesus, that you may live in forever. Now I leave you because it is so arranged. But I do not abandon you. That is impossible. It simply transforms the way in which our relationship will appear while you are in time, for we will always remain united in our holy being and I will continue speaking to your heart every day of your life.

I leave you but I do not abandon you. I leave you, for if I did not you could not receive the grace of words from the sweetest heart of Jesus, which are at the gates of human conscience to be spoken and written. And so it will be done, for that is the will of God. Trust what He tells you. Do what He commands you to do or stop doing, and I assure you that you will live Heaven on Earth and bring before the throne of the Most High an uncountable number of souls. Your brothers and sisters are waiting to receive from you the beauty of your heart. Receive this work as a treasure of grace that creates within you an unimaginable flow of divine love which illuminates your face, making it more serene, smiling and pure.

I assure you that whoever sees you after having received these words with love and breadth of heart, will perceive the transformation of light that has occurred in you. Not a single moment that you spend in divine union with the Love of all love fails to create its effects. Love transforms everything into more love. Holiness transmutes everything into more holiness. And this is not an exception. Your transformation has been accomplished. Now you are not only a new holy being, but you are increasingly united to the heart of God.

This work has fulfilled God's mission in its own way. Remember that the divine Word fulfills its purpose. It is like the rain that comes from Heaven and waters the Earth to germinate the grass that will be food for the living. Similarly, these messages are food for the soul. I invite you to listen to the beat of your heart and let yourself be carried away by what love tells you in unity with reason, that is, with truth. Never forget that love and truth are a holy unity, and that is why it is so necessary to live in the union of heart and mind, so that reason and divine love can act as what they are, the two wings with which spirit flies.

I thank you in the name of Heaven for giving me your time and your souls, to be part of these dialogues of wisdom and truth. You have chosen to spend time alone with your Creator of pure love, and in doing so you have chosen to live love. That choice will pay off. Your life will not be the same because the seed of divine love has germinated in you. You are no longer a cocoon, or a simple grain that, although beautiful, has not yet germinated. Now you are a radiant soul that illumines the world. You are a star that radiates beauty. You enjoy eternal wisdom and the perfect knowledge of where sweetness resides and love dwells. Knowing what is the path to truth and where Christ dwells, you have become creditors of the greatest treasure that exists, the treasure of having found the truth.

Go around the world announcing peace. Join the movement of beautiful love. And stay waiting for the One who is the beloved of your Soul, Jesus of Nazareth. His word will come and do great wonders for you. Join him and you will remain united to me and to God.

I thank you for receiving my messages.

I bless you in the holy union of beautiful love,

Mother Mary, your Divine Mother

About the Receiver

Sebastián Blaksley is a native of Buenos Aires, Argentina, born in 1968 into a large traditional Catholic family. He attended the Colegio del Salvador, a Jesuit school headmastered by Jorge Bergoglio, the current Pope Francis. Although he wanted to be a monk as a young man, Sebastián's family did not consider it acceptable, and the inner voice that he always obeyed spoke thus: "You must be in the world, without being of the world." He studied Business Administration in Buenos Aires and completed his postgraduate studies in the U.S. He held several highly responsible positions in well-known international corporations, living and working in the U.S., England, China, and Panama. He then founded a corporate consulting firm in Argentina that he led for 10 years. Sebastián has two daughters with his former wife.

At the age of six, Sebastián was involved in a near-fatal accident during which he heard a voice, which later identified itself as Jesus. Ever since he has continued to hear this voice. Sebastián says: "Since I can remember, I have felt the call of Jesus and Mary to live surrendered to their will. I am devoted to my Catholic faith."

In 2013, he began to record messages from his mystical experiences. In 2016 he miraculously discovered *A Course of Love* and felt the call to devote himself to bringing it to the Spanish-speaking world. He also now receives, transcribes, and shares what the voice of Christ—the voice of love—dictates. Most recently he has received and shared *Choose Only Love*, a series of seven books.

Sebastián is the president of the nonprofit Fundación Un Curso de Amor, www.fundacionamorvivo.org, through which he shares *A Course of Love* and *Choose Only Love*.

Other Works Received by Sebastián Blaksley

Choose Only Love: Echoes of Holiness (Book I)
Choose Only Love: Let Yourself Be Loved (Book II)
Choose Only Love: Homo-Christus Deo (Book III)
Choose Only Love: Wisdom (Book IV)
Choose Only Love: The Holy Dwelling (Book V)
Choose Only Love: The Divine Relationship (Book VI)
Choose Only Love: The Way of Being (Book VII)

The Age of the Heart: The Birth of a New Heaven
and a New Earth

All books are available as audiobooks on Audible.com,
Amazon.com, and iTunes.
Audiobooks of *Choose Only Love* narrated in Spanish by
Sebastián Blaksley are available on www.beek.io.

The website http://cocreatingclarity.org/CHOL/ offers a
powerful search tool that enables searches for words or
phrases within all of the *Choose Only Love* books.

The website https://www.chooseonlylove.org offers free
chapters and other resources about the *Choose Only Love* books,
the Refuge of Divine Love in Argentina, the Way of Being
program, the Hour of Grace program, additional information
about Sebastián Blaksley, and more.

Information about the Spanish-language books received
by Sebastián, *Elige solo el amor,* and the companion book
Mi diálogo con Jesús y María: un retorno al amor is available at
www.fundacionamorvivo.org

The Truly Beloved Books

Book 1 — Truly Beloved: Love Letters from
the Divine Mother in You
Book 2 — Truly Beloved: Love Letters from the Christ in You
Book 3 — Truly Beloved: Love Letters from an Angel

Other Works from Take Heart Publications

A Course of Love is a living course received from
Jesus by Mari Perron. It leads to the recognition,
through experience, of the truth of who we really are
as human and divine beings—a truth
much more magnificent than we
previously could imagine.

A Course of Love is available in multiple languages.

A powerful search tool is available to search for specific words
in the book, as well as simultaneously in *A Course in Miracles*.

Many dialogue groups consider *A Course of Love*
both in-person and online.

For more information go to www.acourseoflove.org.

Made in United States
North Haven, CT
25 May 2024

52939593R10215